INTERIOR DETAILS

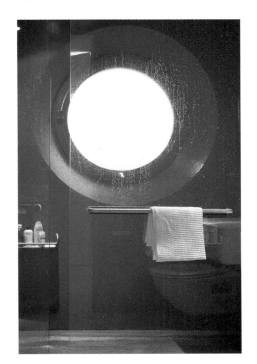

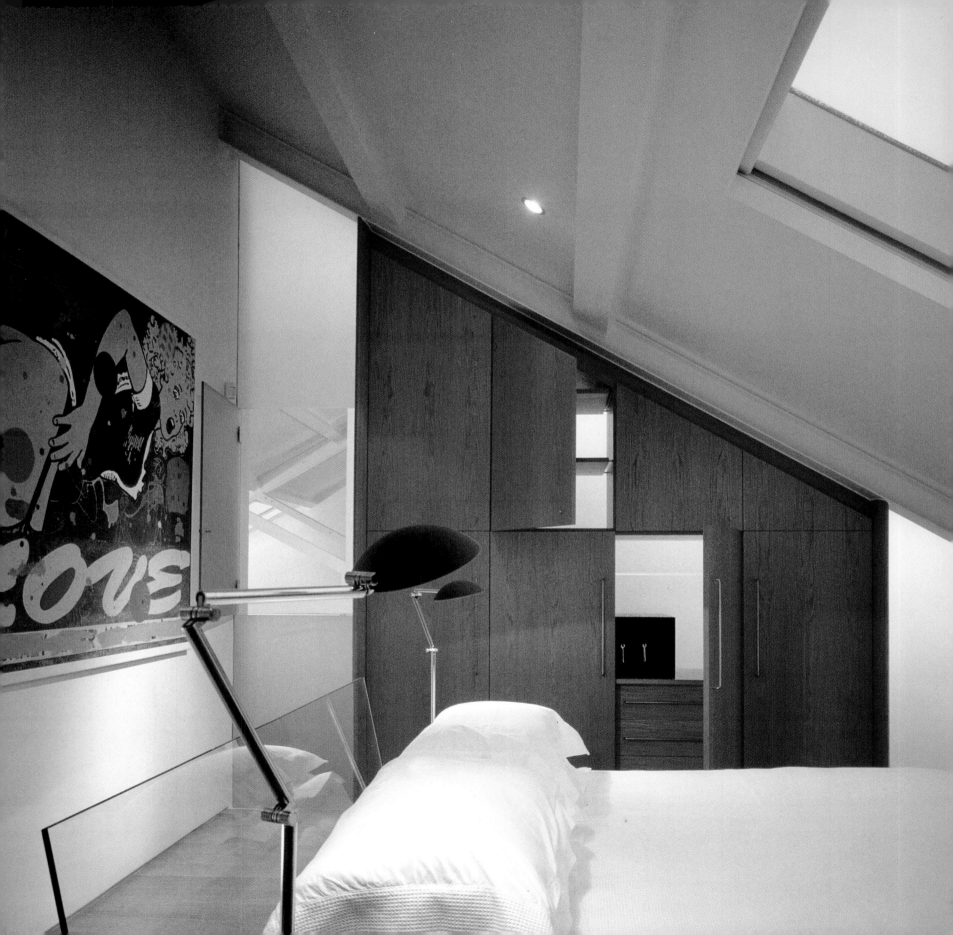

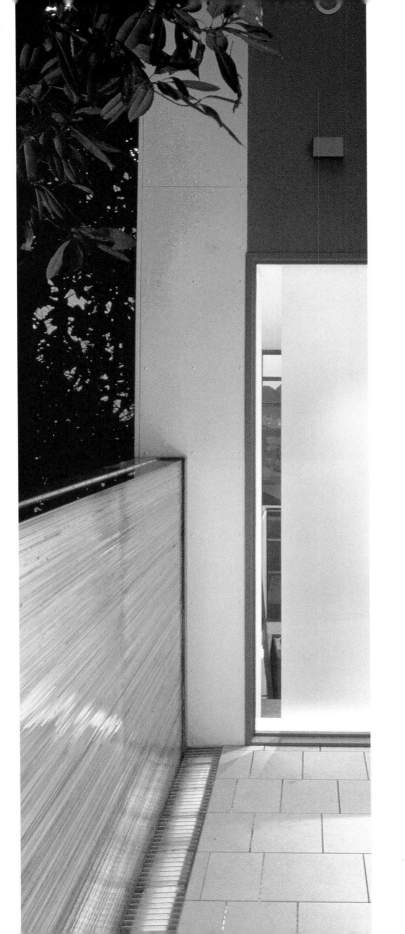

INTERIOR
DETAILS

FAY SWEET

ROCKPORT

First published in the United States of America by

Rockport Publishers Inc.

33 Commercial Street

Gloucester, Massachusetts 01930-5089

Telephone: (978) 282-9590

Fax: (978) 283-2742

www.rockpub.com

First published in Great Britain in 2002 by Mitchell Beazley,

an imprint of Octopus Publishing Group Limited,

2—4 Heron Quays, London E14 4JP

Copyright © Octopus Publishing Group Limited 2002

Commissioning Editor: Emma Clegg
Executive Art Editor: Auberon Hedgecoe
Senior Editor: Lara Maiklem
Editor: Jonathan Hilton
Designer: Emily Wilkinson
Production Controller: Alex Wiltshire
Proofreader: Barbara Mellor
Indexer: Hilary Bird

ISBN 1-56496-803-0

A CIP catalogue record for this book is available from the British Library

Typeset in InterFace DaMa

Produced by Toppan Printing Co. (HK) Ltd.

Printed and bound in China

contents

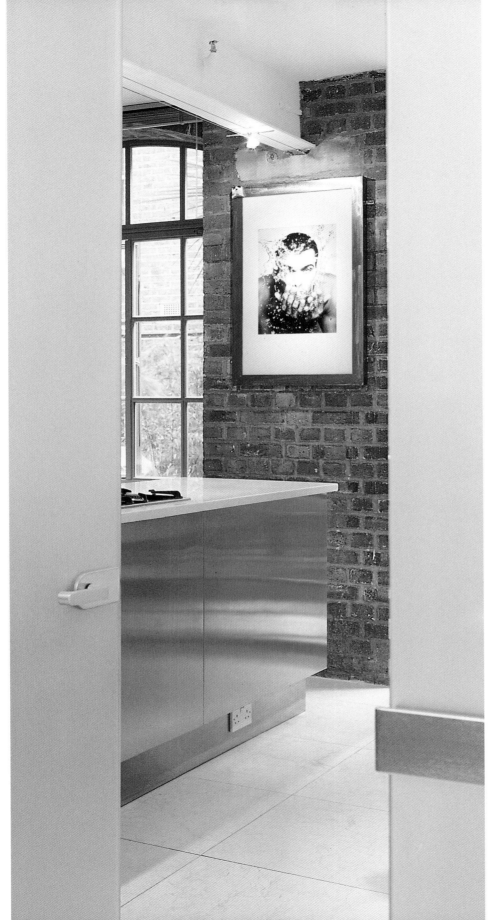

introduction

The importance we place on our homes cannot be overstated. Home is sanctuary, where it is possible to rest and restore ourselves, to take the time to look after the needs of our mind, body, and spirit. It is a place where we should feel comfortable, safe and secure, as well as separate from the noise and clatter, the pressures and demands of the outside world. Here the family is brought up and the company of friends enjoyed. Home is also where it is safe to be ourselves, to feel free to express something of our personalities and shape and decorate a space as we like it. Our urge is to create an environment that appeals to the senses — one that looks good, feels good, smells good.

To satisfy these homemaking needs, *Interior Details* has been conceived as a source book to provide not only inspiration but also practical help in putting together a beautiful home. It features hundreds of carefully selected images from projects by some of the leading architects and interior designers working today all around the world. In addition, there are also many close-up photographs that allow you to see in detail some of the particularly stunning materials and products available from the world's best manufacturers.

As the pictures collected together here demonstrate, the choice of materials and products is now incredibly impressive, and so one of the roles of Interior Details is to suggest ways of putting together ideas and schemes to achieve a specific goal or a particular effect. Once you have been inspired, and to help you find exactly what you are looking for, you will also find an extensive directory of designers, makers, and suppliers starting on page 150.

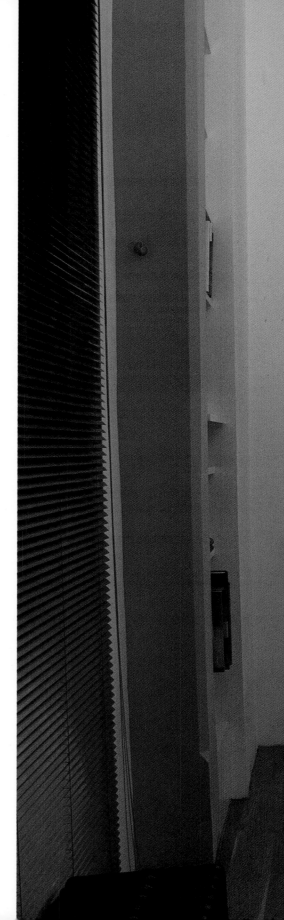

→ A sequence of appealing spaces has been created in this home, designed by The Douglas Stephen Partnership. Materials are used to great effect to distinguish the rooms, with timber floors and smooth plaster walls making a crisp, calm, sophisticated backdrop to the sitting room. This is followed by a change of tempo, with raw brick and industrial lamps for an up-tempo, textured, and rich-coloured finish in the dining area.

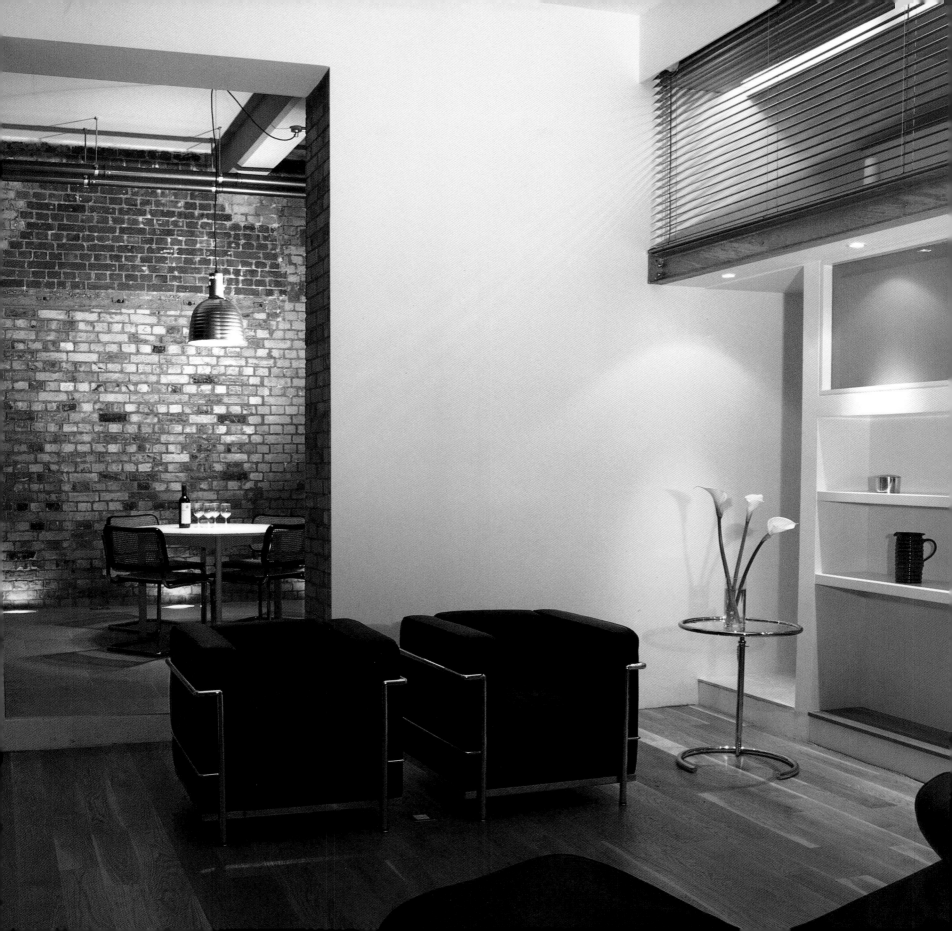

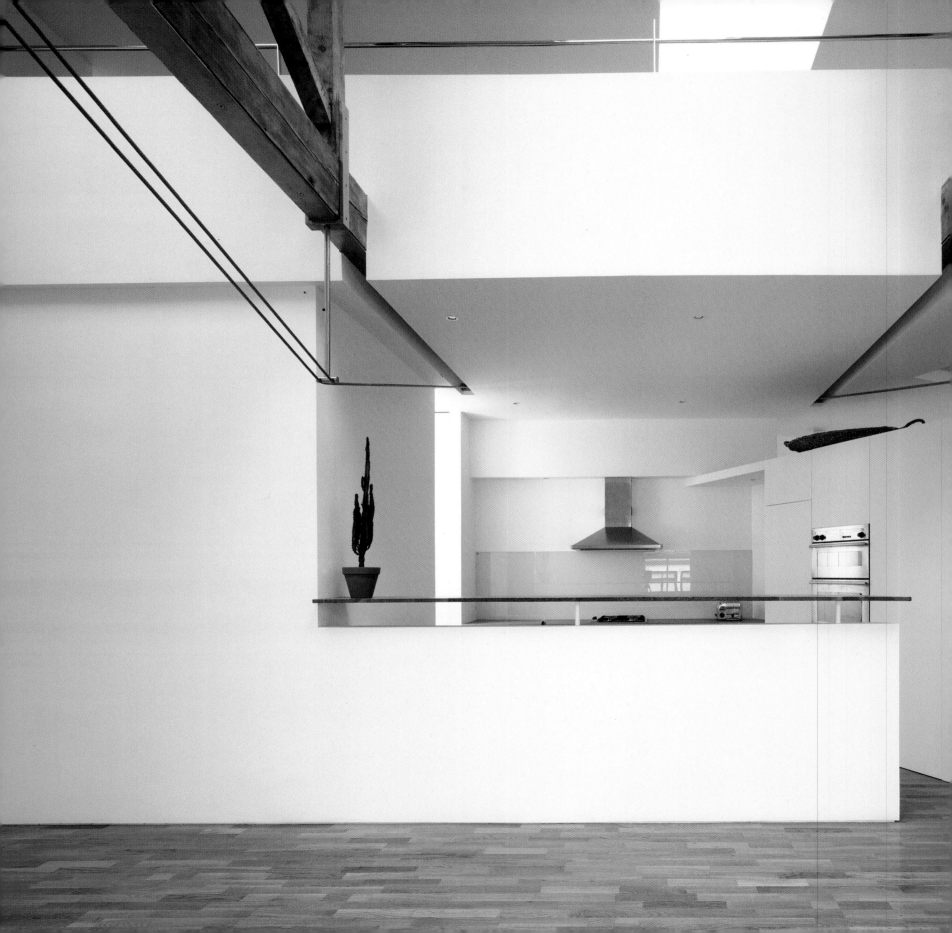

Think of the interior of a home as you might a complex recipe —
a combination of different ingredients that have to be blended together
to provide texture, colour, shape, and light in just the right measures if you
are to create an exciting and satisfying whole. And always, just as in cooking,
it's worth bearing in mind that the greatest success is achieved through
careful attention to detail. Experienced practitioners may make the process
look easy, but often this apparent casualness is the result of years of hard
work and problem solving.

The importance of beautiful finishes and fittings is given extra emphasis
in the contemporary interior, where large, sheer surfaces and well-lit spaces
leave absolutely no room for tatty materials or poor workmanship to hide.
Simple-looking interiors take a great deal of care, both to make and to
maintain. In a pure white cube, for example, the smallest gouge in the wall,
finger mark at the light switch, or scuff of the floor is glaringly obvious.

With this fact in mind, it is a good idea to set aside a comfortable part
of your budget to allow for good-quality finishes and skilled workmanship.
However, this certainly does not mean everything has to be lined with slabs
of expensive marble, hung with crystal, or draped with exotic fabrics — even
inexpensive materials, such as plywood sheeting or cast concrete, can look
glorious and last for years when they are fitted properly and finished with
care. Returning to the cooking metaphor — a diet of *foie gras* and truffles
would be difficult to stomach, while a single fragrant tomato, with a simple
dressing, can wake up the most jaded of taste buds. The answer is to

← A cubist puzzle of interlocking planes has been created in this converted industrial space. Architect Charles Barclay separates the large, open living space from the more intimate cooking area with the intervention of a chest-height counter. A sense of intimacy in the kitchen is created by the lowered ceiling, which is part of the mezzanine level.

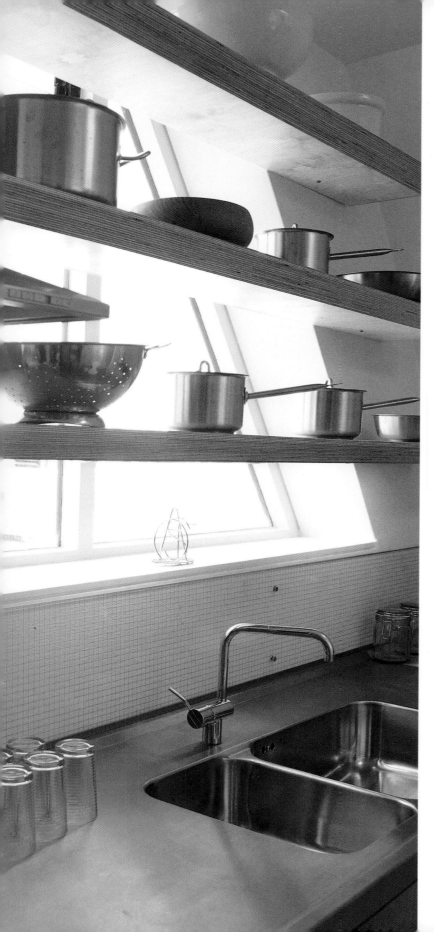

research the available choices widely, choose materials judiciously, experiment with new ideas occasionally, and be prepared to pay a little more sometimes.

However, before spending your hard-earned cash, ask yourself some basic questions so that you can be confident you are doing the right thing. First of all, whether you have just moved or you have lived in your home for a number of years, are you sure that you like the location, neighbours, and property enough to make a substantial investment of time, money, and energy in carrying through the improvements you are contemplating? It could be that it is cheaper to move elsewhere, into a more appealing or suitable home, than to lavish attention on a property you only half like or might move from in the relatively near future.

Second, refurbishment and building work is inevitably dirty, messy, disruptive, and stressful, and nearly always more expensive than you budgeted for — so are you prepared to live in a degree of chaos for a while? There really is no gain without pain.

Third, decide how much change you want to bring about. Sometimes, just moving a door, installing a new lighting scheme, or fitting a larger window can make an enormous difference to the quality of a room or space. Or perhaps you have grander plans to revamp a whole room, knock down walls, add an extension, or completely gut the interior of your home from top to bottom and start over again. Do you need structural, electrical, or plumbing work completed at the same time? If your home is going to be in a mess, it may as well be in a total mess. Perhaps you should move out for a while?

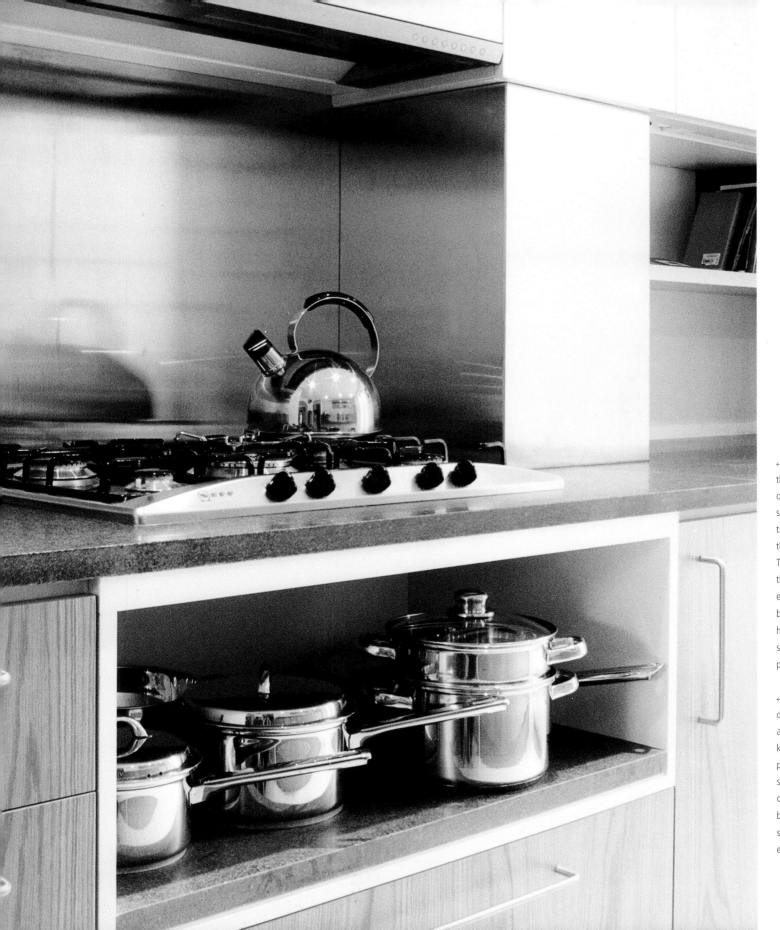

← Here, we can appreciate the stylish combination of a stone counter top, splashback, and the timber-faced doors with their long handles. The kitchen has been thoughtfully and ergonomically planned by AAB Architects, which has added a deep recessed shelf below the hob for pots and pans.

← ← Careful attention to detailing pays dividends, as you can see in this kitchen. The aesthetically pleasing and practical single run of stainless-steel counter top and sink sits below unusually chunky shelves, which feature very elegant chamfered edges.

Is the job you are contemplating one for a builder, or would a supervising architect be a good idea? With the exception of the smallest and most straightforward of jobs, the best advice is always to use an architect — with their years of training and experience, architects are able to visualize how changes will look and work, and they have the skills to reshape spaces, make rooms flow together better, and generally squeeze the most out of any home. Good architects also often have an extensive knowledge of unusual and interesting materials, know who can supply them, and can hire the best craftspeople to install them — so, armed with some of the ideas taken from this book, you can swap notes.

Once you are certain that the envisaged refurbishments and improvements are right for you, next turn your attention to the budget. Do you expect the value of your spend to add automatically to the value of your home? Even if the expected rise in property value does not match the cost of the work, will the changes be worth making anyway in order to create a home that you like better and will live in longer?

To gain some idea of what you might have to spend to realize your ideas, you should start to piece together what the project is likely to entail. Collect together magazines and books and build a picture of the look or atmosphere you are hoping to achieve. If you are embarking on this adventure with a partner, make sure you are in broad agreement on what to do and how to do it. Domestic harmony will help to carry you through the more traumatic moments that may occur during the refurbishment.

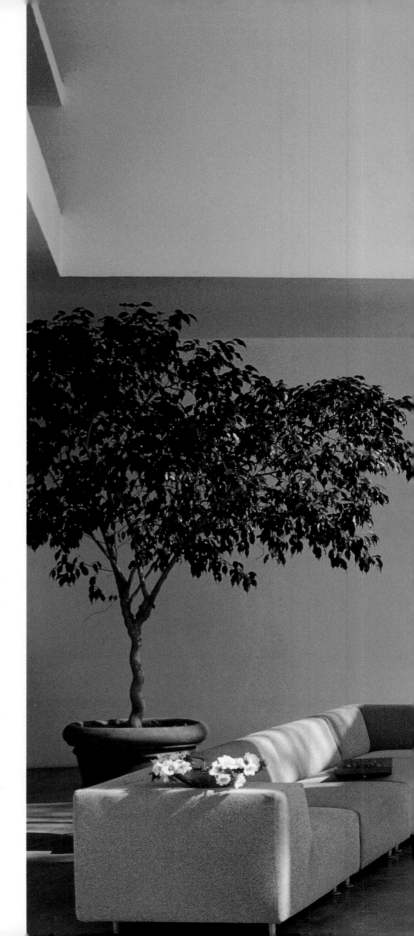

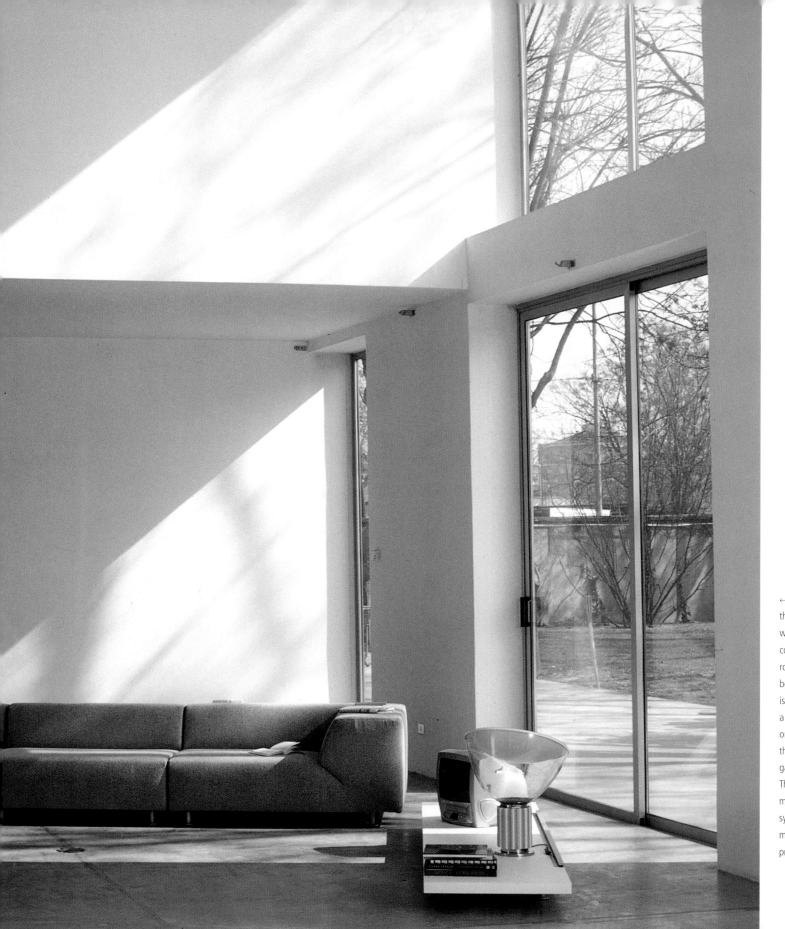

← Sunlight flooding through huge glass doors with windows above contributes to making this room an irresistibly beautiful, restful space. It is easy to imagine reading a book or newspaper here, on the large sofa with the doors leading onto the garden thrown wide open. The L-shaped sofa is made using a modular system called Globe, manufactured by Italian producer Cassina.

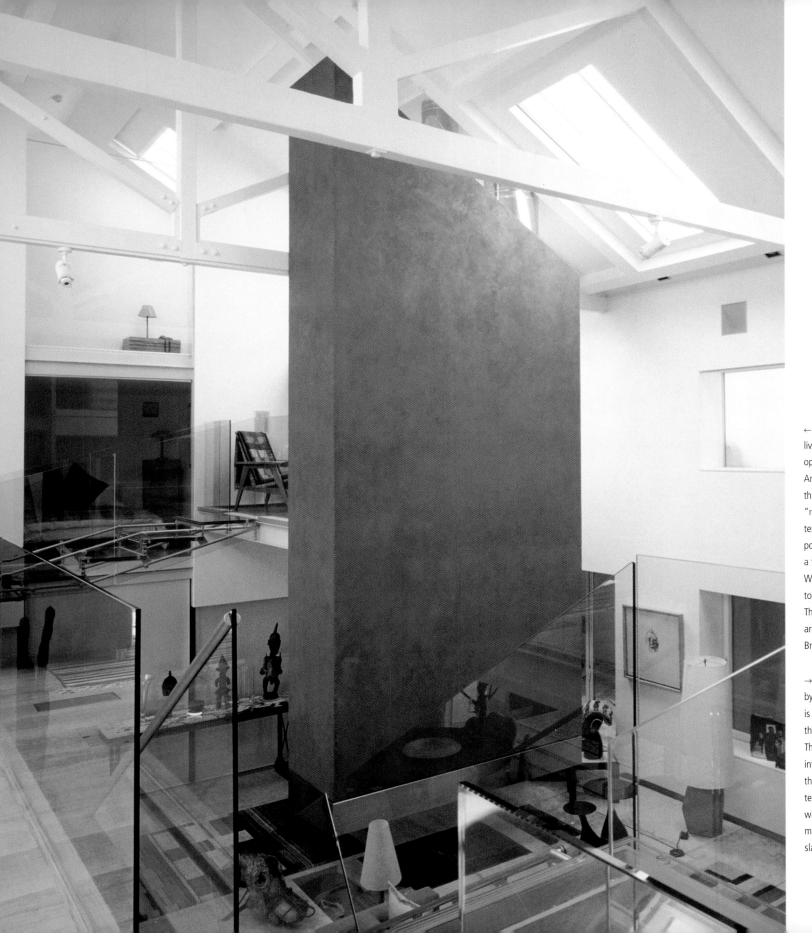

← This highly unusual living space has been opened right to the eaves. And hanging like a banner through the middle is a "red-hot" wall – actually terracotta-coloured polished plaster housing a fireplace at its base. When lit, flames appear to leap out of the floor. The project is by the architecture practice Brookes Stacey Randall.

→ This finely detailed stair, by the Tugman Partnership, is pure pleasure to glimpse through the doorway. The open treads cast interesting shadows on the wall behind, and the tension-wire balustrade with its tubular handrail makes powerful, diagonal slashes through the air.

Sketch some ideas and take your inspiration from a variety of sources.
For example, take a good look at the buildings you regularly visit, check
out hotels, museums, restaurants, banks — anywhere that might have used
materials in interesting combinations or unusual ways. Do some initial
research on how much things might cost — it will insulate you from severe
shocks later — and collect together product brochures or use the World Wide
Web and visit as many relevant sites as you can find.

You might opt for a simple palette, exploiting just a handful of different
finishing materials. This approach not only provides the opportunity for you to
buy in bulk, and so perhaps save some money, it also holds out the possibility
of a crisper result than you might achieve by cramming together a wide
variety of materials. Bear in mind, too, how this new-look space will
accommodate your old-look furniture. The more you know about what
you want, the easier it will be to communicate this to a designer, builder,
or architect, and the less chance there will be of them misunderstanding
or, worse still, improvising.

With a box full of brochures and samples, it is time to find somebody
to see the work through to completion. Ask friends for recommendations
for builders or architects, and perhaps also try professional bodies (in most
countries, you will be able to obtain a shortlist of architects' or builders'
names from the relevant professional bodies or governing organizations).
Before signing up, insist on seeing references, and then take them up; ask for
the names and addresses of clients they have worked for within the last three

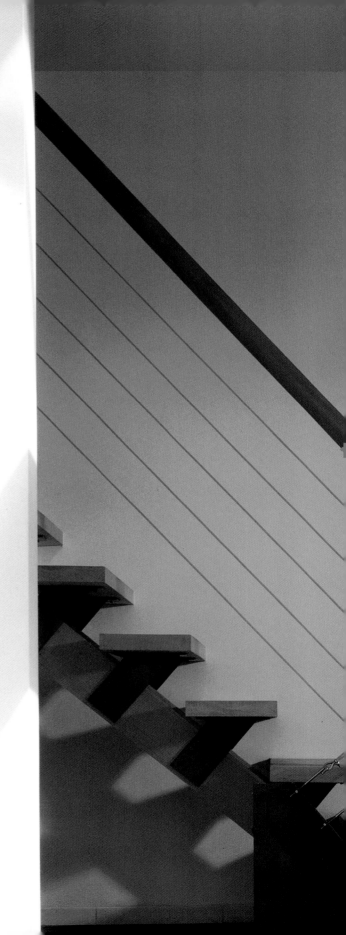

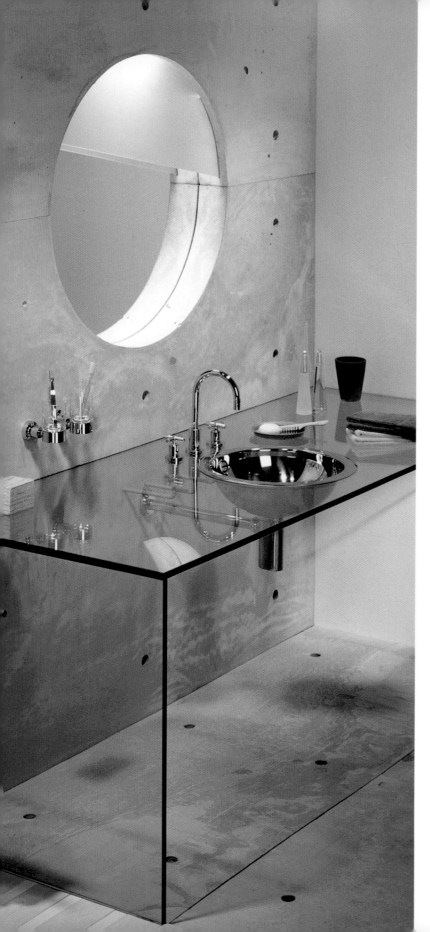

years and ask if you can go and see the work they have done. Be sure to get at least three quotes for the work, but don't automatically opt for the cheapest one — make a judgement on value for money and the quality of the ideas. And make certain that you like the person and that you can communicate easily together — you will be entrusting them with much of your future happiness, not to mention money.

When considering the budget, discuss the finishes and fittings to be used, and bear in mind that good quality always comes at a price. If you are planning on installing stone floors, for example, it is likely to cost considerably more than choosing simple pine floorboards that are suitable for staining and varnishing. Bills have a tendency to mount up at an alarming rate — even putting in something as rudimentary as a kitchen sink can see costs spiral if you select a particularly high-quality stainless-steel unit and a set of well-crafted, beautifully designed taps. If your budget is tight, then decide in advance on your priorities — you might be prepared to save money on kitchen cabinets by opting for a composite particle board for the backs, sides, and any hidden shelves, for example, in order to have exactly the right counter tops, cabinet doors, and drawer fronts. Always build in a contingency sum — perhaps as much as twenty per cent of the total quoted price — to cater for the unexpected. And always expect the unexpected.

One potentially useful way of offsetting huge bills is to buy some items second hand or to visit salvage yards. And you might also choose to spend some time thinking about how environmentally friendly you can or want to be.

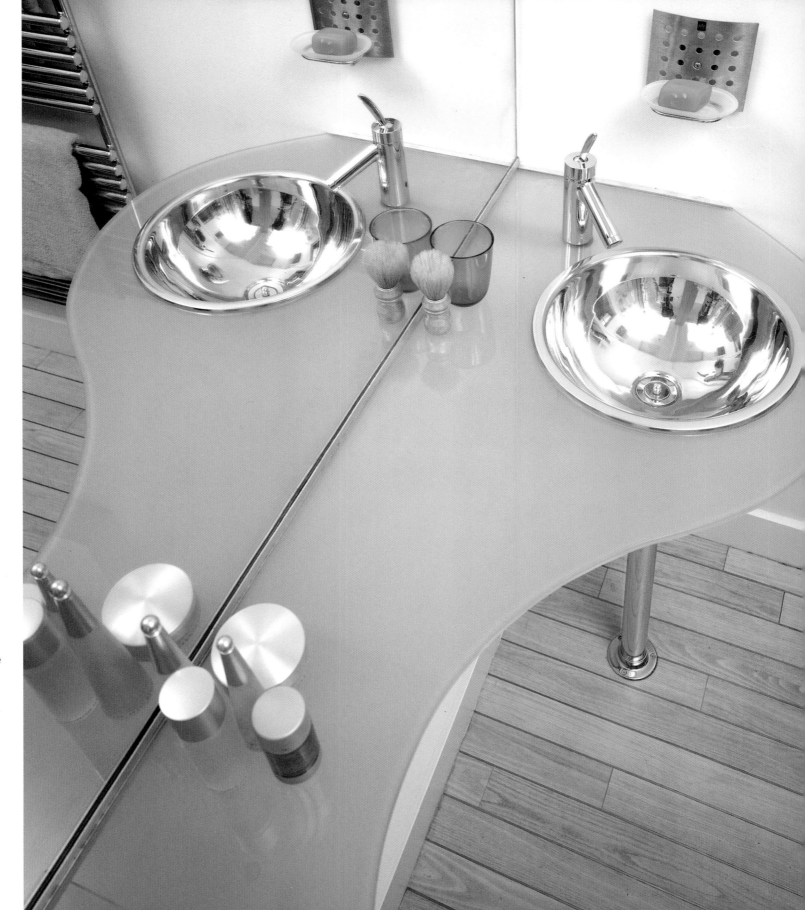

→ Masses of interesting details combine to make this room, by Anne Hunter Interiors, a delight. Where the timber flooring meets the wall, any slight unevenness at the edges has been disguised by the narrow beading strip; the stainless-steel bowl is wrapped around with its curvy, tailor-made, sandblasted glass counter; and the tap is set into the corner to make best use of the confined space.

← In this exercise in precise detailing, a stainless-steel bowl sits in a glass-topped cabinet against a backdrop of sheer concrete. The circular mirror, with its "eyelid" of frosted glass to diffuse the light, echoes the basin shape, and so too does the Dornbracht stainless-steel tap spout from the Tara collection.

The situation has improved dramatically in recent years, with so many do-it-yourself outlets and builders yards now able to supply information on where their products have come from, and offering items that are considered to have a greener bill of health than others. For example, readily available now are products such as low-odour paints and varnishes. These are much safer, and far more pleasant to use than the old-style versions, leaving fewer choking fumes behind. It is also worthwhile asking from where timber is sourced, especially if you are using tropical hardwood, to make sure it comes from recognized, sustainable, and well-managed plantations.

If you want to be a truly responsible consumer and as environmentally friendly as possible, there are now eco builders' merchants in many areas, and there are also vast amounts of information to be found about green building products on various Internet web sites. You might also want to encompass water and energy efficiency by investigating the energy rating of new electrical appliances such as refrigerators and the water usage rates of washing machines and dishwashers, or you might even consider installing solar panels to generate at least some of your own domestic power requirements.

Whatever you are looking for, remember that the small details do matter – so be persistent and optimistic, and keep on looking until you are completely satisfied. Whatever it is you are searching for, it is sure to be out there somewhere.

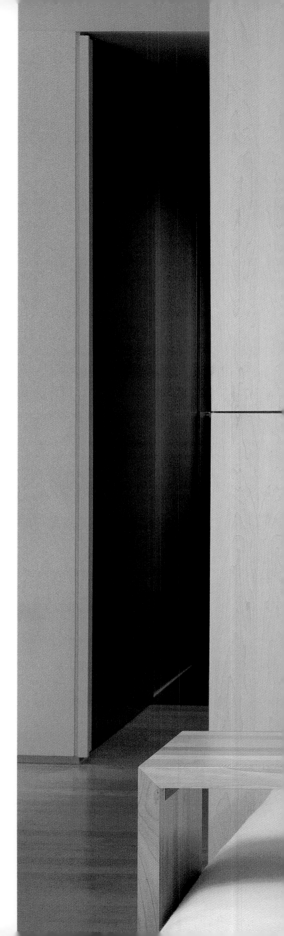

→ A good eye for detail makes the best possible use of this bedroom space, with its built-in storage units and wardrobes, a recessed bookshelf with reading lights, and a simple, full-width table spanning the bed.

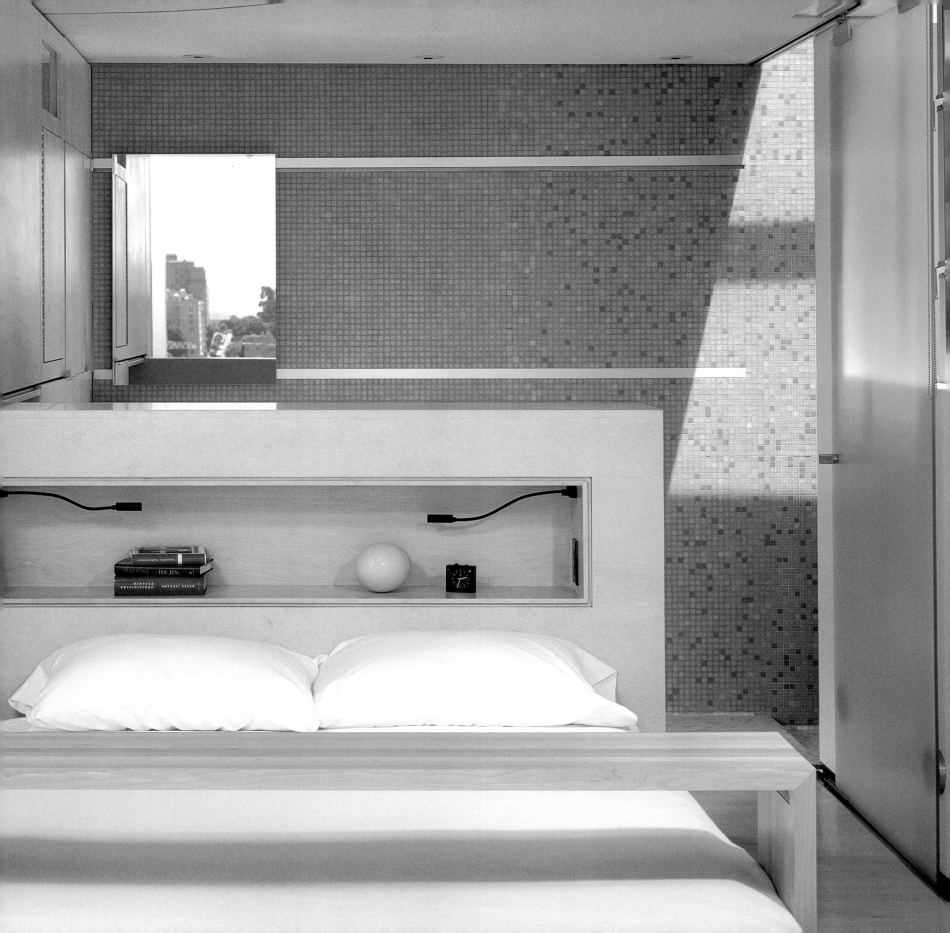

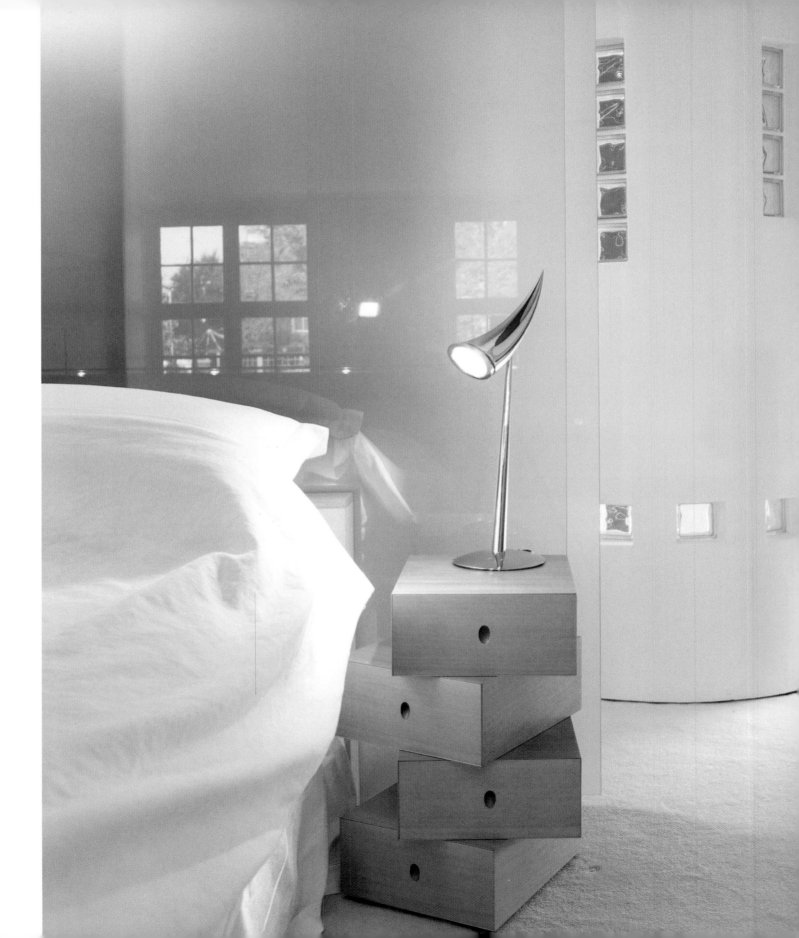

walls

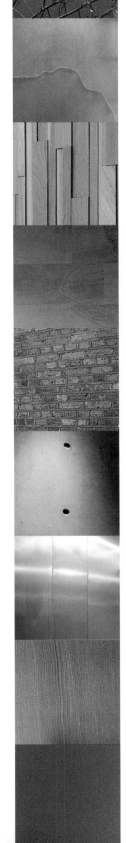

← A subtle combination of shapes and materials adds intrigue to this serene bedroom. The bed is separated from the bathroom space by a simple floor-to-ceiling translucent glass screen and sliding glass door (shown open). The entrance to the bathroom is marked by the curved wall studded with glass bricks. This imaginative use of glass ensures that natural light flows through the rooms.

The modern architecture movement of the twentieth century has almost systematically seen to the demise of the substantial, upright, floor-to-ceiling wall. While the exterior envelope of any building still has to perform the basic functions of providing shelter from the weather and protection from intruders, the familiar masonry and clapboard have gradually been replaced by larger and larger expanses of glass. It has been some time now since this reached its apotheosis in a house with no solid walls — the transparent design comprised glass roof, glass walls, glass floors, glass doors, and, of course, glass windows.

Ever since early twentieth-century architects, including the American Frank Lloyd Wright, showed us the pleasures of open-plan living areas, solid walls inside the home, just as those outside, have fallen from favour. The effect has been to make room "boxes" seem old-fashioned and restrictive. Our urge has been to bust open living spaces and blur boundaries between areas with different functions — the kitchen and dining room, the kitchen/dining room and garden, and, more recently, the bedroom and bathroom. However, despite this, there are still times when the division of space is appropriate, and many occupants of agoraphobia-inducing, open-plan loft apartments have sought ways to mark out different areas and reintroduce new types of wall. Sometimes, a huge sheet of glass will act as a partition; at others, a simple divider inspired by the Japanese paper shoji screen does the trick. Walls no longer have to span from floor to ceiling — a suggestion of a barrier, such as a room divider shelf-unit, is enough. And there are times when we still welcome the idea of enclosure — a waist-height counter to separate a kitchen or perhaps a curved wall to "embrace" a dining area.

transparency

Along with our ready acceptance of open-plan domestic interiors, two major factors have been at work in shaping and forever changing the inside of our homes: the long quest to bring ever more natural light into our homes, and a fascination with transparency.

In the second half of the twentieth century, the fashion for picture windows, for light and views, was accompanied by an enthusiasm for knocking down interior walls, for light and space. More recently, the allure of transparency has been pushed to new extremes, with whole areas of exterior wall being replaced by massive plate-glass panels or glazed doors that fold back to dissolve the barrier between inside and out.

Alongside this development, manufacturing and building technologies have advanced to such an extent that fewer walls are needed to make buildings stand up, with the result that many internal walls can disappear altogether, or be reduced to a slender screen of glass or Perspex. The response to this change has been inventive, with the imaginative exploitation of panels of glass brick, sheets of transparent and translucent glass, and rigid plastic sheeting. These all perform a range of different functions, from separating spaces and making internal windows, to opening up long internal vistas, or perhaps creating exciting shimmering screens.

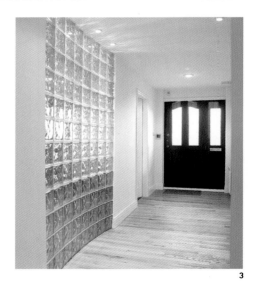

2

← In this project, the frosted glass walls have an ethereal quality, shimmering under the artificial light and providing an intriguing backdrop to the seating area. Through the glass are hints of colours and shapes – even the structural beam supporting the upper floor.

↓ Our desire to open up and create vistas constantly tests the ingenuity of architects and designers. Here, architect Mark Guard adds a two-panel glass balustrade to a flight of stairs. With glimpses outward as you climb, there are reminders of the continuity of the space with the linking colour scheme and chunky structural, studded steel post.

→ Panels of glass bricks can be an exciting intervention in a domestic space. In this example, the glass wall makes the hall appear larger, and certainly lighter, than would be the case with masonry. And interior glass bricks also provide enticing glimpses through to the space beyond. The artificial lighting is interesting here, too – recessed ceiling fittings provide a wash of illumination down the wallface, which makes it appear to glow when seen from the inside.

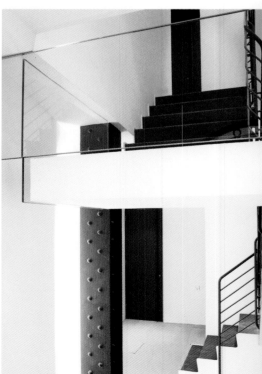

3

4

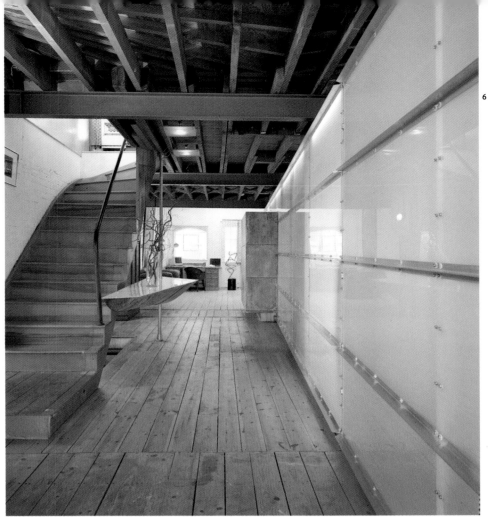

6

← Opal polycarbonate panels sandwiched between horizontal aluminium "T" sections have combined to form this long wall. The architect, Fraser Brown McKenna, chose polycarbonate over glass because the plastic is cheaper, lighter, and easier to handle.

↓ The beauty and strength of glass are explored in the exterior wall of this garden room by The Architects Practice. To make strong corner posts, small strips of 18-mm (¾-in) glass were laid horizontally in a tower and laminated together, and toughened glass was used for the windows.

5

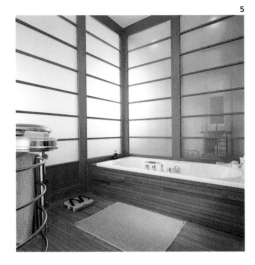

↑ In this contemporary interpretation of the Japanese shoji paper screen, an elegant glass and timber enclosure wraps around the bath, providing privacy as well as the suggestion of light and space beyond the barrier. The pattern of long, horizontal divisions in the screen is echoed in the timber panelling along the side of the tub, endowing the interior with a sense of peace and calm.

→ Floor-to-ceiling sliding glass screens are used to separate the kitchen and dining areas. The glass is held top and bottom in aluminium frames, which glide open and shut in ceiling and floor channels. The architecture practice D'Soto has employed a glass theme throughout the space, with a thick, plate-glass table top, glass kitchen splashback, and glass canopy over the extractor vent.

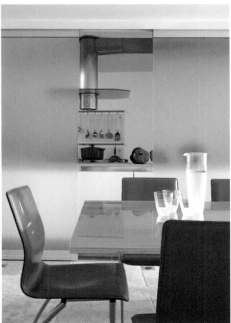

7

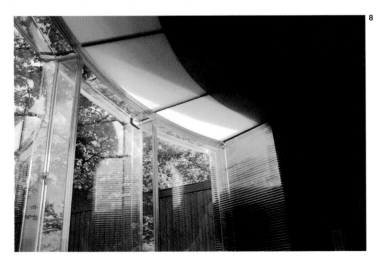

8

9

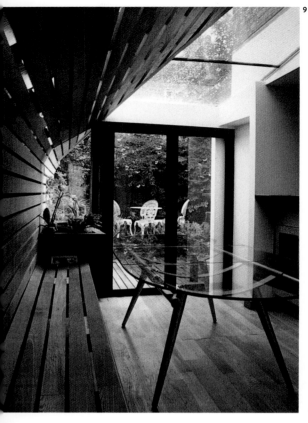

← From floor to seat to wall to ceiling, this sweep of oak planking wraps the garden room extension before bursting upward to the sky through a glass-panel roof. The oak continues outside to link the interior with the exterior deck. The architect is Frankl + Luty.

→ Even when it is painted, wood imparts tremendous warmth and character to a room. Here, interior decorator Ann Boyd lines the walls of the bathroom entirely with white-painted vertical boards. These stand in contrast to the dark-stained deal floorboards, their grain still visible.

→ The hard-edged industrial tone of this apartment is offset by the use of natural materials. Architect Renato Benedetti, of McDowell & Benedetti, created an entire kitchen wall of strips of African walnut in different thicknesses to create an irregular effect. The dining table and bench are made from a composite material of softwood chips bonded with resin that is usually used for structural beams (see picture 12).

10

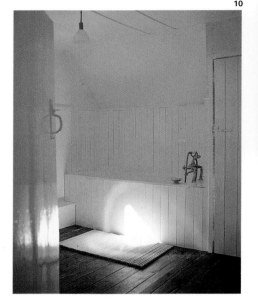

11

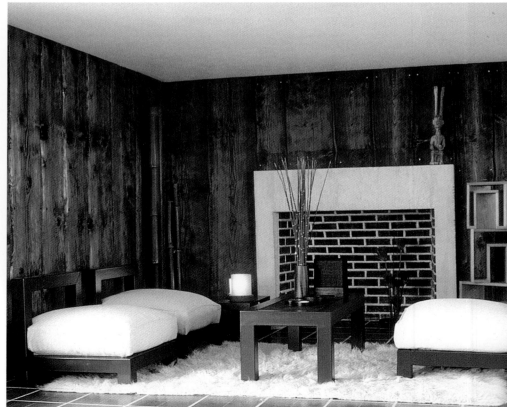

↓ In such an apparently controlled and precise interior, the intervention of the vividly patterned raw timber lining the walls has an almost shocking effect. The broad planks of wood stand in complete contrast to the highly finished, black-lacquered furniture and the grid of floor tiles, but they find a companion in the unruliness of the shag-pile rug. The whole effect is of a modernist log cabin.

13

→ A close-up of the McDowell & Benedetti use of pale African walnut (see picture 11). The wood was prepared in strips 40, 50, and 60 cm (16, 20, and 24 in) long, and also in thicknesses of 3, 9, 12, and 15 mm (⅛, ⅓, ½ and ⅝ in). It was then fixed to the wall to make this intriguing subtle, abstract, bas-relief effect. The walnut was left in its natural cut state and remains untreated.

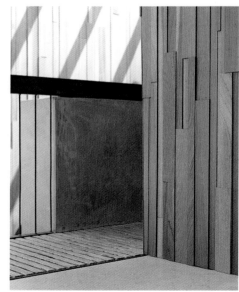

12

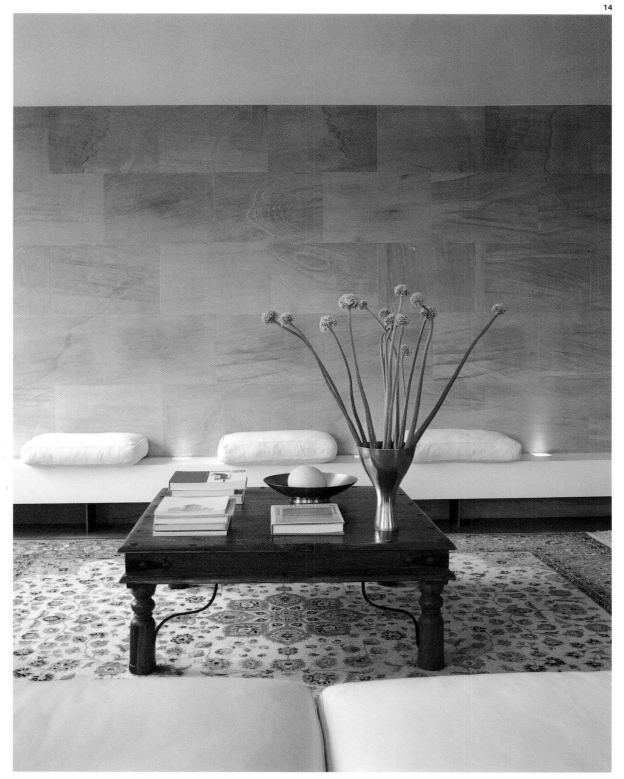

14

wooden walls

In an age when there is so much around us that is synthetic and manufactured, it is reassuring to see and feel and smell real wood. Perhaps our imaginations are stirred because wood is a reminder of a simpler past; maybe it is the knowledge that this beautiful and intriguing material was once a living, growing thing; or perhaps it is a nostalgia for the hand-crafted log cabin or timber-framed house.

The creative potential of using wood in our homes is in no doubt — whether it is for lining walls or laying as floors, there is vast palette of colours and beautiful patterns ranging from vivid, flaming, tropical hardwoods to subtle, finely-grained American and European timbers. They can also be used in a variety of ways, with finishes ranging from rough and untreated to those that are highly polished or painted.

However, because the choice of wood on offer is now so wide, including a large number of unusual hardwoods, it is advisable to ask about its source before buying. For years we were told to avoid tropical hardwoods, for fear that the lucrative, and often illegal, timber trade was destroying ancient rainforests; now, however, it is possible to source well-managed, sustainable supplies, where trees are replaced for future generations.

← The low-level seating, table and lighting in this room by architect Ian Chee create a powerful sense of serenity. The neutral colours help the overall effect, as does the low-level uplighting recessed into the bench. The natural texture of the Indian sandstone wall, free of artwork, also underlines the tranquillity of the space.

special features

The enthusiasm for replacing walls with glass, or for removing many of them altogether, has had the unexpected effect of giving extra significance to those walls that remain. Where there are walls, why not make the most of them — they are, after all, the backdrop to our everyday life and activities?

The main considerations for wall treatments are colour, pattern, and texture, and all three have an important contribution to make to the mood of a room. For serenity and calm, expanses of plain, neutral shades are difficult to beat, while interest and accents can be added with items such as paintings and furniture. For drama, choose intense, rich colours.

However, the extra dimensions at our disposal through the use of pattern and texture remain to be fully explored. In this regard, experiments with interesting materials should not be overlooked, especially when they can be used in unexpected ways. A panel of colourful ceramic or glinting mosaic tiles can add an exotic element to an interior, while stone and marble bring grandeur, and wood panelling a sense of luxury. But we should not feel restricted just to the familiar themes — the palette extends far beyond these finishes. For example, a leather-clad wall is intriguing, warm, and sophisticated, while sheets of riveted metal create a hard-edged, industrial feel. Other possibilities include sheet plywood, textured wallpapers, cloth, and even entire wall-sized installations of light panels that glow and pulsate through the colours of the spectrum.

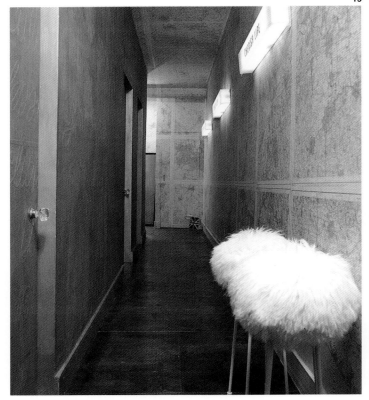

15

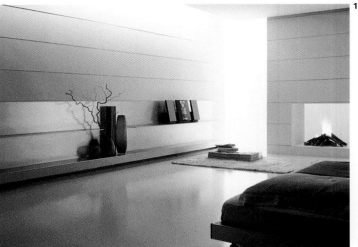

16

↓ Architect Hawkins Brown converted a former glassworks into apartments and, as a reminder of the building's industrial past, a single exposed-brick wall has been left, complete with its cast-iron tie disc — a device used to brace structures that are potentially unstable. The earthy textures of the brick offer an appealing contrast with the wholly domestic interior furnishings and white-linen bedclothes.

↑ In this flamboyant apartment, which was created by a film and television producer, even the circulation areas are given lavish treatment. Since this passageway provides a route to and from different places in the apartment, this theme has been enhanced by smothering one entire wall, and the ceiling, in the detailed graphics of British Ordnance Survey maps. On the facing wall, the gold finish features beautiful oversize copperplate calligraphy.

17

↑ Long horizontal lines of benches, cupboards, or seating really do create a laid-back, serene atmosphere. Here, the neutral colours and use of stone and glass contribute to the creation of an atmosphere of intense restfulness. The fitted cupboards are by EmmeBi.

↓ Using leather to line walls is a reinterpretation of an ancient idea. Here, the leather bears the incised and painted pattern of an intricate map. The use of an expensive material such as leather creates a tremendous sense of luxury, especially when it is enhanced by flecks of gold leaf.

18

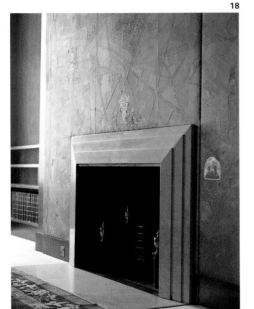

→ The fashion and interior designer Bill Amberg is renowned for his use of leather. Here, an entire sweep of corridor wall is lined with rich chestnut-brown, rectangular leather tiles. The dramatic effect is enhanced by lighting inset at the top of the wall and washing down over the face of the leather.

↓ Centralizing the bath is dramatic enough, but lining the side of the tub and the wall behind with jade-green mosaic tiles makes bathing a real event. A fetching detail is the use of a random sprinkling of tiny gold mosaic tiles in the upper section of the wall.

19

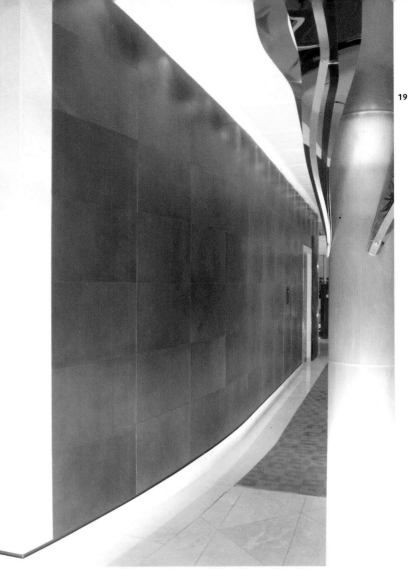

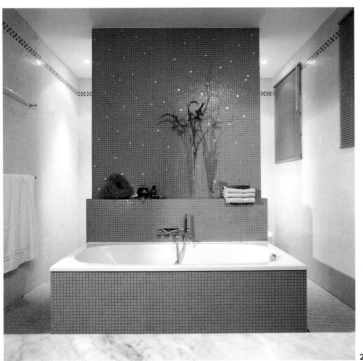

20

→ Designer Bill Amberg uses traditional oak-bark tanned leather, which can be coloured to suit the client's preferences. Just about any surface can be covered, including walls and doors. Where two pieces of leather join, they are simply "laced" together with stitching, which in this example, produces a meandering trail across the surface.

21

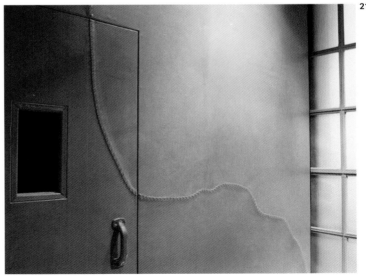

22

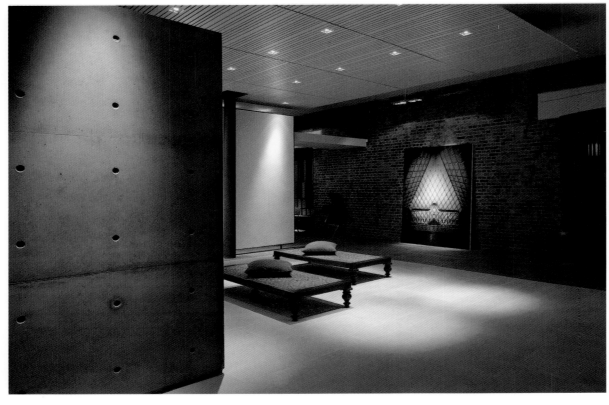

23

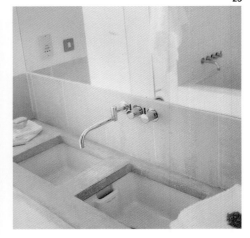

↑ Raw, exposed concrete is not usually associated with domestic interiors – and particularly not with bathrooms – but this converted school house project by Studio MG Architects incorporates a skilful piece of concrete casting to make a counter top for two deep sinks.

25

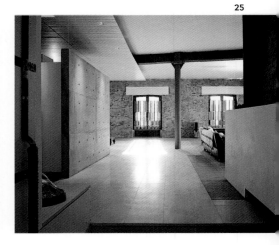

↑ Despite being championed by many modernist and brutalist architects, concrete was until recent years associated only with decaying public housing, and remained a thoroughly unloved material. Squalor is now replaced by high sophistication. Architecture practice Patel Taylor demonstrates the beauty of smooth, cast concrete in this highly controlled interior. The satin-sleek finish stands in contrast to the rough brickwork opposite, and dramatic downlighting lends the concrete wall a brooding presence.

→ This vista is reminiscent of an abstract monochrome collage, featuring large expanses of glazing wrapping around the exterior wall, a concrete post by the entrance, metal-mesh balustrading, and a half-height, white-plastered wall. All of these details and elements are set against a stunning blue-grey slate floor.

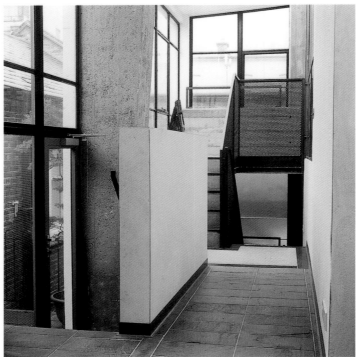

24

↑ With this clever use of three-quarter- and half-height internal walls, the architects at Patel Taylor have demonstrated how a large, open-plan space can be organized into different areas. Even with the partitioning, plenty of natural light is drawn into and through the deep space.

→ In this sumptuous bathroom, the thick cast-glass sink, by glass artist Jeff Bell, sits almost like a modern font on top of a square-hewn block of Kirkstone silvergreen slate. The plinth is made of the same material as the walls in this project by architect Fiona McLean, of McLean Quinlan.

27

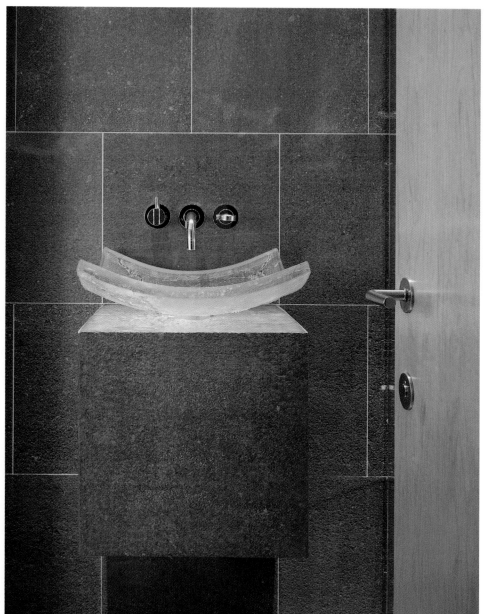

→ In their own house, German architects Gerhard G and Yong Sun Feldmeyer have built a stairway that incorporates a mixture of materials to filter and reflect light. At the foot of the stairs, the wall has been opened up with a full-length panel of glass bricks drawing light into the stairwell, which has a concrete wall on one side and delicate steel mesh on the other. The mesh takes the place of a balustrade.

26

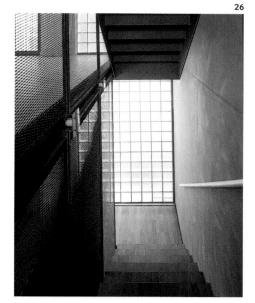

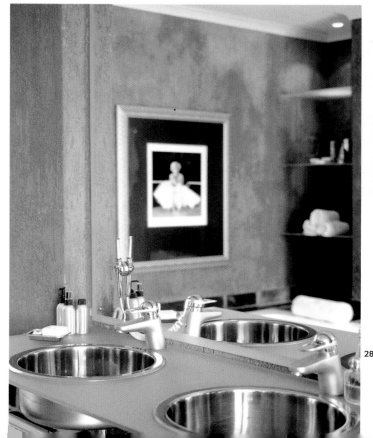

← The rough texture of the concrete walls provides an interestingly tactile backdrop to the exquisitely finished stainless-steel wash basins and their etched-glass counter top. The restricted colour palette is very subtly handled, with grey walls and inset glass-block window, a large mirror, complete with its reflection of a black and white picture, and the chromed taps and washstand.

28

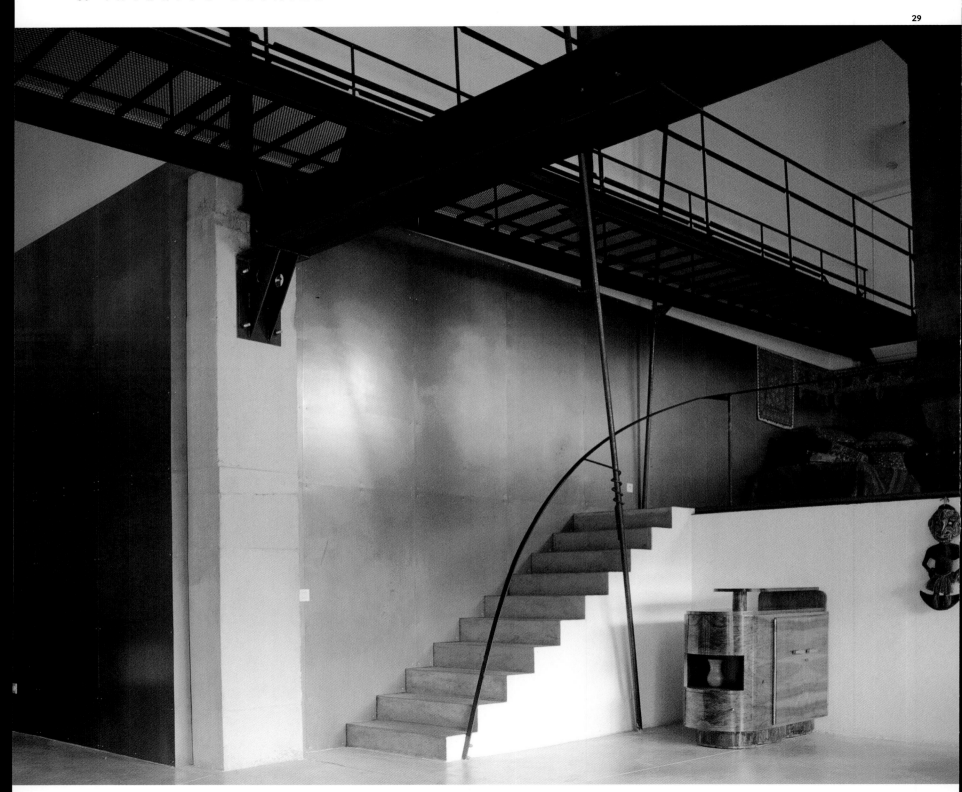

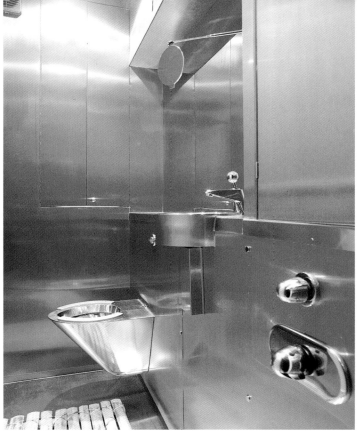

↑ The almost clinical finish of stainless steel is used to great effect in this lavatory and shower room. The walls are entirely lined with sheet stainless steel, but secreted behind the flush surface are the cupboards and plumbing. Designer Martin Walker has only once broken the stainless-steel spell – with the addition of a bamboo shower mat.

← A cavernous industrial-style interior is given detail and texture to draw the eye through the space. Walls are clad in enormous sheets of riveted, matt-finish metal, there are huge exposed girders, and a metal walkway spans the space.

30 ↓ A playful theme of circular shapes features in this bathroom. The white porcelain basin, made by Duravit, has been set against a wallpaper background printed with a repeat pattern of tiny circles. And above this is fixed the bathroom cabinet with its rounded corners and off-centre circular mirror.

31

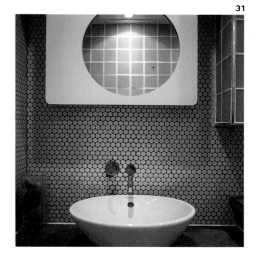

unusual materials

The impact of unusual materials can be powerful and rewarding, as well as being an expression of your personality and individuality. However, in order to use these materials successfully, it is essential that they are professionally applied or installed.

Of course, with ideas such as using maps as wallpaper, the pitfalls are likely to be fewer than when it comes to cladding an entire wall in metal sheeting. But in most instances, style innovation requires a measure of research and a great deal of preparation.

In practical terms, this means allowing time to source your material, to find out whether and how it has been used before, and to be certain that it will produce the desired effect. Some metal finishes, for example, may be susceptible to rust in damp environments. This may be exactly what you want, but it is just as well to find out before installation. Another consideration is maintenance, for example stainless steel, especially when used in a kitchen or bathroom, will collect unattractive limestone blemishes. The advice here would be to choose another material, fit a water softener, or be prepared to invest plenty of effort in cleaning. These may be rather mundane considerations, but an uninformed choice will almost certainly result in an expensive and disappointing mistake.

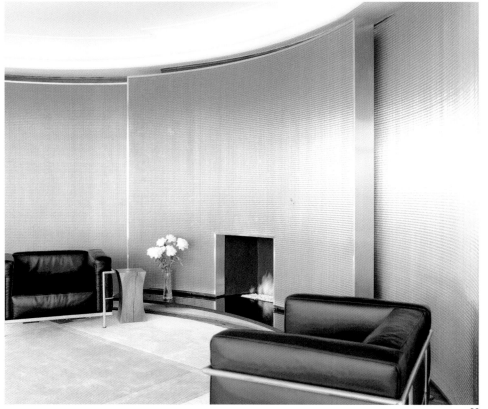

← A highly unusual effect by architecture practice Munkenbeck + Marshall is this finely woven metal-mesh cladding with its seductively soft sheen, which wraps itself around the gently curved walls.

32

→ This white-upholstered chair sits against an unusual textured backdrop of rust-coloured cord-effect paint by United Colours of Benetton Paint Colours and Effects. The effect is achieved in a two-stage application: the base colour is applied then dragged into raised lines with a cord brush.

↓ The revival of interest in wallpapers means that makers have been trying new finishes and textures. Here, Muraspec has created a speckled silvery paper called Meteor Storm – a vinyl material with real sparkling metal fragments.

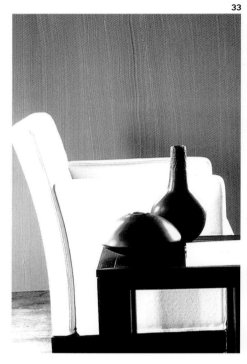

33

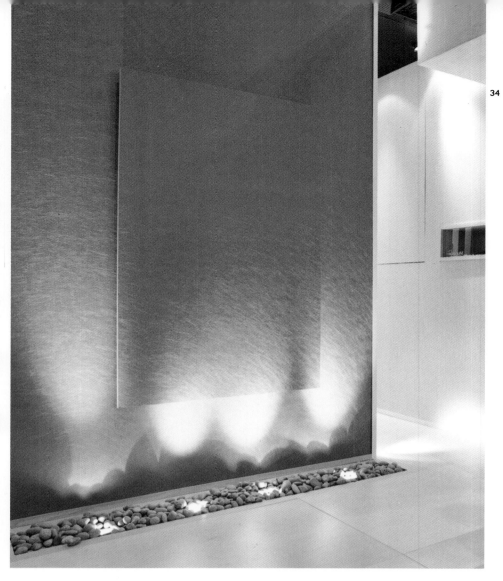

34

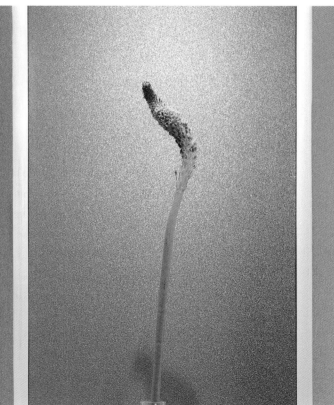

35

↑ This textured wallcovering is called Fusion and comes from the specialist manufacturer Muraspec. It is laminated for extra rigidity and has been given an intriguing printed metallic finish.

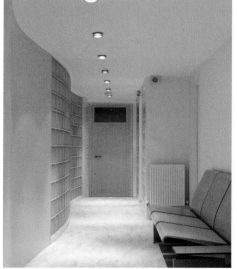

36

← When architect Peter Thomas de Cruz was asked to introduce interest and light into this dark basement corridor, he added a wavy wall inset with a panel of glass bricks. The wall opposite also features glass bricks and is at the bottom of a lightwell. Now light flows across from the well to the other wall and then into the area behind. A sunny yellow paint was chosen to give the whole space a lift.

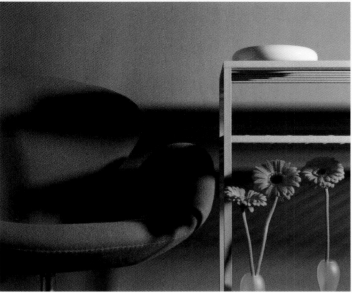

37

← Lewis and Wood has achieved this lovely soft, matt-surfaced wall finish using a rich-coloured paper-backed felt material. The period look is completed with the 1958-designed Swan chair by Danish designer Arne Jacobsen.

↓ Elements is an entirely natural wallcovering material composed of paper and finished in woven grasses. This retro look, from the manufacturer Muraspec, conjures up textured wallcoverings from the 1950s and 1960s.

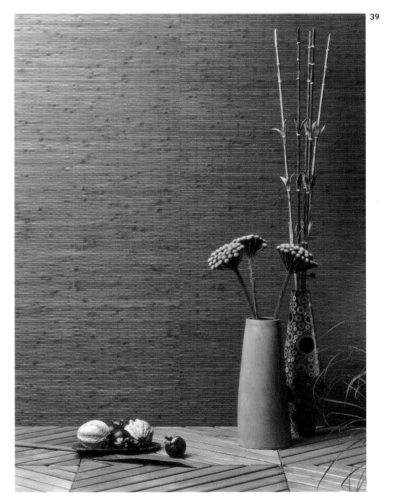

39

← Demonstrating that walls don't have to be upright and true, architect Michael Wilford has added a bizarrely shaped, sculptural, lilac-painted larder into this kitchen. The walls incline inward and then wriggle around the corner before making an exciting junction with the ceiling.

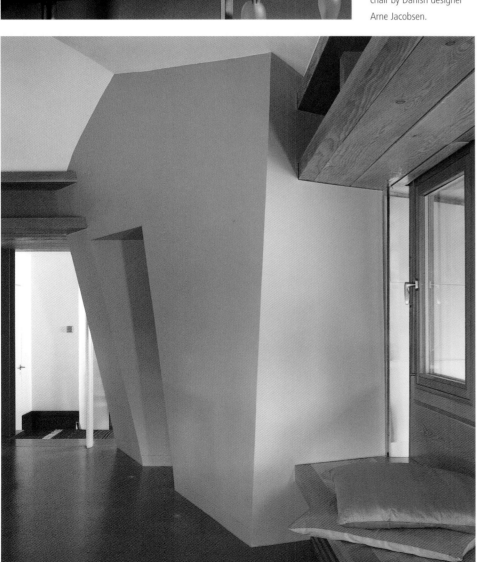

38

ceilings

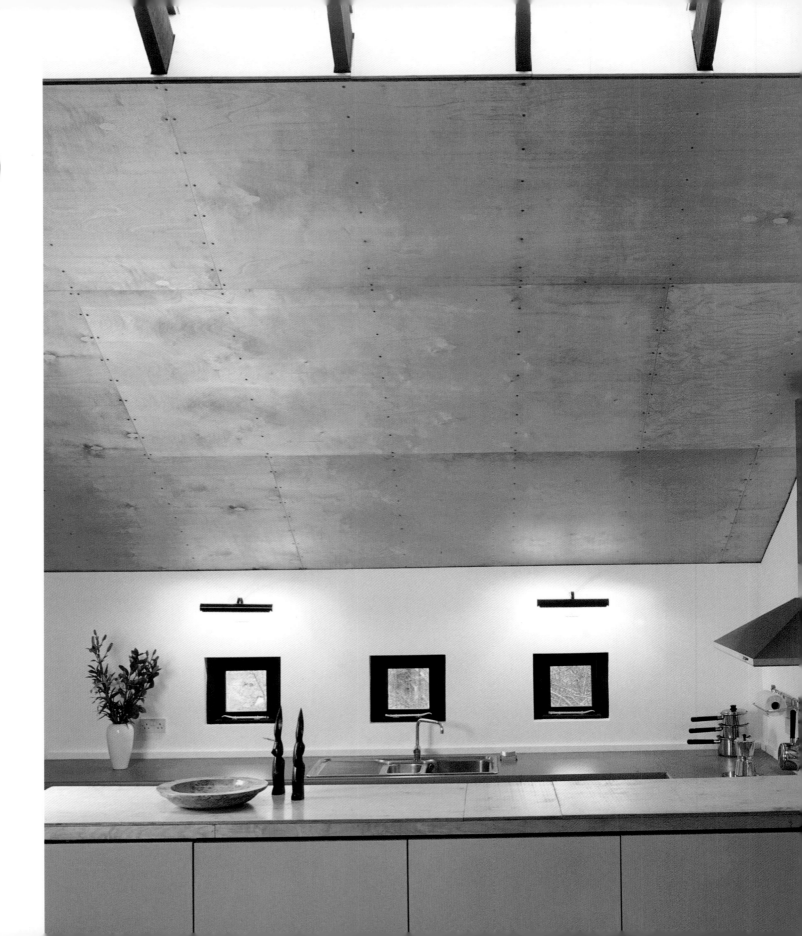

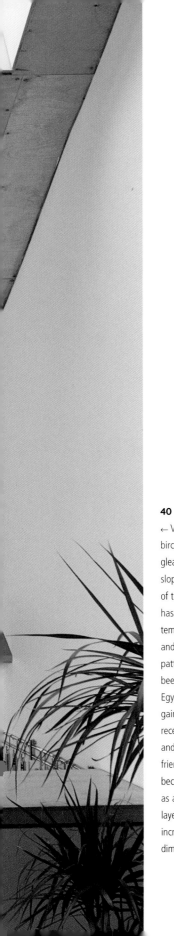

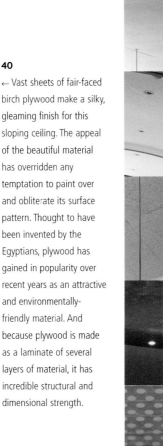

O nce a surface embellished with elaborate plaster mouldings and adorned with richly painted decoration, the ceiling has become the real Cinderella of the modern interior. In most homes, look up and you are greeted with a blank white sheet. It is modest, attracts almost no attention, and functions as little more than a barrier between floors and as a useful reflective surface for bouncing light around the interior.

Even in the most highly finished rooms, there is rarely any attempt to re-create the glamour and glories of the past. However, in recent years designers and architects have experimented with manipulating the shape and form of ceilings to change and enhance mood. To take two extreme examples of how ceilings can be used: high ceilings are immediately associated with grand spaces, great halls, or rooms intended for entertaining; low ceilings are used more to create a sense of calm and intimacy.

In between these two extremes, there are plenty of variations to be explored. The high, barrel-vaulted ceiling has a structural tension that is excitingly unusual, for example, and high ceilings may incorporate lowered sections for interesting internal landscaping or to act as rafts studded with recessed lighting. And as the upper parts of buildings are opened up to the sky and the traditional dingy attic disappears, in its stead are found sloping ceilings that echo the shape of the roofline and are studded with windows.

40

← Vast sheets of fair-faced birch plywood make a silky, gleaming finish for this sloping ceiling. The appeal of the beautiful material has overridden any temptation to paint over and obliterate its surface pattern. Thought to have been invented by the Egyptians, plywood has gained in popularity over recent years as an attractive and environmentally-friendly material. And because plywood is made as a laminate of several layers of material, it has incredible structural and dimensional strength.

glass ceilings

Even a small panel of glass in a ceiling can draw a welcome stream of sunlight into the interior. Of course, direct light at roof level is ideal – whether it is the roof of an extension or an upper floor of a building – but, increasingly, interior design schemes include glass panels set into floors so that light can flow down through the entire height of a house.

The main considerations when adding glass ceilings are weight and heat gain. Glass is a deceptively heavy material, especially when used in large, laminated panels – it takes a lot of effort for an adult to carry a single square metre (square yard) of laminated material, even at a thickness of only 12 mm (½ in).

Thus, when incorporating large expanses of glass it is vital to make sure the building structure can support the extra load. Take advice from an architect, engineer, or the local authority's building regulations office on the types of glass recommended for your project. Regulations vary from country to country, but there are important safety distinctions between toughened and laminated glass. There are also recommended thicknesses for different jobs.

And finally, where there is more sunlight, there is bound to be more heat. Glass is now produced with a range of coatings that are designed to reduce heat gain while preventing heat loss, thus avoiding great temperature swings inside the building. Another option is to select glass that with photovoltaic panels, designed to convert light to electrical power – so you will be able to make the most of the sun's light and energy.

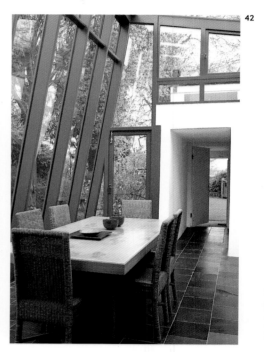

41

↓ The glass wall of this contemporary-style dining room extension turns the corner at cornice level to become the room's sloping ceiling. The use of the same glass-and-steel system for both the wall and ceiling produces a pleasing aesthetic continuity.

42

↑ To provide natural light over the kitchen working area, the designer removed the top corner of the wall and replaced it with a lightbox of glass. It is an ideal solution where light is important but you do not want to be overlooked.

→ This townhouse, by 51% studios, culminates in a bedroom where the ceiling and roof have been removed and replaced with sheet glass. The result is a light-filled "sky room", which can be used all year round.

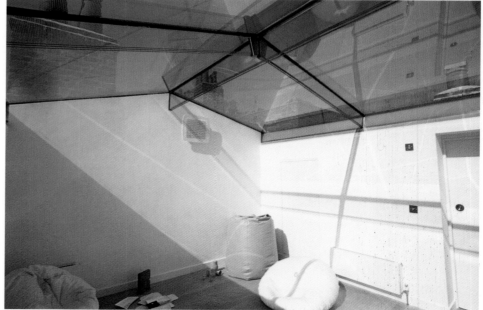

43

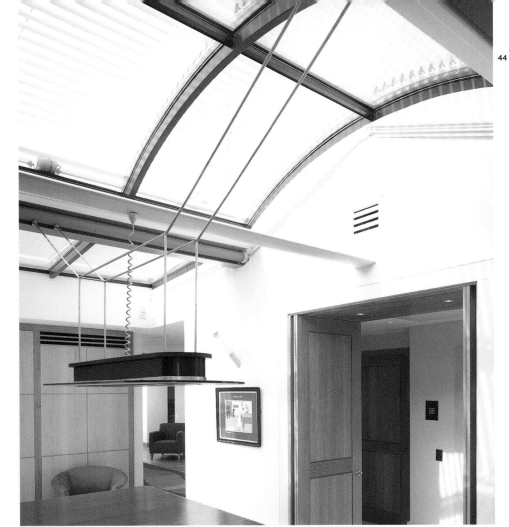

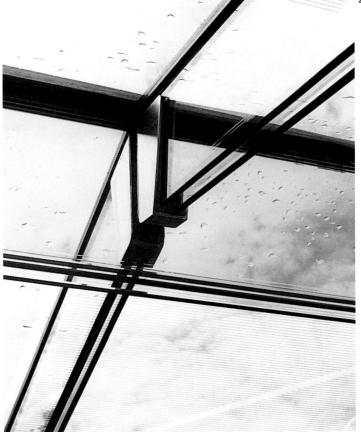

↑ In this large apartment, The Architects Practice has designed a dramatic vaulted ceiling using two layers of laminated glass. The surface has a solar coating to shield the interior from the hot sunshine, while externally-fixed slatted blinds offer extra protection.

→ To bring useful natural light into this kitchen, architect Peter Bernamonta has designed a large ceiling panel made with long, slim, obscured-glass beams.

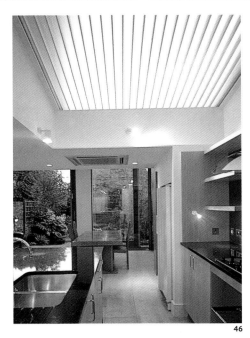

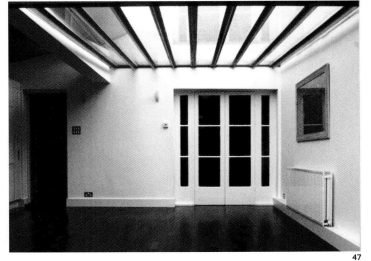

↑ This glazed ceiling, made with glass panels fixed in long, slim, rectangular frames, brings welcome natural light deep within this building. The architect was Arthur Colin.

46

47

↑ This detailed shot shows the glass sheets and rafters forming the roof of The Greenhouse (see picture 43). This roof is of a traditional design, except that glass rather than timber has been used. The 10mm (0.4 in) toughened glass is made in frameless double-glazed units and the rafters are hung by custom-made stainless-steel joist hangers. This is the family home of architects Catherine du Toit and Peter Thomas, of 51% Studios.

48

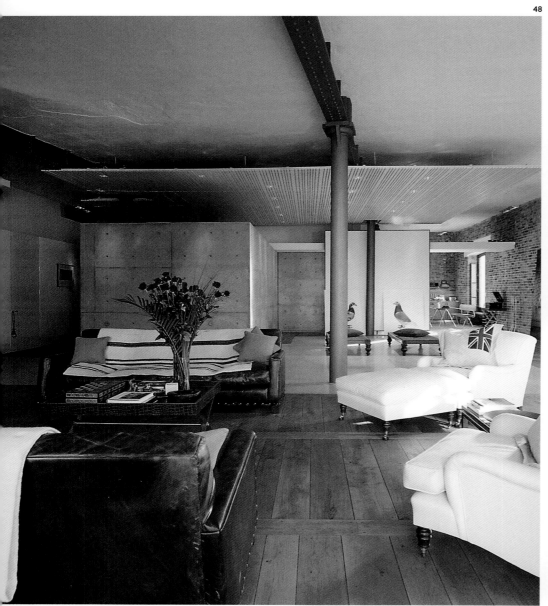

49

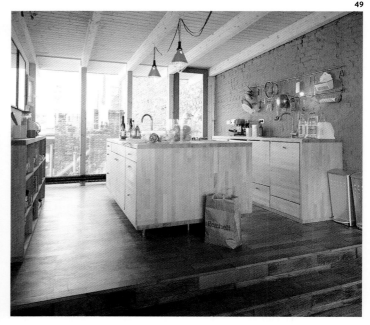

↑ Natural wood is a major feature in this modern, light-filled kitchen. In tune with the pale timber of the floor-standing storage units and work surfaces, the wood-beamed ceiling has also been left in its natural state. To achieve a satisfying visual effect, care has been taken to ensure that the ceiling beams follow the line of the upright posts used for the window.

50

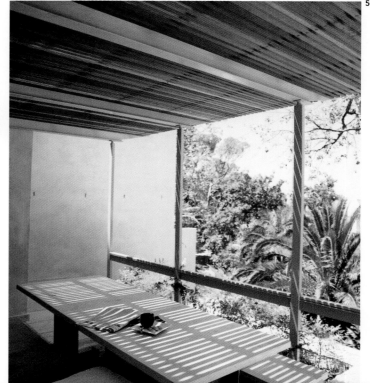

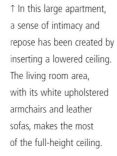

↑ In this large apartment, a sense of intimacy and repose has been created by inserting a lowered ceiling. The living room area, with its white upholstered armchairs and leather sofas, makes the most of the full-height ceiling.

→ This small verandah is given extra protection from the effects of bright sunlight by the panels of slatted timber that make up the ceiling. A pleasing pattern of dappled light falls on the table and diners below.

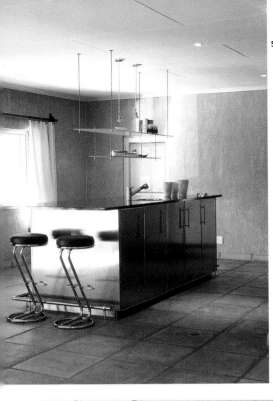

51

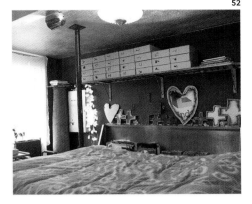

52

← What might have been a plain, unremarkable white ceiling has been given a more interesting treatment with this finish of large rectangular panels. The ceiling also features recessed, low-voltage, halogen lighting, and from the centre of the space, an elegant lighting raft has been suspended directly over the island worktop area to provide task lighting.

← The gothic style of this bedroom, with its blue-black walls, rugged metal shelving, and blood-red bed cover, has been carried through with an appropriately unusual ceiling finish of silver metallic paint.

colours and finishes

The ceiling is just about the last major element in the modern interior to have attracted the attention of the designer. Although it is not always possible to introduce interesting and unusual shapes when the ceiling is a fixed, horizontal plane, there are nevertheless opportunities to introduce beautiful finishes.

Colour and finish are no longer restricted to just plain, white-painted plaster. Light colours give a bright and airy feeling, even in fairly small rooms and a pale wall colour can often be continued across the ceiling, instead of breaking into plain white. However, in larger rooms, a more daring palette can be accommodated. Why not, for example, experiment with rich wall colours – perhaps a burgundy or purple – continued on the ceiling? This creates the effect of being immersed entirely in colour. Colour can also alter the perceived dimensions of a room, with a dark ceiling teamed with light-coloured walls having the effect of lowering the apparent height.

When it comes to ceiling finishes, natural timber works well in contemporary-style rooms. Try cladding the ceiling with boards, sheets of ply, or tiles of variously coloured and grained hardwood veneers. Metals are another unusual intervention – an entire covering of sheet steel might be oppressive, but a shallow copper dome set into a hallway ceiling can hardly fail to delight. Or consider borrowing ideas from the past, such as a ceiling-sized fresco – images can be digitally printed on paper to match the exact dimensions of a room.

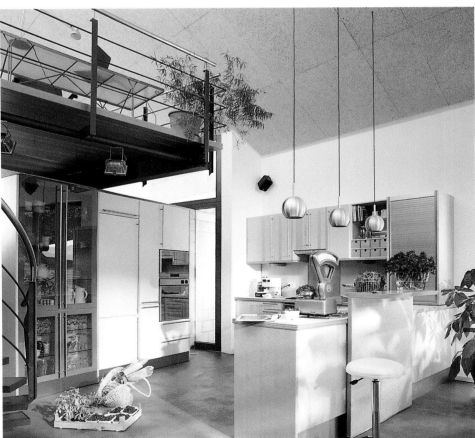

53

← Large-scale panels of an industrial type of particleboard make a very practical and hardwearing finish for the sloping ceiling above this elegant and spacious, double-height kitchen area.

height variations

We are so used to the simple, flat plane of a ceiling that it is easy to overlook its potential in shaping or enhancing an interior space. A clear, glazed ceiling offers a window onto the sky as well as admitting more natural light to the interior, but solid ceilings can also have a role to play in creating a variety of different moods.

Where it is possible to alter the ceiling level — on the top floor of a building, for example, or in a single-storey extension — the most dramatic effect is achieved by removing the ceiling altogether and opening the room right to the roof. While this obviously does not give any more floor space, the room will feel much larger as a result. The addition of rooflights will introduce more light and the space immediately has an eye-catching and unusual shape. There may even be room to add a mezzanine level.

If you already have a high ceiling and want to introduce some features, then consider stepping down the height over areas, such as a dining table, sofas, or a bed. You can achieve this by making a lightweight box to the desired dimensions and suspending it from the existing ceiling. This has the effect of making subtle distinctions between different areas. Another version of this idea is to suspend a horizontal panel over a sofa or bed. Both the box and panel can incorporate light fittings as required.

→ In this house extension by architect Peter Bernamont, the detail of the beamed ceiling continues through to the outside, in the form of a beamed canopy. By extending such details, you can visually link inside and outside spaces and so create an illusion of blurred boundaries.

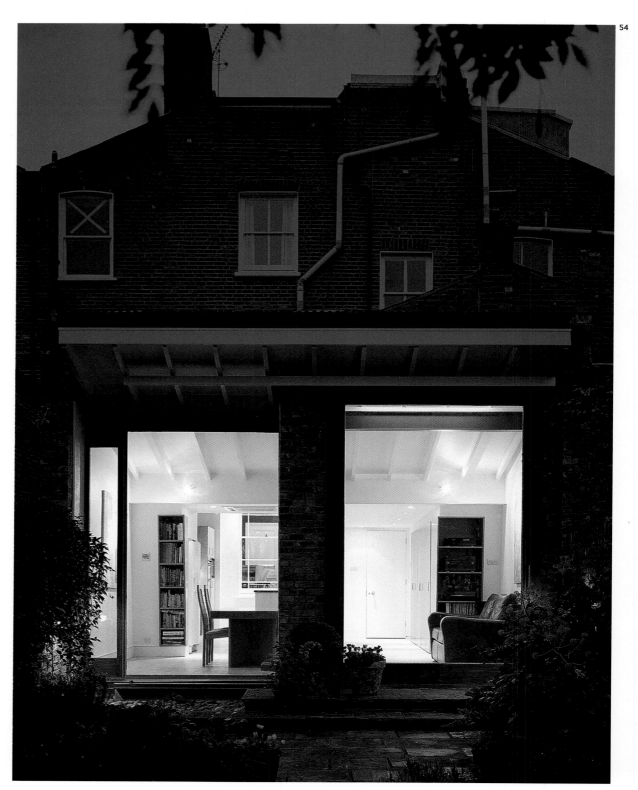

→ The shape of this ceiling, by architect Peter Thomas de Cruz, is much more than a whim. The highest point of the wave shape opens up the space above the door and at the top of the wall to allow for the band of clerestory windows, thereby delivering extra sunlight to the inside.

↓ To echo the oval shape of the dining table and to add to the intimate atmosphere of the space, architect Hawkins Brown has designed a suspended oval ceiling with built-in lighting. The coziness of the space is emphasized still further by the embracing rust-coloured curved wall.

55

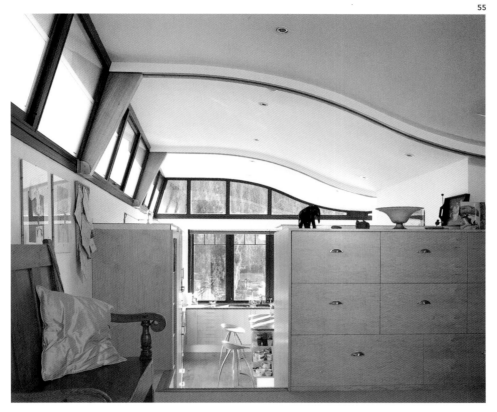

56

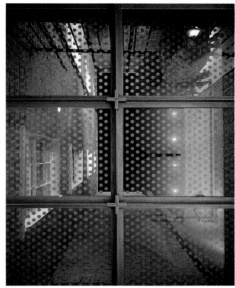

↑ This photograph has been taken looking upwards through a lightwell with a ceiling composed of a six-panel frame, designed by Belsize Architects. The glass has been screen printed with large dots, which serve the double function of obscuring the view from outside and providing dappled shade inside (see picture 58).

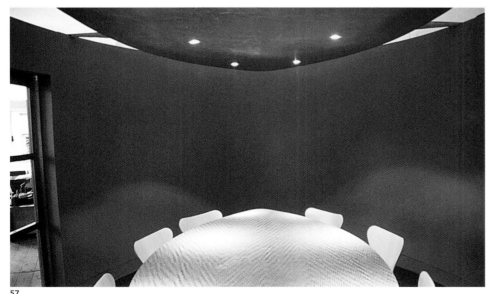

57

→ An inside shot of the Belsize Architects room created beneath the glass-panel ceiling shown above (see picture 56). An ideal space has been created for taking it easy in this inviting-looking lounge chair.

58

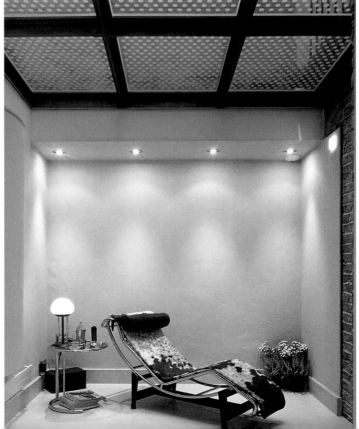

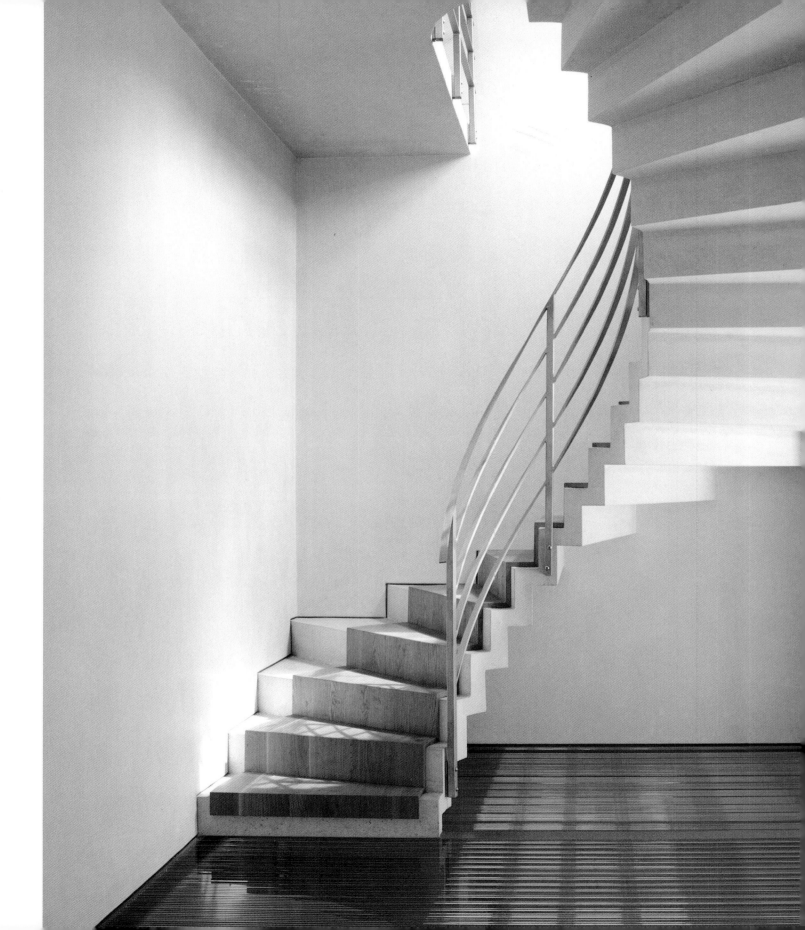

floors

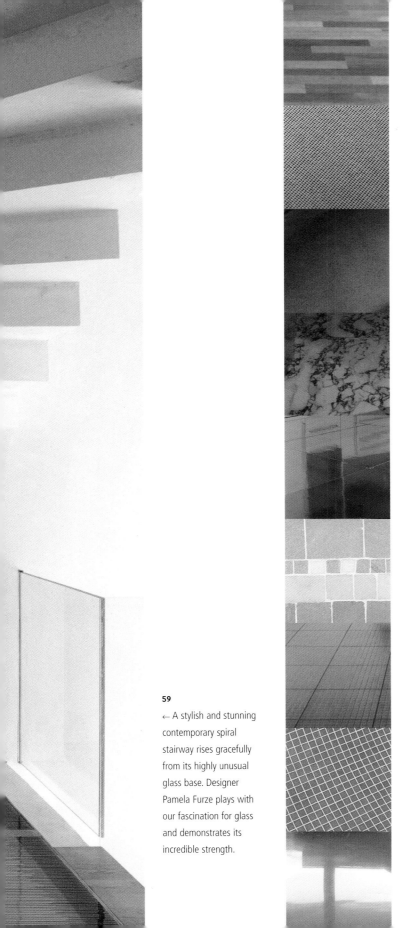

← A stylish and stunning contemporary spiral stairway rises gracefully from its highly unusual glass base. Designer Pamela Furze plays with our fascination for glass and demonstrates its incredible strength.

The floor is the base upon which interior design schemes are built, and these expanses of surface can be responsible for setting the tone of the entire interior environment. Traditionally, where there is money to lavish on interior design, a substantial proportion of it is spent on flooring. In the past, designers and craftsmen were commissioned to produce magnificent inlaid marble patterns, exquisite rugs, or timber floors with decorative multicoloured panels. Only the poor would resort to the humble finishes of clay tile, brick, or floorboards. As in so many areas of design, modern architecture has turned these notions on their head, relinquishing pattern and ostentation, and instead honouring materials in their purest and simplest forms.

Floorboards, parquet, plain stone, and ceramic tiles have all been incorporated in the pared-down new architecture of the twentieth century. Meanwhile, a proportion of public taste has continued to hanker after ornate tiles, decorative linoleum, and patterned carpet, preferably of the type that is fitted from wall to wall. Now, in the twenty-first century, we have already moved the story on again, and have taken an entirely eclectic approach to flooring. The choice on offer is vast, and a single household might be finished in just one material or feature a highly varied range, which could include aluminium sheeting in the kitchen, patterned marble in the bathroom, carpet in bedrooms, timber up the stairs, and limestone tiles in the living room.

timber floors

Crucial to the success of any flooring is starting with a level and sound base. A further consideration is how that base has actually been built. Essentially, a concrete floor gives greatest scope, as just about any finish can be laid on top. Even if the floor is in an upper part of a building, it is likely to be substantial enough to withstand the additional weight of ceramic or stone tiles. However, in older, traditionally built homes featuring timber joists and floorboards, it is possible that the floors will be uneven and unsuitable for the considerable extra weight of tiles. If you are in any doubt, obtain advice from a professional, such as an architect or a structural engineer.

Timber flooring is available in a wide range of finishes – from raw, untreated, solid wood planks to highly sophisticated, factory-made, wood-veneer laminate panels with a hardwearing and protective vinyl coating.

The less finished the material, the greater the options available. If the timber is a good-quality hardwood, you might want to emphasize its qualities and finish it with a polish. Although polish takes considerable time and effort to maintain in areas where there is high foot traffic, it should improve with age. Alternatively, you might consider applying a low-maintenance, hard-wearing varnish.

With cheaper materials, such as pine boards, you could use a colour stain, varnish, or even paint. Natural options are now also widely available, including Danish oil or tung oil, which soaks into the surface and then hardens to produce a durable, waterproof finish.

↑ With a beautifully finished wood floor, a room looks partly furnished from the start. In this project by The Douglas Stephen Partnership, the elegant timber flooring is complemented by classic black leather and stainless-steel furniture by modernist architect Le Corbusier.

→ This South African home, designed by James Gubbins, features an unusual flooring comprising large, cast-concrete panels set in a mid-tone hardwood frame. The finish has an attractive waxy sheen and it is hardwearing and easy to clean, making it ideal for a high-traffic area such as a hallway.

↓ To show off the natural variability in wood colouring, this lively and intriguing pattern of variegated tones can be found in a walnut strip floor from the Wicanders Wood-O-Floor range. The attractive pattern of narrow wood strips has been made into a laminated board, finished off with real wood veneer and a tough, clear vinyl for durability and ease of maintenance.

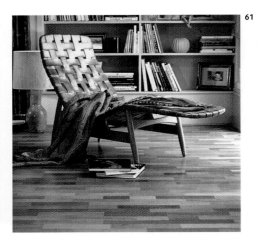

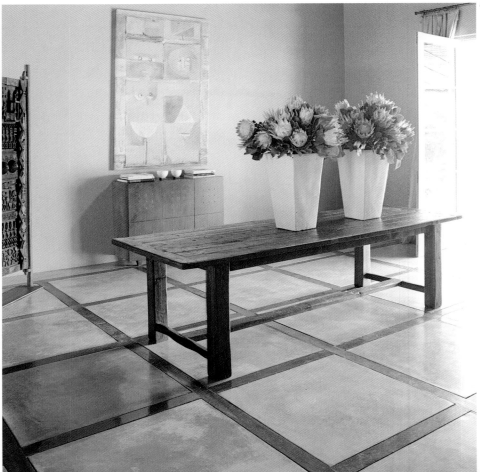

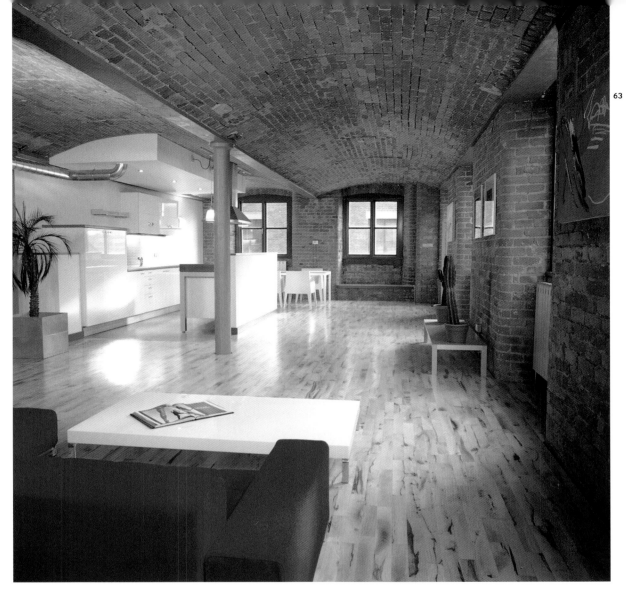

← Timber flooring suits this type of converted industrial space incredibly well. This particularly lively patterned, rustic beech floor, from Junckers, has been used throughout the apartment and succeeds brilliantly in uniting the many different spaces.

↓ When you want a visual link between inside and outside spaces, installing a continuous expanse of wood flooring can be a successful solution. However, because of the effects of the weather, be prepared for the exterior wood to wear and age differently from that inside.

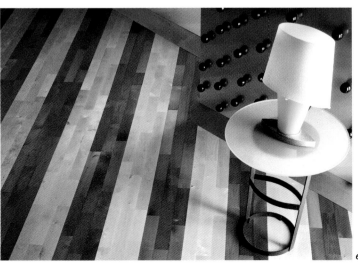

← This eye-catching, zebra-striped flooring has been constructed using boards of contrasting birch woods. The pale version is the wood's naturally light colour, while the darker shade is a heat-treated version. Both woods are available from Upofloor.

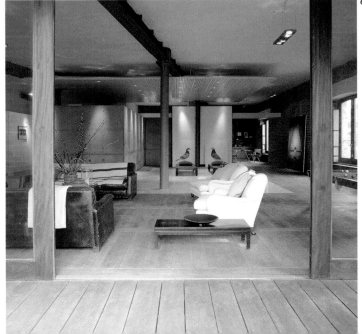

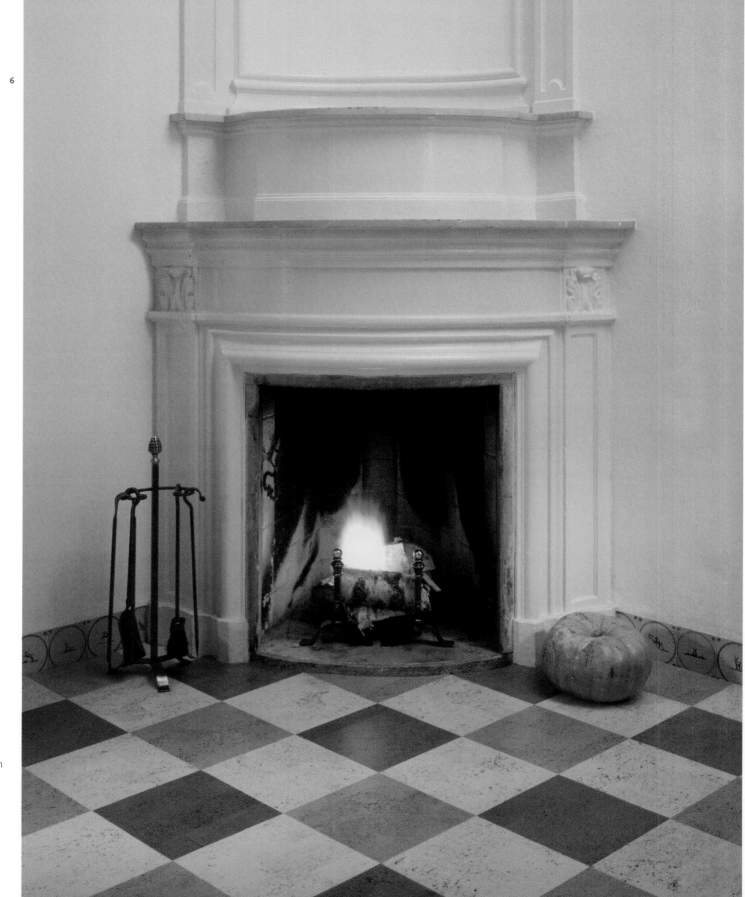

→ Although this chequerboard flooring could be mistaken for a stone finish it has in fact, been achieved using three colours of cork tile – Land, Olive and Salt – from the master range of W canders Cork. This natural, renewable materia is warm to the touch, incredibly resilient and hardwearing, and provides a decree of sound insulatior.

67

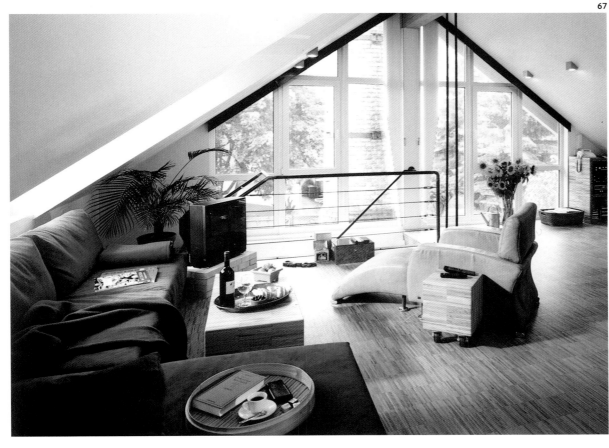

← Bamboo might sound like an unlikely material from which to make a f oor, but it has won many admirers in recent years. This s not only because the narrow strips create a highly unusual-looking and tough finish, but also because it is a rapidly growing and plentiful product — one that is considered to be an environmentally-friendly material if it is sourced from well-managed plantations.

68

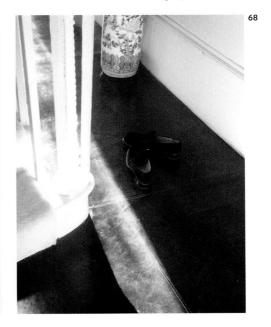

→ It certainly takes courage to use a modern material, such as this white concrete, in the setting of an ancient, timber barn — and here the architect has taken the bold step of introducing not only a concrete floor but also a built-in sunken seating area made of the same material.

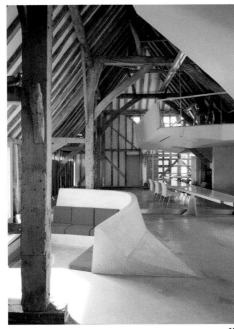

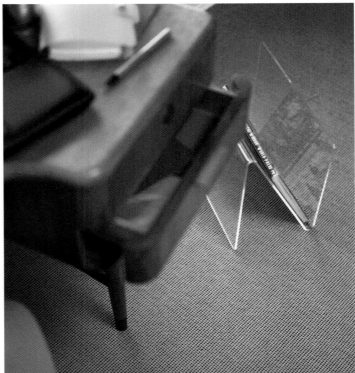

↑ Leather flooring might at first seem impractical, but designer Bill Amberg demonstrates that it is hard-wearing and improves with age. He recommends treating leather like a timber floor — waxing and polishing it every three to six months.

← Where a warm finish is required, few materials are better than a carpet. This stone-coloured carpet, by Kersaint Cobb, is given extra depth by incorporating a dark weave.

69

70

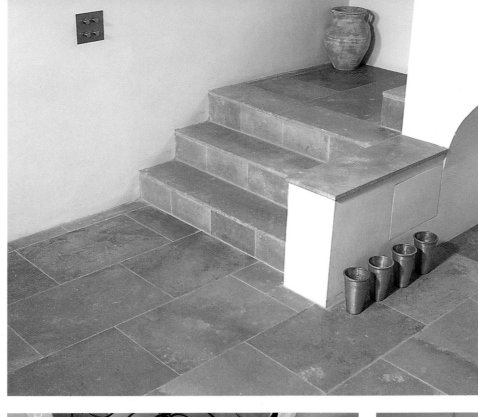

71

← This elegant, cool, and practical area of stone flooring is part of a project by designer Samantha Sandberg. In it, she uses subdued, pale honey-coloured Buffieres limestone tiles, supplied by Kirkstone Quarries. The stone has an attractive, multitone colouring, with blends of dark and pale patches, giving the material an obvious natural quality.

73

→ The creamy, even-coloured quality of this honed, Gascogne beige limestone was seized on by architect Barrie Tankel for use in this area of hallway. The stone was supplied by Kirkstone Quarries.

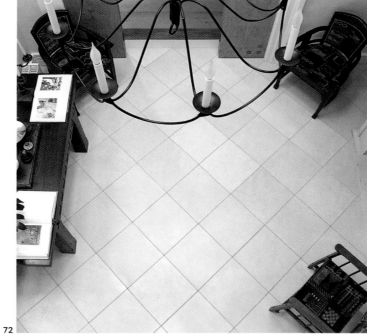

72

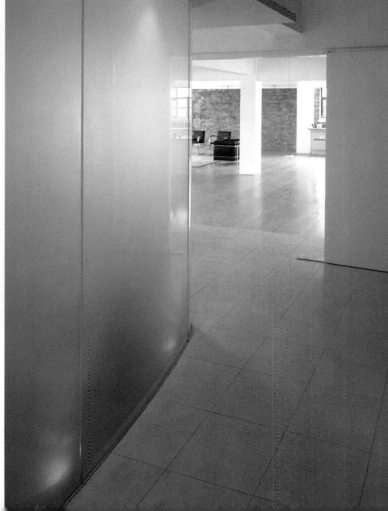

→ Using flooring materials to delineate different areas of usage, this large apartment, designed by architect Brookes Stacey Randall, features a hardwearing limestone tile in the main hallway circulation areas, which then changes to a softer timber finish in the living space.

→ This unusual and stunning tiled floor in amber slate is from Fired Earth. The rich pattern is produced by the combination of a wide spectrum of shades – from a deep chocolate brown through to soft green, rose pink, and cream. It looks particularly handsome with the colours of the hall rug.

↓ The warm, firey red colour of terracotta tile is unmistakable. Here, these 30cm (12in) square handmade tiles, from Natural Tile, show off their natural variation in colour, which is produced as a result of random stacking in the kiln before firing.

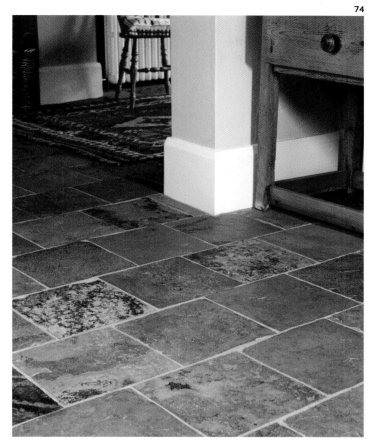

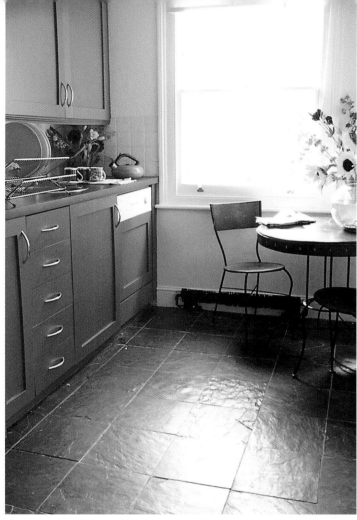

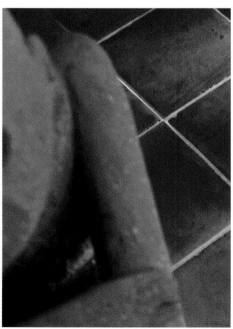

→ Kirkstone sea-green and silver-green stone tiles have been used by The Architects Practice on this floor. The green tiles look particularly effective when they are shown alongside the stainless-steel and chrome detailing. This English volcanic stone is quarried in the Lake District, in the far north of the country.

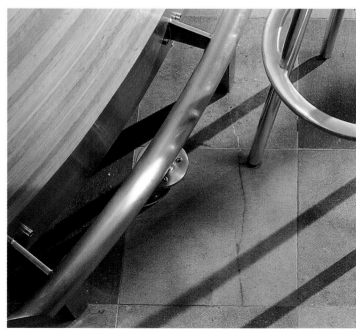

↑ The lustrous quality of slate is shown to its best advantage in this kitchen, where it is washed with sunlight from the window. The colour of the slate looks particularly smart when set against the sage-green, floor-standing kitchen cabinets.

78

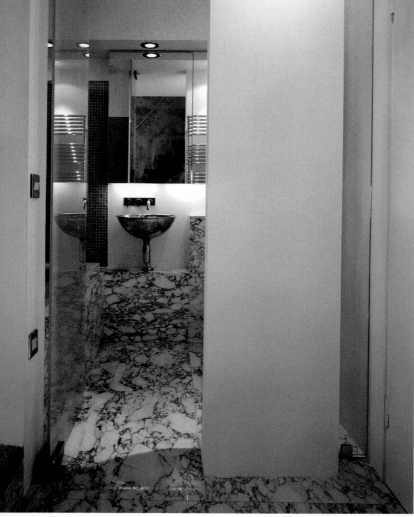

79

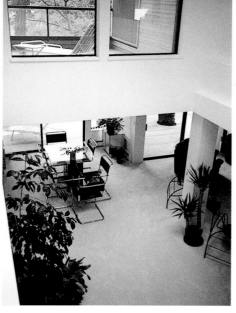

→ Demonstrating the possibility of using flooring to unite a space, John R Kay has given the entire ground floor living area over to a pale grey base that links the different living areas. The grey is also a perfect foil for the chrome and glass furniture.

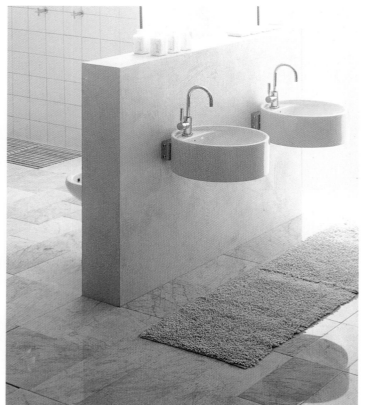

← This all white and cream bathroom is built up from its pale marble tiled flooring. The perfectly circular basins are from the Flaminia Work in Progress collection, designed by Giulio Cappellini and Roberto Palomba, and are available from Original Bathrooms.

→ Unusual long, rectangular marble tiles have been laid in the busy traffic area at the base of these open, timber-tread stairs. The tiles have been cleverly staggered to meet the timber flooring in the living room beyond. The change of materials defines not only the change of mood between these two areas of the house, but also the change of use from high-traffic to a low-traffic living area.

81

↑ The wild pattern of white and black in this Italian Arabescata marble makes a stunning bathroom floor. Although this marble is typically found with a more modest pattern, architect Procter Rihl was delighted to find this unusual variety. The designers liked it so much, that they also used it on the side of the bath and part of the wall.

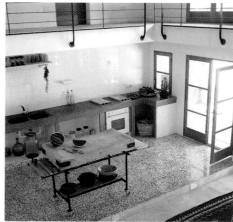

← The dalmatian-spotted composite floor tiling in this kitchen is made using black stone chips in a white base. The composite theme is picked up in the work counter, which is a thick slab of dark grey composite stone.

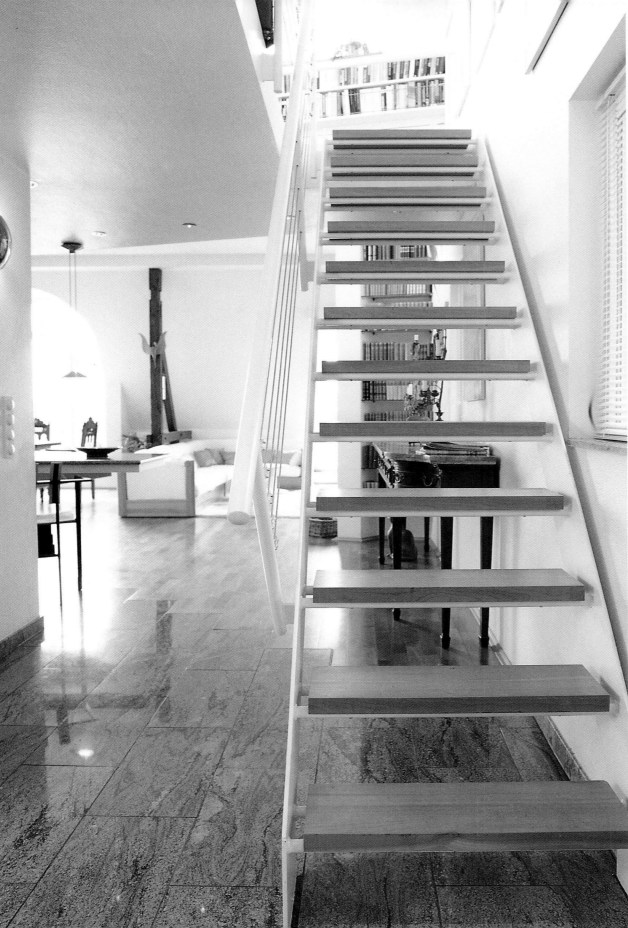

stone floors

There is no avoiding the fact that stone flooring is expensive to buy and to install. Even going to a salvage yard does not guarantee a bargain, but the reward for investing your hard-earned money is a finish that is stunning and should last for years. Taking account of the fact that stone is so expensive, it can be used to great effect even in small areas. It is ideal for use in high-traffic routes around the home, such as hallways, but it also performs well in wet areas, such as kitchens and bathrooms.

The first step in planning a stone floor is to make sure that the base surface – concrete is usually the best material – can bear the weight. If the structure is sound, you then have the choice of a huge array of stone, marbles, and slates in every colour and pattern. Unless you know what you are doing, however, it is always best to have a stone floor professionally laid.

For unusual effects, it is often possible to order the stone cut into non-standard sizes – unusually large or small panels. In this way, you avoid the familiar tiled look. It is also important to make sure that the stone or marble is finished in a way that is appropriate to its intended use: for example, large expanses of white limestone flooring might look absolutely stunning when they are first laid, but unless the material is expertly sealed, it will quickly absorb stains and start to look shabby. Due to their porous nature, even dark-coloured stones and slates will absorb stains unless the surface is protected. Suppliers should offer full details on appropriate finishes and advice on maintenance.

83

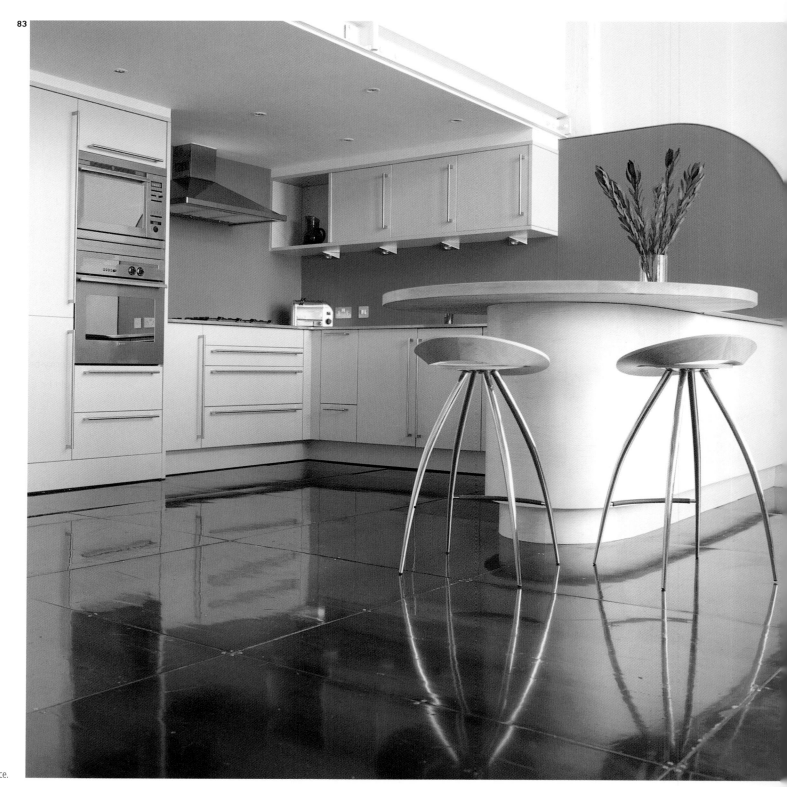

→ This blue-and-white kitchen stands above a beautifully glossy metal floor composed of large, square metal tiles with neatly finished rivets to hold them securely in place.

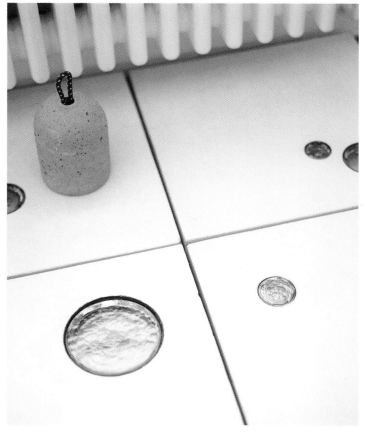

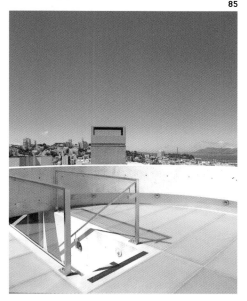

↓ A high rooftop deck with a floor composed of inset panels of obscured, sand-blasted glass looks its best under the cloudless blue of a Californian sky. The deck, which was designed by architect Jim Jennings, also features glass-panel balustrading to the flight of access stairs. Being made of clear glass, the balustrading and flooring helps as much natural daylight as possible to penetrate into the living spaces below.

↑ This sleekly smooth, white concrete slab flooring has been given an intriguing finish by the inclusion of inset glass discs, which act as lenses for recessed lights set beneath the floor.

→ This kitchen borrows an industrial style of design. Its stainless-steel splashback panels and doors are complemented by the hardwearing — almost indestructible — industrial-type ridged-metal flooring. Wherever there is danger of moisture accumulating on floors, such as in a kitchen, a textured surface helps to provide extra grip underfoot.

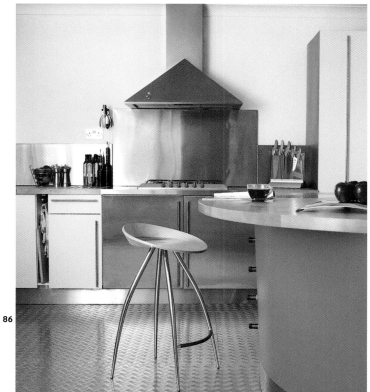

metal floors

Metal flooring for the home is a fairly recent innovation, which is strange since it has performed so well in industrial settings for so long. Although its use in the home tends to be confined to kitchen areas, it could be employed just about anywhere.

The success of the finished look of a metal floor is dependent on careful fitting. Metal flooring tends to be sold in large sheets or tiles, and like any flooring it requires a solid and level base. If the floor is solid concrete, the material can be stuck in place. First, you must abrade the back of the tile or sheet with a wire brush to give the surface a "key" for the glue, which is usually an epoxy-based adhesive. The adhesive should be spread evenly and finished off with a bead running around the outer edge. When the material is pressed into place and abutted to another tile, the excess adhesive can be removed with a cloth.

The second option is to fix the tile or sheet to a timber substrate, such as ply sheeting. In this situation, metal screws can be used to hold it in place, although again it is a good idea to run a bead of adhesive around the edges to seal the tiles and prevent water penetration.

Some tiles may need to be cut to shape, and for this manufacturers recommend a jigsaw with a fine-tooth blade. Rough or sharp edges that result should be finished with a file.

As a safety measure, always make sure that the metal flooring is completely isolated from the risk of electrical contact. If you are in any doubt about safety, have the work carried out or inspected by a professional.

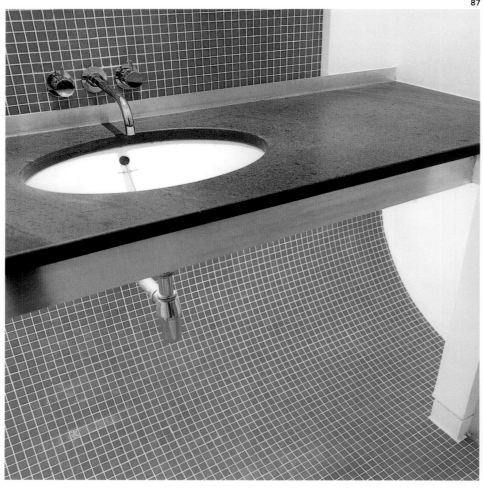

↓ Architect Brian Housden has introduced flooring in a particularly thoughtful way in this project, in order to define the different areas of activity in an open-plan living space. In the main living area, a hardwearing dark blue, mosaic-tiled floor changes to a sunken disk of white limestone in the dining area, while a white and gold mosaic strip to the right forms an informal seating bench.

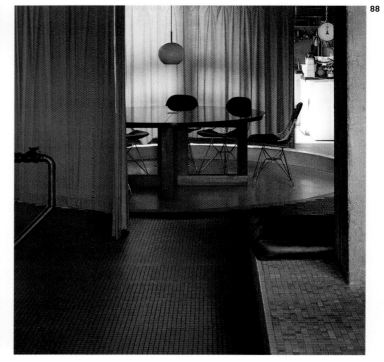

88

↑ A great wave of tiny green mosaic tiles washes up from the floor and onto the wall in this beautifully detailed bathroom, designed by architects Littman Goddard Hogarth.

→ Amazing glinting gold and glass mosaic tiles make an absolutely beautiful floor. The whole area of flooring is one large reflective surface that catches the light and always returns a sunshine glow. The tiles are by the Italian company Bisazza.

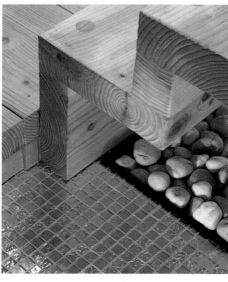

89

→ Delicate white mosaic tiles are a calm, cool presence on the floor and bath panel in this bathroom, adjoining the bedroom of an Australian house designed by architects P Stronach and T Allison.

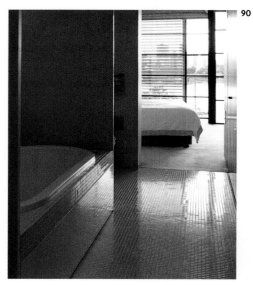

90

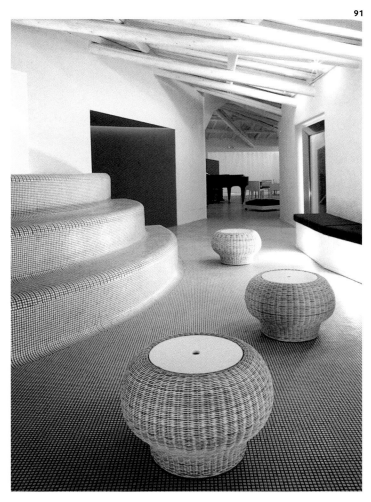

91

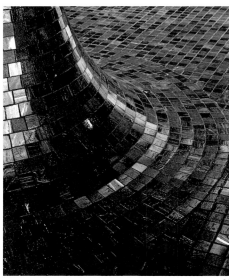

93

← The contrast of pale mosaic tiles with a dark-coloured grouting is shown to good effect in this remarkable interior. The tiles are by Bisazza, and the light and dark blue scheme is continued in the decoration on walls.

→This bathroom uses an unusual but well chosen collection of materials: a silky stainless-steel shower tray, multicoloured blue mosaic wall tiles, and a solid floor of subtly patterned marble.

→ Rich and varied shades of blue have been brought together to make this tiled flooring, by the Italian tile maker Bisazza. The versatility of the mosaic-form of covering is displayed in the way the small tiles wrap themselves around the column rising out of the floor.

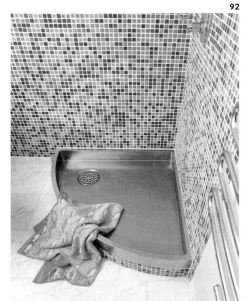

92

↓ A variety of blues, from dark aquamarine to near-white, in tiles of several different sizes has been brought together to make an attractive pattern on floors, bath panel, and walls in this bathroom.

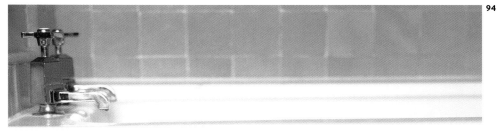

94

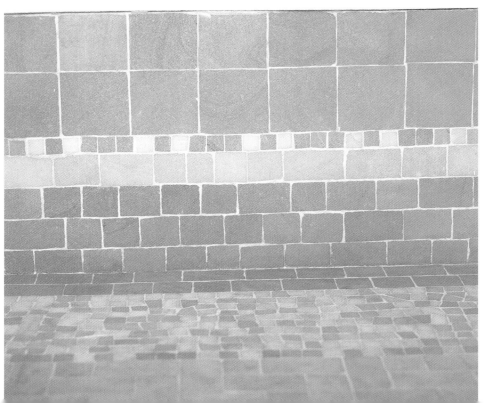

vinyl and linoleum

Sheet and tile floor coverings offer great creative opportunities. They are relatively inexpensive to buy, available in wonderful colours, and most manufacturers even incorporate printed patterns and images.

When deciding on this type of flooring, you will have a choice of a vinyl or linoleum material. The first is a petroleum-based product; the second is made of a mixture of materials including cork, linseed oil, and chalk. Both are warm to the touch, extremely hardwearing, and relatively easy to lay.

The very good news about these types of flooring is that they can be forgiving of slightly uneven floors. To start, prepare the area and lay a substrate of plywood or hardboard sheeting, if necessary. The flooring can then be stuck to this surface using the adhesive recommended by the manufacturer. Laying sheets of flooring, once the material is handled into the space, is usually fairly trouble free. However, when you are dealing with an usually shaped floor, or when there is a considerable amount of cutting around doors or cupboards, it is advisable to make a card or thick-paper template. You can then cut the sheets outside the room and bring them in ready to stick down.

The secret of success in laying tiles is to measure the room and mark a cross at the exact centre of the space. Then place four tiles in a square, with their centre over this cross, and continue laying tiles outward, toward the edges. The logic behind this is that in the centre of the room all the joins will run in parallel, even if the walls are out of true.

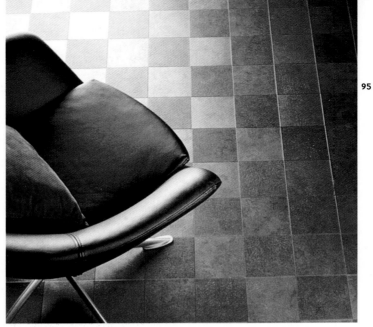

← This subtle palette of plum and slate grey offers an interesting retro chequerboard effect. The flooring is a warm, hardwearing vinyl from Amtico's Astral range.

↓ The appearance of this grey, short-pile carpet could have merely been smart but unremarkable. The effect the floor covering generates, however, has been totally transformed and uplifted by the addition of a random pattern of inset carpet circles in subtly toning colours of purple and magenta.

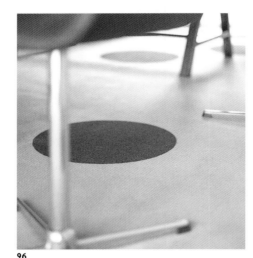

96

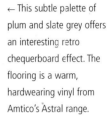

→ This wild pattern of black and white circles and squares makes a floor with tremendous retro impact. The tough, decorative sheet material is part of the Retro range from Amtico.

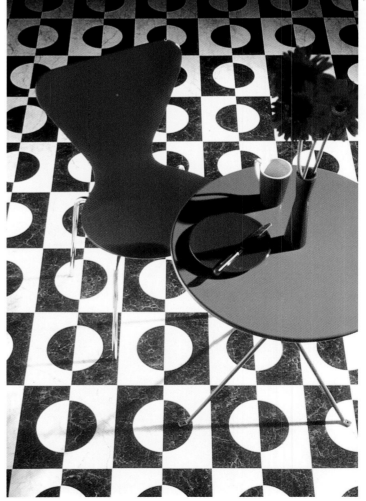

97

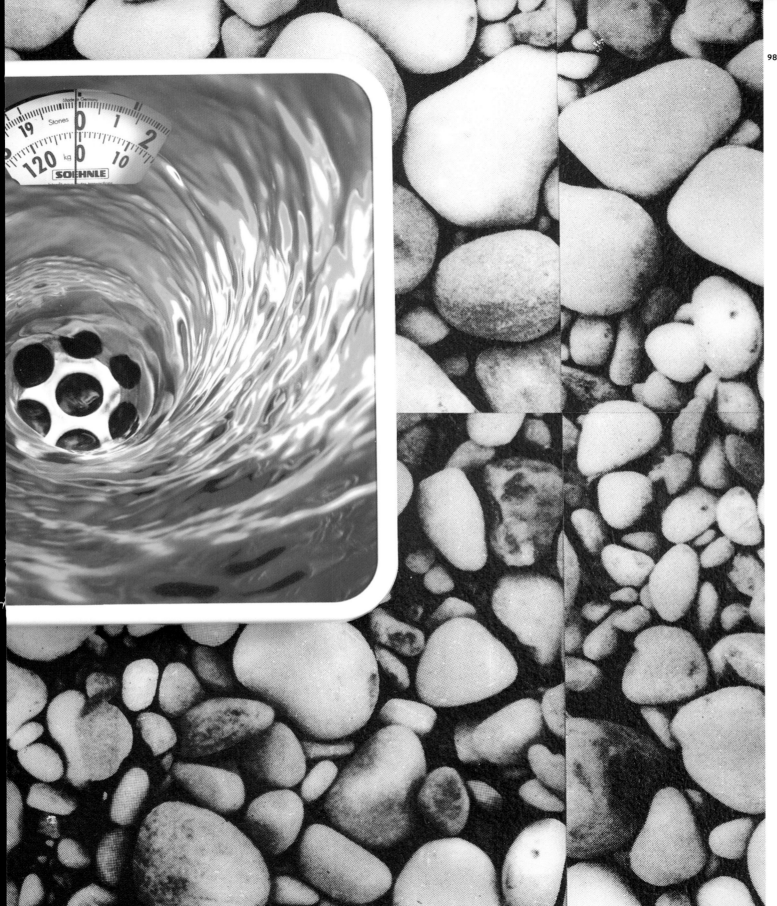

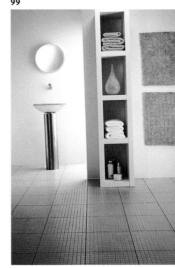

↑ In such a restrained
interior you might expect
a perfectly sheer finish to
the floor, so this beautifully
dimpled texture, called Iced
Glass by Amtico, comes
as a welcome surprise.

← The pebble pattern
on these tiles is a
photographic image
sandwiched between
a cork base and a tough,
PVC-laminate topcoat.
The designs, by tile
maker Harvey Maria,
are enormous fun and are
part of a range that also
includes grass and leaves.

101

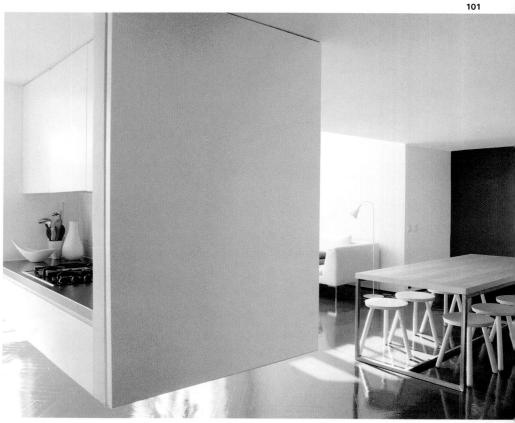

100

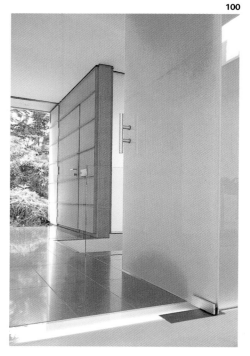

← The transition from room to room is marked at the threshold by a floor-recessed trough of light. The change of space is also marked in the flooring, which alters from pale honey-coloured stone to a high-gloss grey.

→ In this apartment, architect Voon Wong wanted to make sure light could flow through the whole space – so rather than sit the kitchen on the floor, he suspended it from the ceiling. The floor is hardwood parquet painted with a type of white paint designed for use on floors.

102

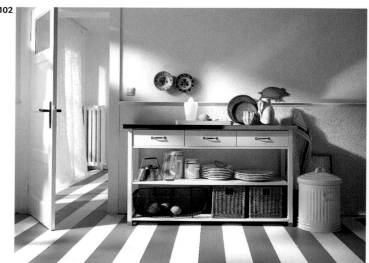

↑ Instead of the more predictable floor painting pattern, which divides the space into squares, this scheme takes individual floorboards and paints them alternately white and bright blue.

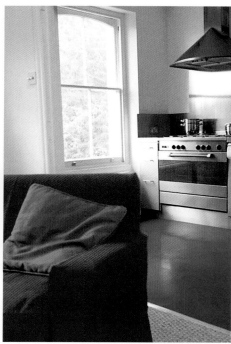

← Because it was used mostly for industrial applications in areas such as workshops, concrete floor paint used to be available in only a limited range of dull, uninspiring colours. Fortunately the palette is now considerably wider, and includes this lively cobalt blue.

→ The concrete floor in this apartment has been polished and varnished to such an extent that it now looks like one enormous slab of marble. It makes an elegant and simple base running throughout the entire apartment.

103

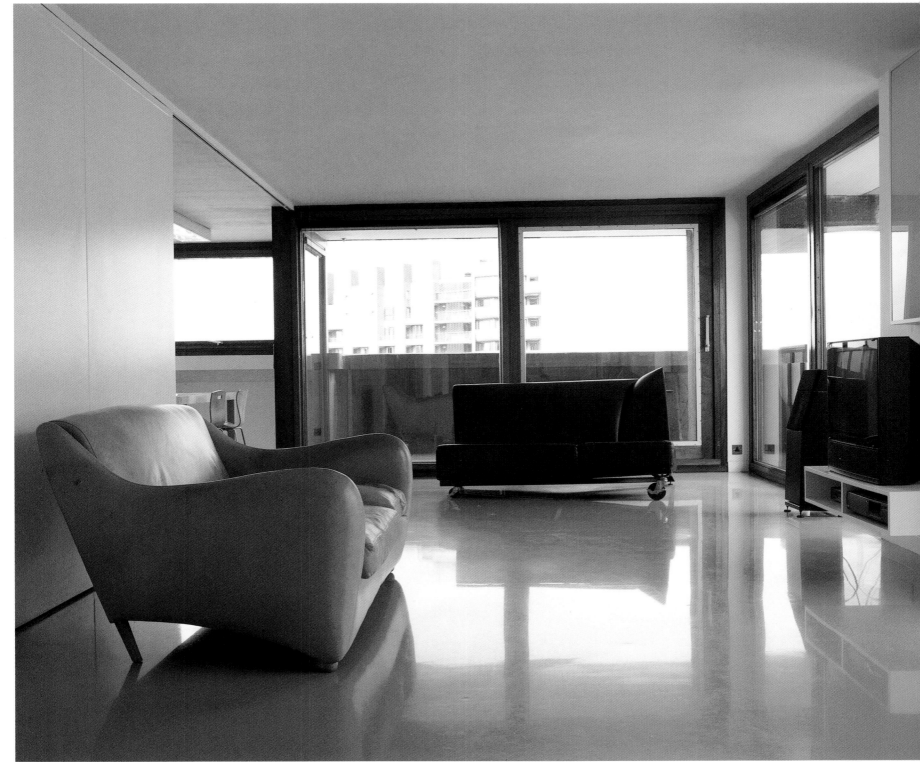

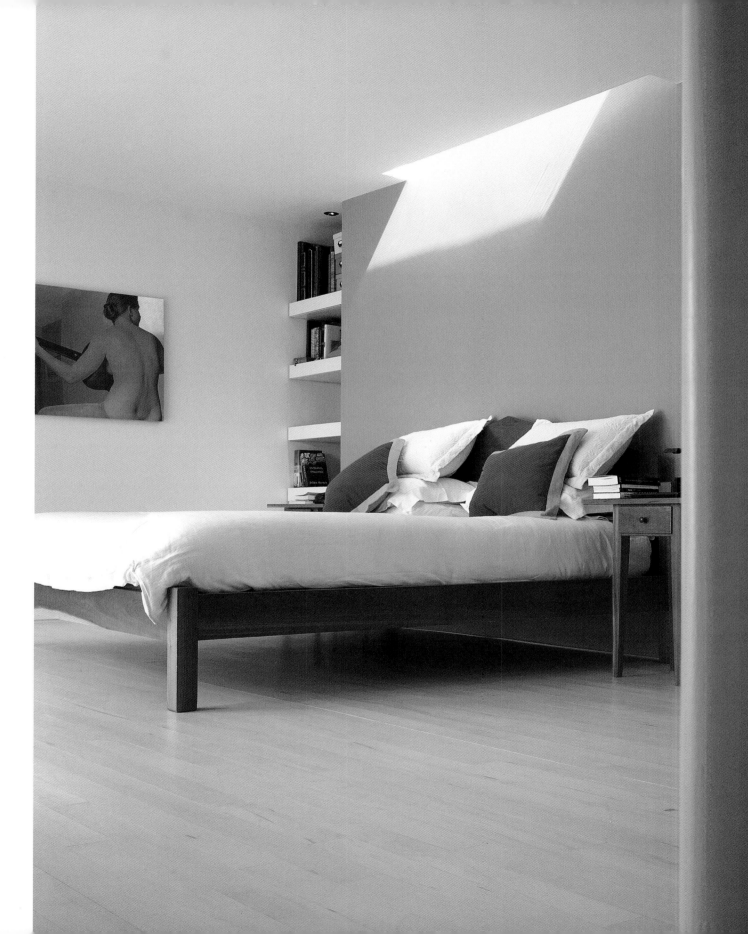

windows

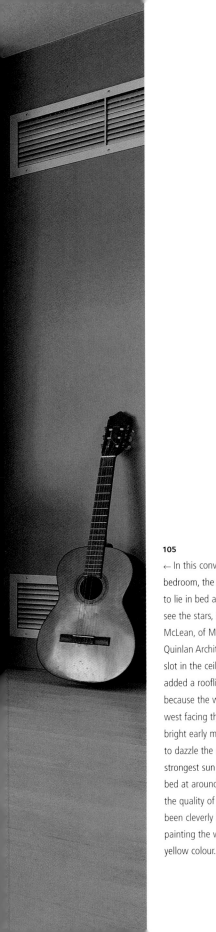
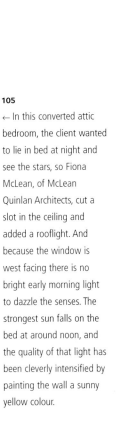

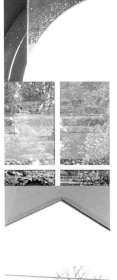
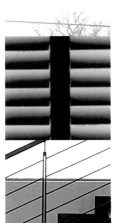

105

← In this converted attic bedroom, the client wanted to lie in bed at night and see the stars, so Fiona McLean, of McLean Quinlan Architects, cut a slot in the ceiling and added a rooflight. And because the window is west facing there is no bright early morning light to dazzle the senses. The strongest sun falls on the bed at around noon, and the quality of that light has been cleverly intensified by painting the wall a sunny yellow colour.

B right, light-filled interiors are among the key features that define the modern home. In a powerful reaction against the suffocating carpets, drapes, and heavy, dark furniture of the nineteenth century, the modernist architects of the early twentieth century set out to free us all from a grim and shadowy past. Light and translucency were pursued relentlessly. Advancing technologies produced bigger and stronger sheets of glass, and designers demanded more and yet more from the manufacturers.

The change of pace has been startling. Where once buildings were made in massive stone and brick, walls have been gradually reduced and refined to little more than a skin of glass hung on the frame of a steel skeleton. Interiors changed, too – open-plan homes evolved to suit our increasingly informal lifestyles. And in the quest for more and more light, rooms have been stripped of their heavy curtains, and windows have burst out of their frames to become whole walls or ceilings – and even floors – of glass.

Not content with bigger windows, we have more recently moved toward the blurring of boundaries between inside and out. Perhaps, in an increasingly unnatural and polluted environment, there is a wish to remain in touch with the natural world by at least being able to see it, to keep an eye on it. At last we have realized the modernist dream of being protected from the elements and yet also being at one with nature.

difficult spaces

Few of us have the luxury of designing a home from scratch and inherit spaces that are often far from perfect or in need of updating. The challenge here is to make the most of every space and in achieving this, natural light is key.

When an awkward space is remodelled — a cellar, basement, or attic, for example — the space remains dead where there is no natural light, However, architects and designers have risen to this challenge by devising ingenious ways of introducing daylight. In difficult cellar and basement areas, if there is room to dig outward from the perimeter of the house, it may be possible to create a lightwell. External walls can be replaced with large glazed panels, or glass extensions can be added to draw more light inside. In other cases, areas of floor can be removed and replaced with glass panels, enabling light to fall through the building.

To unlock the potential of areas at the top of the house solutions are often easier, with rooflights available to suit any type of sloping ceiling, Alternatively, the whole roof can be replaced with glass. But even the smallest of openings can transform a space, and several manufacturers now supply "sunpipes" — lengths of pipe with a glazed cover that can be inserted into a roof. Often these pipes are no more than 15 cm (6 in) in diameter, but the light they deliver can transform a dark stairwell, shower room, lavatory, or other dingy corner.

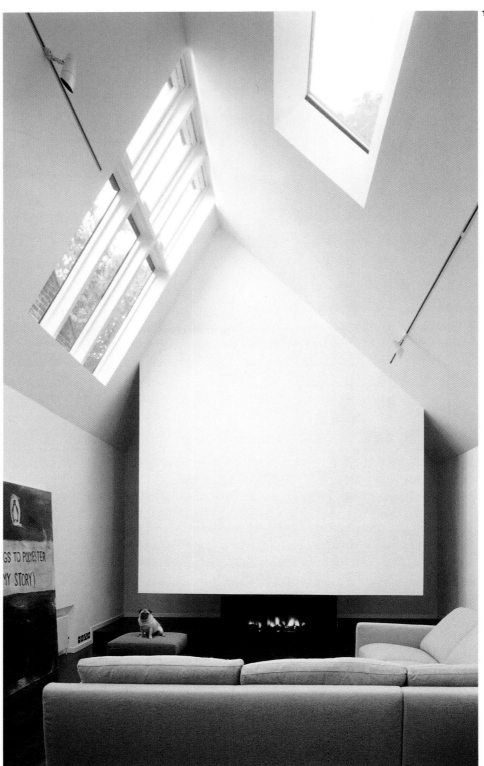

← Architect Stickland Coombe was unable to install windows in the walls of this converted artist's studio, where they might normally be expected, because it is landlocked by adjoining properties. Instead, the room was opened to the very apex of the roof and two large windows were inserted into the sloping roofsides. It is an unconventional space, but any risk of claustrophobia has been banished by the addition of these generous areas of glazing.

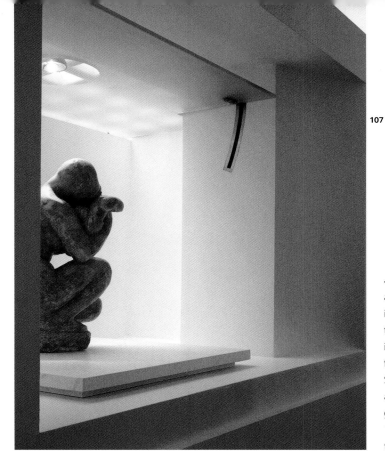

107

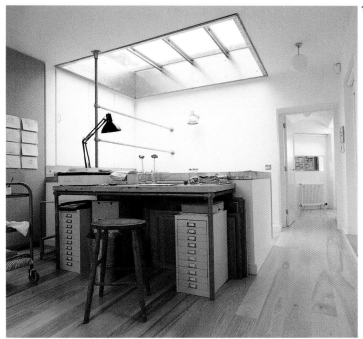

108

← In this basement apartment, extra light is drawn into the space through glass blocks set into the street above. To filter this light, architect Stickland Coombe has added this unusual plate-glass panel (see picture 109). There is an inset light to illuminate the sculpture.

→ This horizontal panel of glass can be tilted downward for cleaning and runs in these beautifully detailed stainless-steel tracks (see also picture 107).

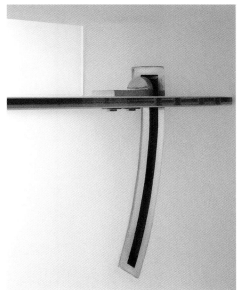

109

↑ Diffused sunlight is the best illumination for most work environments. In this home office, a glass ceiling panel draws in generous light onto the desk beneath. Coming from above and in front, this light leaves the work surface shadow-free.

← To make the most of the light in this bathroom, a horizontal window slot has been inserted near the roof ridge, with a vertical slot added at the fa, gable-end wall. The space has been painted in pale colours, and a wall panel fitted with a mirror reflects more light for exciting uplighting.

110

111

112

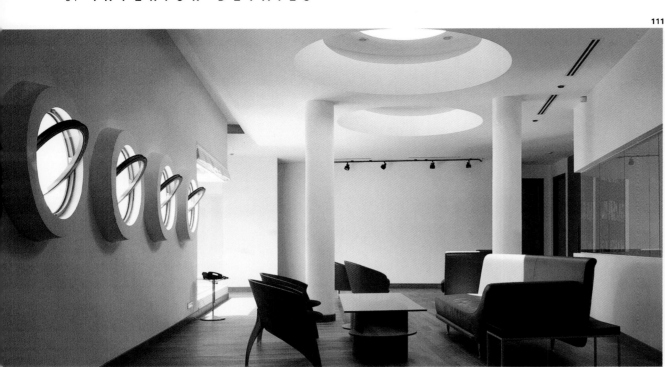

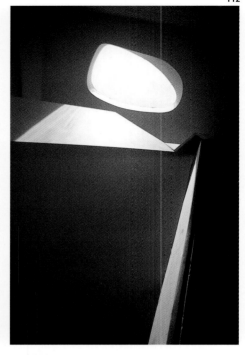

↑ Looking just like the lounge of a luxury liner, this Singapore house has been given an unmistakable nautical theme by the practice of KNTA Architects. Not only is there a neat line of portholes set in the outside wall, the designers have taken advantage of the room's top-floor location by adding a pair of circular rooflights above the seating areas. The columns, white-painted walls, and timber flooring all add to the shipboard theme.

113

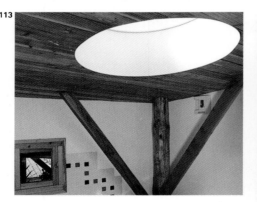

↑ The timber-lined ceiling might have been in danger of making this space look and feel slightly oppressive, had it not been for the inspired addition of a large, circular rooflight to dispel any hint of gloom. The window has been stamped through the deep roof space like a cookie cutter through pastry, and by painting the deep frame off-white, to match the walls, light is reflected around the room.

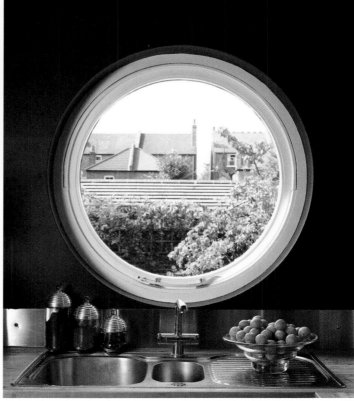

↑ Architect Peter Barber used a standard roof window fitting here, but he created the egg-shaped rooflight by cutting the plasterboard ceiling to the desired shape. The light admitted by the window makes a dramatic intervention into the stairwell beneath.

← Circular windows have enormous appeal – but because they are more unusual than square or rectangular shapes, they can also be more difficult to install. However, the extra effort reaps rewards. Here, the disc of glass sits above the kitchen sink to frame views of the garden and neighbourhood.

114

115

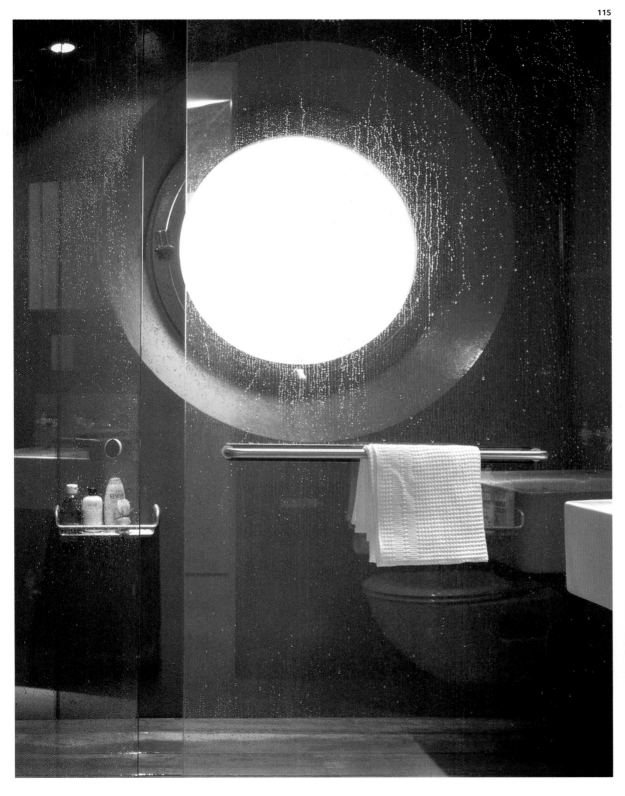

← Circular windows can look great in bathrooms, as this oversized opening demonstrates. The apparent size of the frosted-glass window is exaggerated by the splayed reveal, which, along with the wall, is painted a rich cobalt blue.

↓ Even a small rooflight can draw good amounts of natural light into a space when it is combined with a deeply angled frame, as in this project by architect Dennis Mires. The white-painted, conical reveal reflects light into the space below, which is coloured a deep red.

116

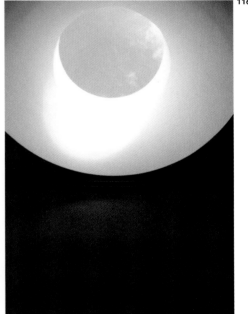

size and shape

The desire to dissolve the boundaries between inside and out has produced countless ingenious window designs. And the ability of manufacturers to produce ever-larger sheets of glass continues to be an inspiration. In some situations, entire exterior walls can be removed and replaced with glazing; in others, there are designs that incorporate unusual shapes of openings.

Since building work is nearly always messy and glass is not cheap, it is always worth spending some time looking at all the options before deciding precisely what you would like to achieve. Do you, for example, want to make a dramatic design statement; provide access to the outside; improve your views; or simply admit more light to a particular room?

In some cases, the wisest course of action is, in fact, to limit the size of opening. This is particularly so when there are cost or security considerations, or where the opening would be sun-facing and receive the full force of hot, direct sunlight. In this situation, consider installing smaller windows, ones incorporating some form of canopy to prevent an excessive build-up of heat indoors.

There may also be structural considerations to take into account. Removing a wall and replacing it with a sheet of glass may sound exciting and daring – however, it's a wise course of action to consult a building engineer before starting any work of this nature. Removing a supporting wall, or even punching a hole through it, will be certain to have serious structural consequences.

117

↑ This large, high-ceilinged, open-plan room is radiant with natural sunlight, brought in through an end wall composed entirely of windows. The screen is composed of six floor-to-ceiling panels of glazing, which incorporate a pair of double doors as well as a single door. The choice of pale wood flooring, white walls, and minimal furnishing adds to the open, light quality of the space.

1 1

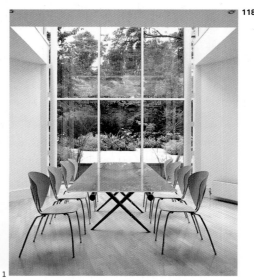

↓ The ceiling above this glass-topped table has been completely removed in order to create a tall, double-height dining space. And to emphasize further the sense of openness this produces, the end wall of the room is now a huge plane of glass offering views into the garden. The elongated proportions of the space are echoed in the tall, rectangular panels of window glass.

118

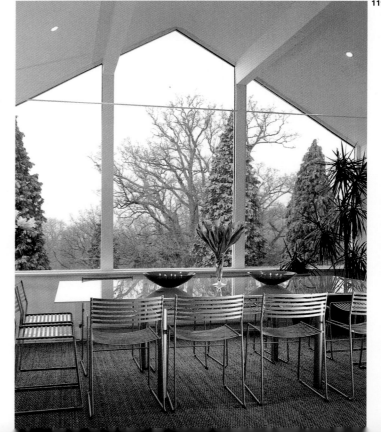

119

→ It is visually exciting to substitute a window for an entire wall of glass, particularly when it appears to be suspended in space with virtually no supporting frame. In this room, the glazing stretches from wall to wall and then right up to the apex of the roof. Thoughtful detailing includes the two solid posts, which run continuously up and over the space to support the roof, and the fact that the window ledge sits at precisely the same level as the table top, giving unhindered views of the trees and landscape.

→ When this home owner wanted to open up her living space into the courtyard beyond, the architecture practice Thinking Space devised this ingenious pivoting window. The design borrows from garage doors, and is a metal frame inset with toughened, laminated glass. The whole slab, weighing around ¾ tonne, is counterbalanced with lead weights. The opening and closing movement is electronically controlled, and when open the window locks in place.

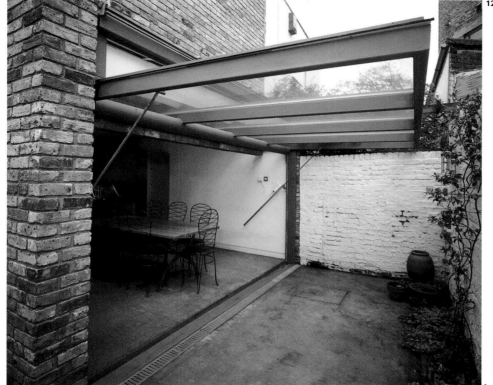

120

↓ If sunlight is very strong, or where a degree of privacy is required, different types of obscured glass can be used in windows. In this Californian project, vertically ribbed glass has been installed between deep wood fins, and the combined effect of glass and fins offers some protection both from onlookers and from the intensity of the sunlight.

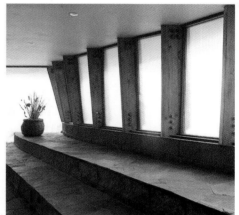

121

← The design concept of this Singapore house is that it wraps around its swimming pool. And in order to give easy poolside access from the crescent-shaped living room, the architects at KNTA have designed floor-to-ceiling windows each hung on a central pivot. On warm days, the windows swivel open to connect the inside and outside spaces.

122

123

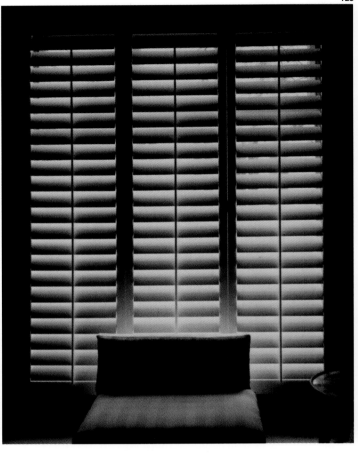

→ To provide privacy at the windows of this street-level mews house, architect Arthur Colin added these handsome wooden louvre shutters with unusually deep slats. Light can be drawn in by holding the central spindle and moving the slats up or down. Each panel is also side-hinged to open fully.

↓ As well as its hanging bed, this room also features an unusual window. The upper portion of wall has been glazed in four long, horizontal panels. Because it is set so high, this is clearly not a window that offers great views, but it does bring plenty of light into the room.

124

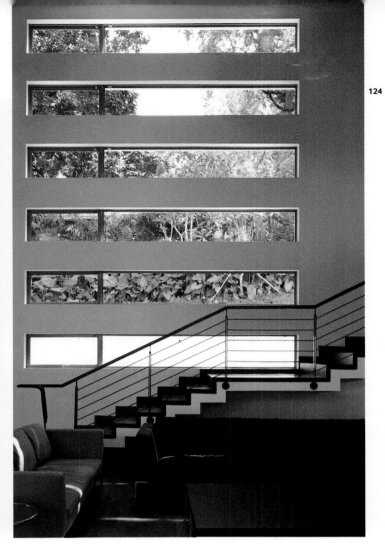

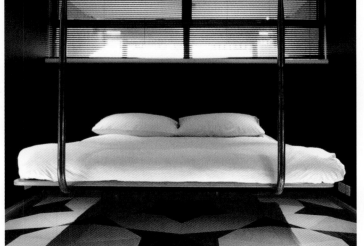

125

→ The idea of the perforated wall has been used in different forms for centuries. It is sometimes built with open holes for ventilation; sometimes for dappled light. In this London house, the planning authorities were unhappy about the inclusion of a large window, so architect Fiona McLean, of McLean Quinlan, devised this screen where the solid wall is punched through with holes containing glass bricks.

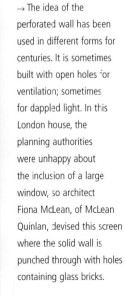

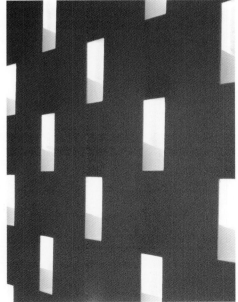

↑ The horizontal lines of the furniture and slow-rising stairs echo the horizontal slots making up this window. The design, by KNTA Architects, has tremendous impact, with its six oblong panels looking like a sequence of panoramic pictures. In a tropical climate such as Singapore's, this window is a clever way of bringing light in and providing views out, while at the same time giving protection from excessive sun and heat.

126

using light

The subtle handling of small packets of natural light can make an even greater impact inside the home than light that is available in great quantities. To this end, windows can be shaped and glazed and shuttered in a huge variety of different ways. Understandably, there is a temptation — whenever building technology and local planning authorities allow — to opt for generous, plain expanses of glass. However, modulation does prove that less can sometimes be more.

When choosing and installing new windows, be imaginative — the biggest window might be rejected in favour of a window that perhaps perfectly frames a view or aspect of the garden. A long, horizontal slot at the base of a room will provide an unexpected glimpse of the outside, while a similar slot in a top-floor ceiling opens up views of the sky and stars.

Homes in hot climates can provide lessons for us all. Here, windows are used sparingly — sometimes reduced to just small perforations in a wall — to infuse the inside spaces with dappled light. In other examples, a series of small openings punched in the walls of a room can be designed to scoop up sunlight at different times of the day. And where you don't want views, but you do want the light, then windows finished with sandblasted glass or sheets of plain-coloured glass can provide intriguing, glowing panels of illumination.

127

↓ Internal windows offer glimpses through a space. In this bedroom, an entire wall has been replaced by a slender glass screen overlooking the stairwell. The Japanese decorative theme is emphasized in the screen, with its shiny black, geometric-pattern frame. The grid is picked up in the distance with the drop of square windows through the stairwell.

128

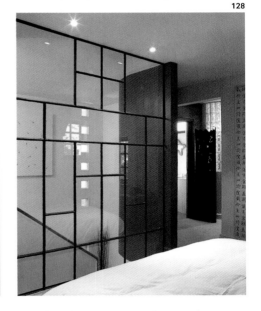

↑ Among the attractive features of those industrial buildings that have been converted into homes are their very large windows. In this project, the imaginative conversion avoids the need for opening the entire window by building a small hinged panel into the much larger area of glazing. The grid of squares in the window is a motif repeated in the tiny mosaic tiles on the walls and the floor.

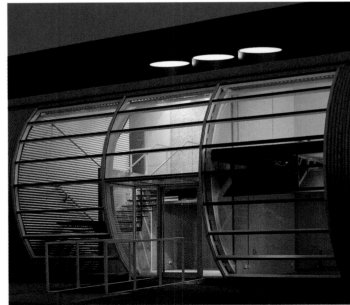

← This project features a reinterpretation of the bay, or bow, window. This time the bow works from top to bottom instead of from side to side. The space inside is filled with light, boosted by additional light from above falling through a trio of cylindrical windows. Architecture practice Studio Baad takes the theme of the horizontal bands in the windows and continues it inside the room, introducing horizontal, corrugated walls panels.

129

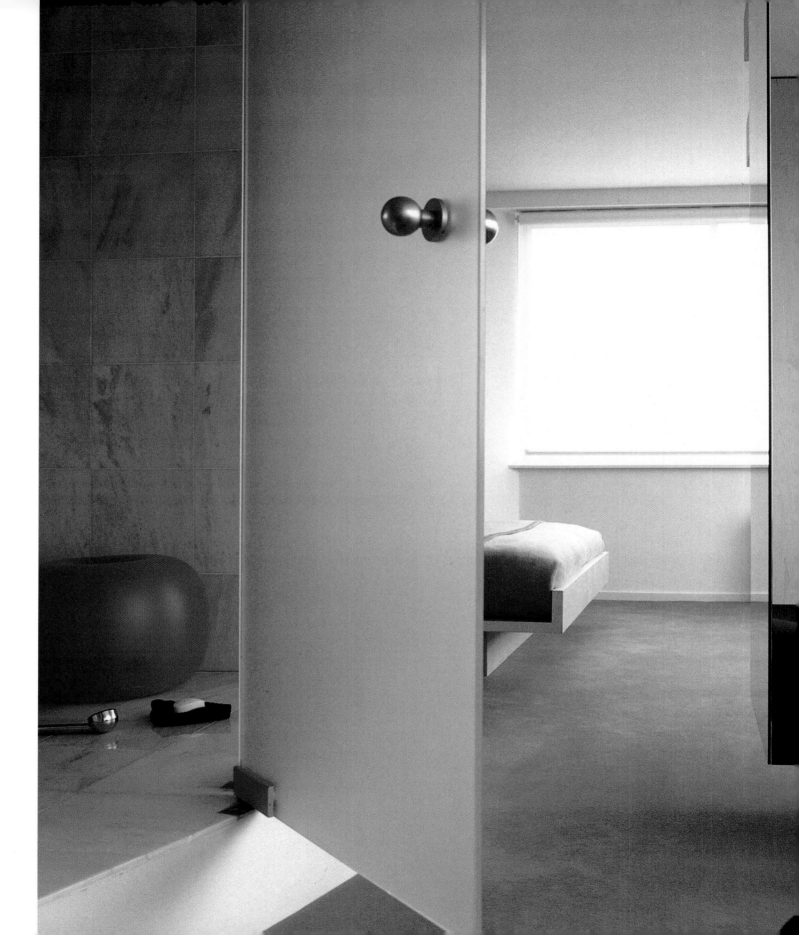

doors

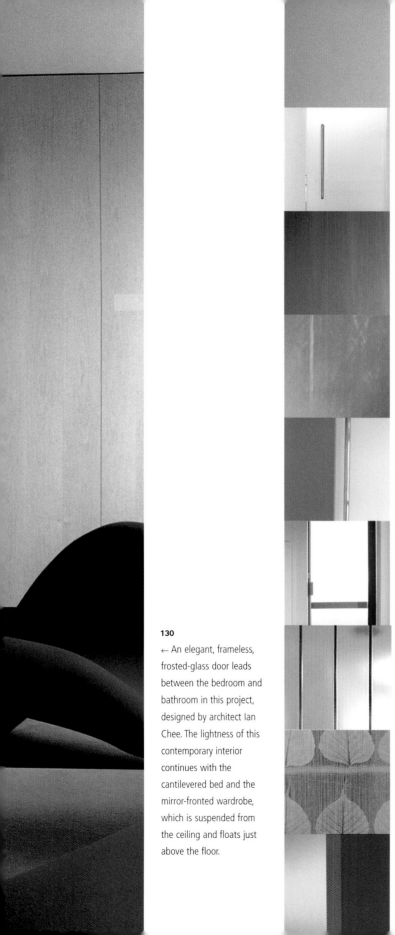

130

← An elegant, frameless, frosted-glass door leads between the bedroom and bathroom in this project, designed by architect Ian Chee. The lightness of this contemporary interior continues with the cantilevered bed and the mirror-fronted wardrobe, which is suspended from the ceiling and floats just above the floor.

The role of the door has remained virtually unchanged over the centuries. Doors have always stood for security and seclusion, and also occasionally for ostentation. First of all, they mark the very threshold of the home; then they are posted along the main circulation route inside the house, closing off the private spaces within. It is interesting to note that the door even played a particular role in the minefield of Victorian etiquette in nineteenth-century Britain — doors were always hung on hinges in such a way that, when opened, they obscured part of the view of the room. In this way, servants could not suddenly swing open a door to reveal a view of the whole interior. Instead, they had to walk round the door so that those inside had a few seconds to compose themselves in preparation for the encounter.

From more recent times right up to the present day, the entrance door has remained steadfast and, if anything, has become even stronger and more imposing than ever in order to withstand the attentions of burglars. In contrast, however, inside the home, as rooms have been joined together or opened up, doors have come to be considered almost as unnecessary obstructions. Nevertheless, there remain locations in every home where an internal door is not only desirable but also essential — either to provide privacy or to act as a sound barrier between different spaces.

glass doors

The traditional panelled, solid-wood door has put in tremendous domestic service, but as homes have evolved during the past century, so too have the style and materials used for doors. No longer do we always need a door to provide total, slammed-shut privacy, separating family from servants or adults from children. In the informal atmosphere of the contemporary home, space is shared and accessible to all.

In this changed social climate, there has been a tremendous growth in the popularity of translucent or transparent doors – those featuring glazed panels or made entirely of a single sheet of glass. Special toughened glass must be used to withstand the inevitable knocks that it is likely to receive. At first, glass doors appeared in frames, but gradually these have disappeared, leaving the sheet wholly unencumbered – apart from the handle and fixings for a hinge or sliding mechanism.

If you are choosing or commissioning this type of door, take into account the fact that glass is incredibly heavy – so make sure that the fixings can take the weight. In addition, if you have young children, you might opt for glass doors only in predominantly adult areas, such as between the bedroom and bathroom.

→ Two glass drums, one containing a shower and the other a WC and basin, have a glowing, surreal quality in the living room of this apartment. Designed by architect Simon Conder, the cylinders are constructed from toughened glass, which has been sandblasted and then rubbed with white powder. With the doors fully open, the two pods become connected. Each contains a circular skylight, and at night the pods are illuminated by recessed ceiling lights.

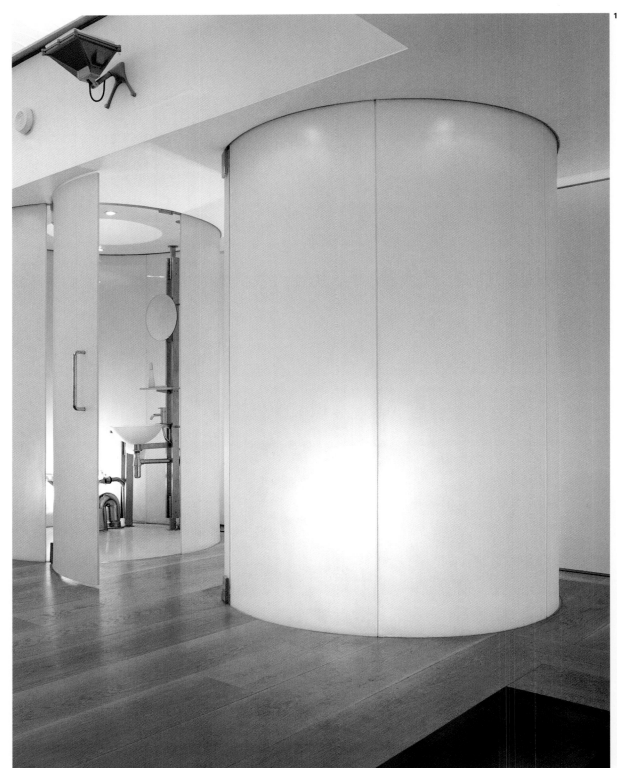

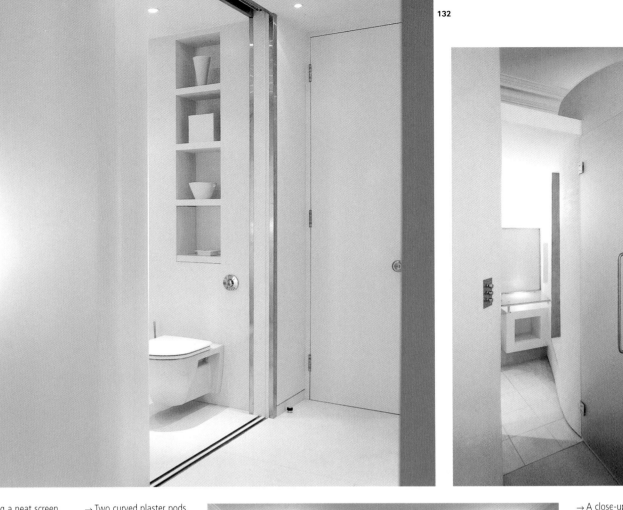

133

← This view is of the inside the pods illustrated below (see picture 134). The glass door opens to reveal a simple interior – the wall on the right curls around to envelop a shower, and directly in front of the door is a basin set into a glass counter with storage shelving below. The lowered false ceiling adds a sense of intimacy.

↑ Providing a neat screen between the bathroom and bedroom, this glass door sits in a sturdy sliding-track frame recessed into both the floor and the ceiling. The door is held in place by a runner situated at the top of the frame.

→ Two curved plaster pods have been built into this apartment, remodelled by architect John Kerr, to provide a bath on one side and shower with WC on the other. Between these two elements is a semi-transparent glass door with a long stainless-steel handle. The pods have been given an unusual finish in textured Venetian plaster. This exterior roughness stands in deliberate tactile contrast to the smooth, sleek, finely polished surfaces of the interiors.

→ A close-up shot reveals the elegant detailing of a sliding glass door in this project by Anelius Design. The glass panel is hung on a slender, wall-mounted, stainless-steel track. Two tiny rubber buffers are fitted on the pole support to make sure that the glass is stopped in its tracks and does not overshoot into the adjacent stainless-steel door.

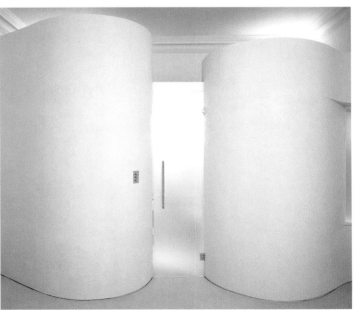

134

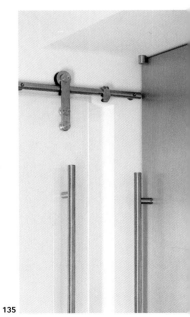

135

→ In confined areas, sliding doors are a great deal more space-efficient than regular hinged types. In this Melbourne apartment, designed by architect Andrew Parr, the en suite bathroom is screened from the bedroom by a pair of frosted-glass, timber-framed sliding doors. The use of glass doors, instead of solid wood, allows light to flow freely between the two rooms.

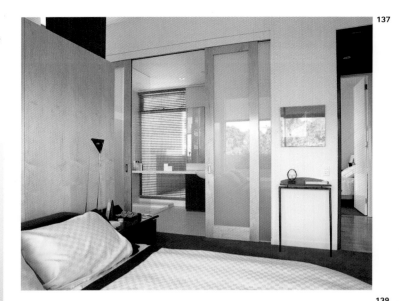

137

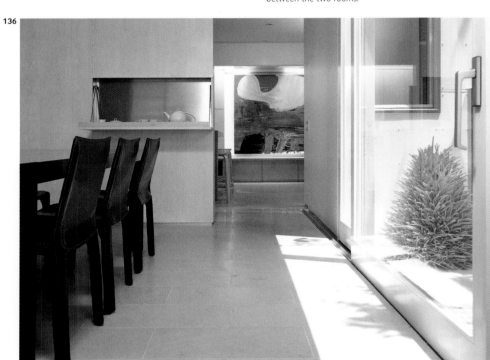

136

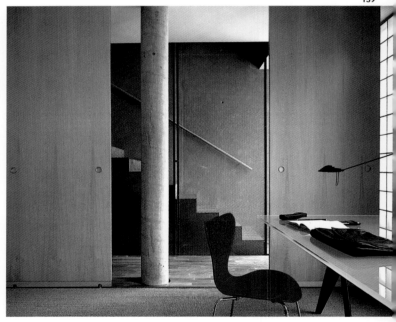

139

↑ Where we enjoy the luxury of a terrace or a garden, most of us want to make the most of that space by blurring the distinction between inside and out. With this large, sliding plate-glass door, architect Kuth/Ranieri succeeds in linking the dining area with the terrace beyond.

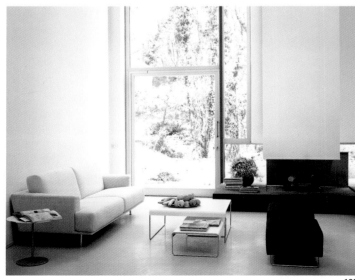

138

← In this living space with its high ceiling, an extra-wide door has been installed to lead onto the garden. A smaller door would have failed to complement the proportions of the space. The sofa is by Cassina.

↑ In order to provide a flexible way of screening the corridor and stairs from their home office, architects Gerhard and Yong Sun Feldmeyer have installed enormous floor-to-ceiling blond wood doors in their home in Germany. Because doors of this size and construction are extremely heavy, they need to be hung on sturdy tracks that are fitted at both top and bottom.

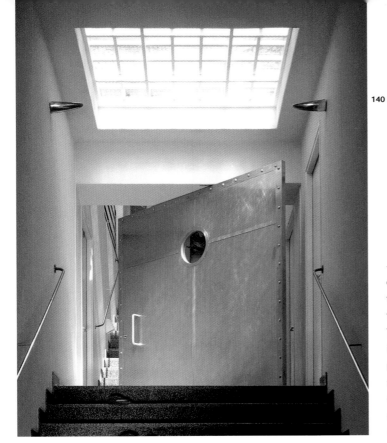

140

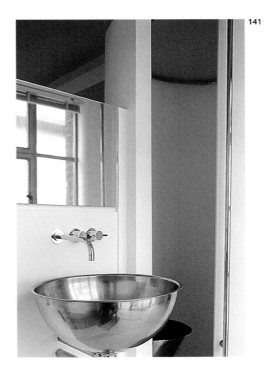

141

→ In this stylish and very contemporary bathroom, the circular lavatory cubicle features a curved door. This runs on a track and is swung into place by pulling the unusually long stainless-steel handle. The circular theme is picked up and carried through in the deep metal washbasin.

↑ Resembling the door to a vault, this heavy, riveted metal door, complete with porthole, makes a dramatic statement. This effect is heightened when the dark stone steps pause at the door shimmering in a shaft of light cast by the large ceiling panel of glass bricks. An unexpected detail, from architect Douglas Roberts, is that the door swivels on a central pivot.

→ In remodelling this property, architect Charles Barclay has united house and garden by installing specially designed metal-frame doors that fold right back out of the way to link the inside and outside, both physically and visually.

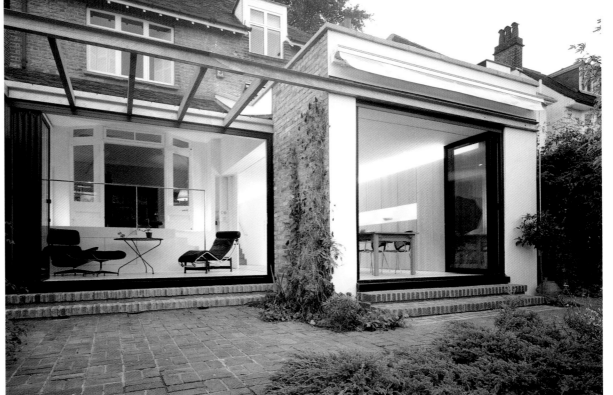

142

sliding doors

In most modern interiors, the best type of door is one that fulfils its function of separating one space from another, yet hardly makes its presence felt. In order to maintain a sense of openness, all-glass or part-glass doors are a good choice. Sliding doors are also becoming increasingly popular, particularly where space is in short supply or where a hinged door would intrude unhappily into the available space.

When choosing sliding doors, the key detail to check is the hanging or sliding mechanism. When sliding doors first captured the public imagination in the new homes of the 1960s and 1970s, they were considered to be unusual, even glamorous. However, their appeal was soon dimmed when the tracks and bearings failed and the doors started to jam or even fall out of their frames.

Modern sliding door designs are far more substantial than their earlier counterparts, but the best advice remains to buy really high-quality fittings. This advice also holds true for fold-back, concertina doors, particularly when they incorporate two or more panels. The weight of a multipanel door will certainly take its toll on insubstantial fittings.

→ Built-in cupboards and shelving provide essential storage space, which is particularly useful in compact apartments such as this one, refurbished by architecture practice Sergison Bates. There is generous natural light flooding into the room through the large external doors, which open onto a balcony. However, the sense of light and space is magnified by the bold use of floor-to-ceiling, mirror-finished doors on the storage cupboard.

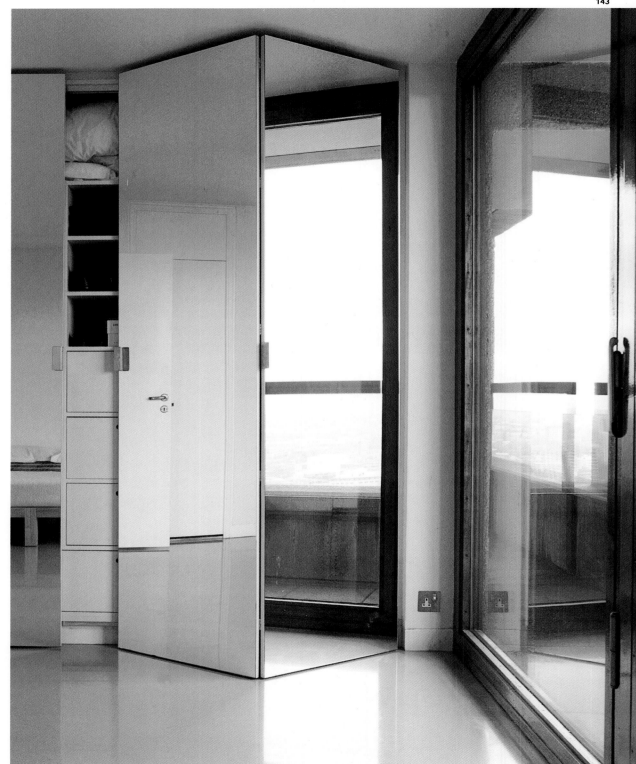

→ An unusual hybrid of door and window has been created in this home, by architect Chris Cowper. The tall, double-glazed, three-panel opening has a central panel that is independently hinged, and provides air, sunlight and great views of the garden.

↓ This en suite bathroom is visually linked to the bedroom by a panel of vertical glass girders. The glass brings natural light into both the bedroom and bathroom, and the sequence concludes in a blond timber door with glass porthole.

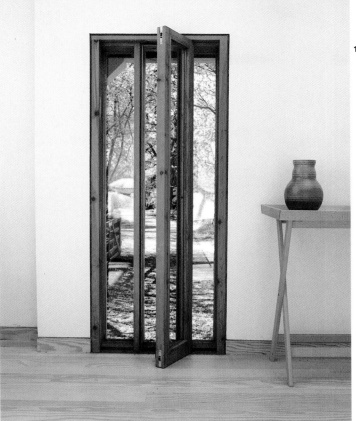

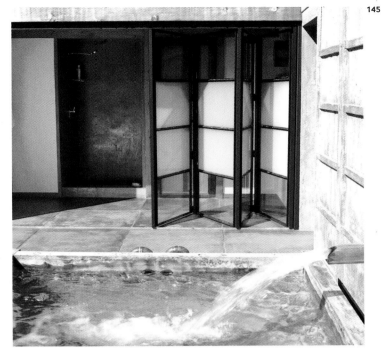

↓ This extension features a wall of metal-framed glazed doors opening onto a stone-flagged terrace and timber decking. Architect Walters & Cohen designed the doors in such a way that a single panel can be opened, as shown, or all six panels can be folded back out of the way.

↑ These folding concertina doors with their etched central band borrow from the design of free-standing folding screens. They open to reveal the luxury of a small private pool constructed in wood and fed by water gushing from a wooden spout. Inside is a simple shower room. The interior and exterior spaces have been linked by the continuous use of large square flagstones.

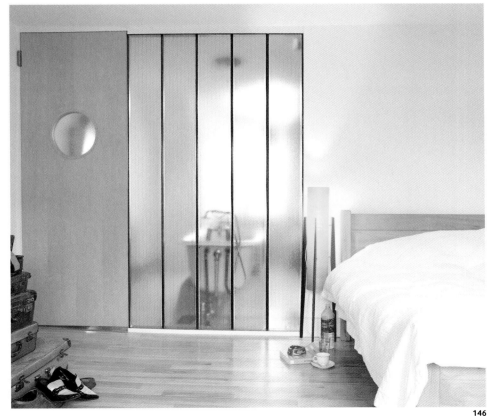

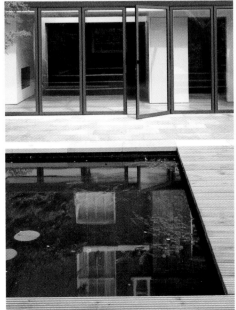

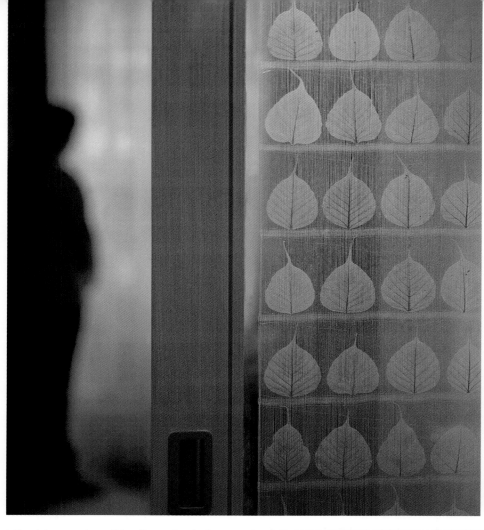

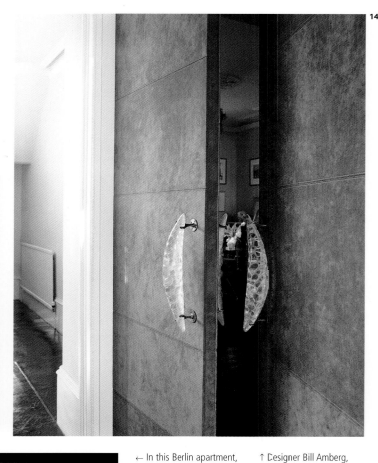

↑ Glazed doors are given additional interest here by the inclusion of a fine panel of open-weave cloth featuring a leaf pattern. The effect is almost as if the pattern has been etched into the glass itself. The cloth is decorative as well as practical, since it provides a little essential privacy for anybody in the room beyond.

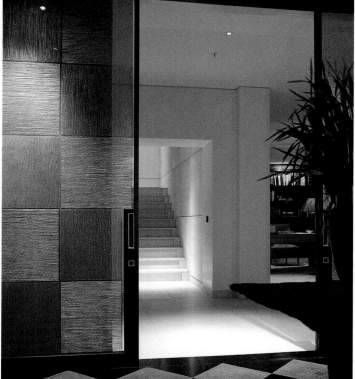

← In this Berlin apartment, the contrast between light and dark is marked at the threshold by dark hardwood-framed glass doors with unusual chequered panels. The designer of the apartment – Jonathan Reed, of Reed Creative Services – used glass from France that has been hand engraved and then finished with gold leaf let into the grooves. The pattern of squares, grained in opposing directions, reflects the basket-weave motif that is found throughout the apartment.

↑ Designer Bill Amberg, who is noted for his inventive uses of leather, has not only designed leather flooring for this hallway, but has also covered the door in stitched panels of soft suede. The tactile quality of the finishes in the space is heightened by the unusual crystal handles.

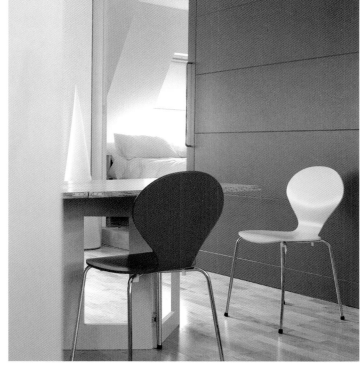

↓ Creating new circulation space in older buildings can be a challenge. In this project, by architect Will White, two adjacent flats have been joined, but to prevent the main living room from becoming the principal route through the home, an extra passageway was created. Here, the hall seems literally to burst into the corner of the bedroom through this exciting curved doorway.

← Where space is at a premium, sliding doors, such as this huge orange-coloured panel, are a useful alternative to the more traditional hinged door. In this compact apartment, even the furniture folds away – the desk top and legs are both hinged and fold back against the wall.

↓ A combination of glass and stainless-steel doors has been used by Anelius Design in this bedroom space. The glass doors lead to the bathroom, while the stainless steel fronts a storage cupboard.

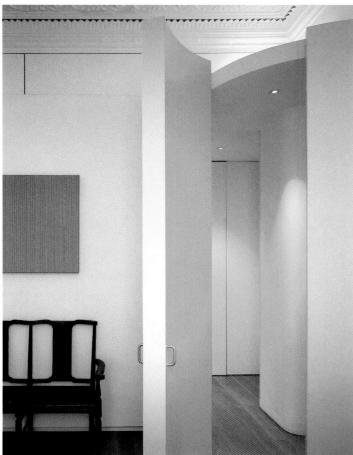

152

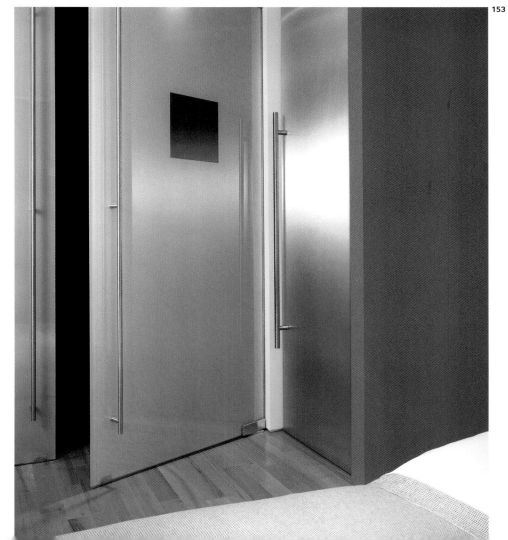

153

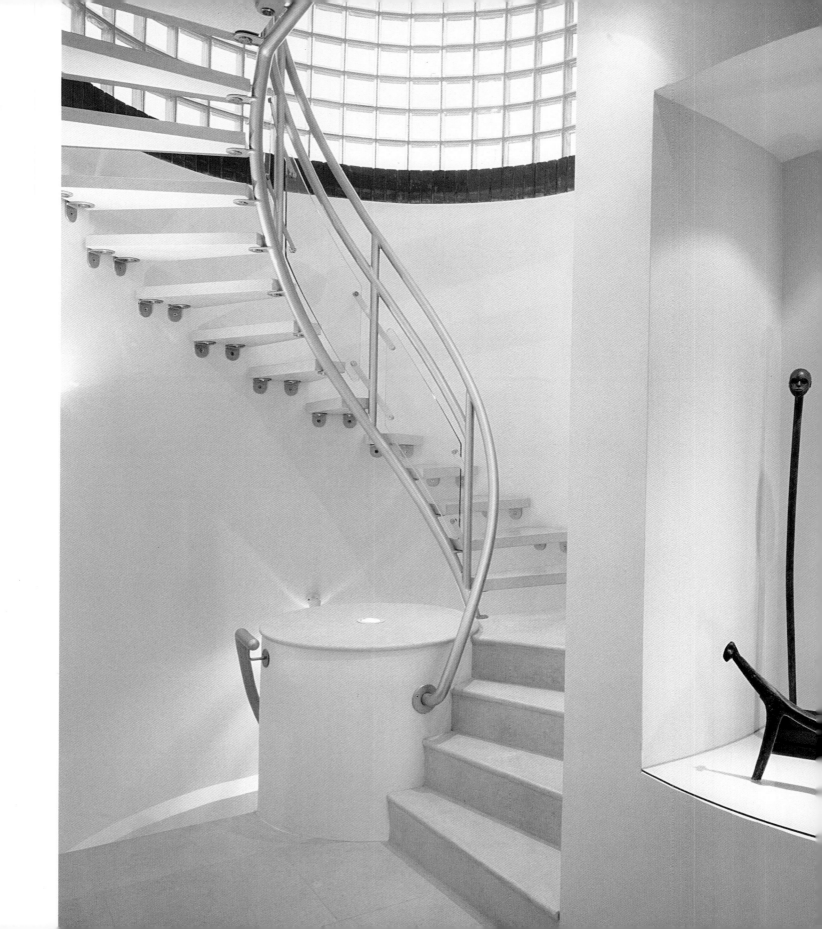

stairs

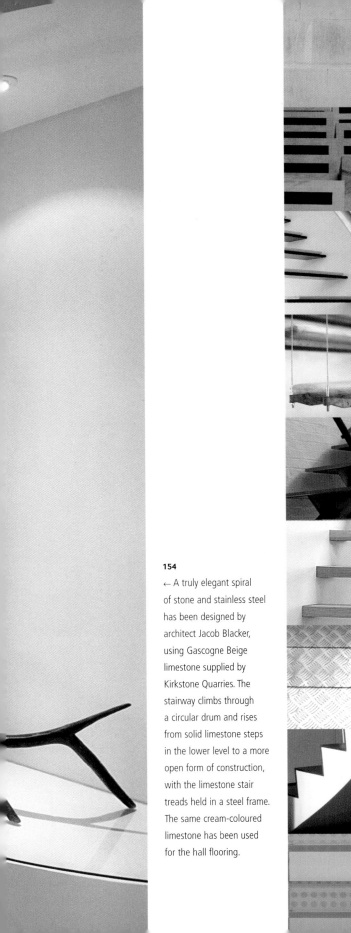

← A truly elegant spiral
of stone and stainless steel
has been designed by
architect Jacob Blacker,
using Gascogne Beige
limestone supplied by
Kirkstone Quarries. The
stairway climbs through
a circular drum and rises
from solid limestone steps
in the lower level to a more
open form of construction,
with the limestone stair
treads held in a steel frame.
The same cream-coloured
limestone has been used
for the hall flooring.

They are the ultimate flights of fancy, triumphs of balance and poise as, step-by-step, they pirouette and leap and zig-zag their way through space. There can be no doubt that stairways are in the ascendant.

Far from the familiar carpeted and heavily balustraded wooden stairways of the past, contemporary designs are lighter and altogether more elegant. And instead of greedily occupying a huge vertical shaft of valuable space within the home, they can now be integrated into living areas. Stairways have sprung free of the walls; they have been stripped back and transformed into daring sculptural masterpieces that now take centre stage in the home as feats of engineering brilliance.

Long fascinated by the challenge represented by this area of design, architects and designers alike are taking the stair to new heights. While every project has its own set of constraints and opportunities, an enormous palette of materials is now being called upon — from glass and stainless steel to stone, timber, and even acrylic — to create stairways that are almost at the point of dissolving in space. But while the possibilities are endless, a balance must always be struck between aesthetics and engineering.

shape and form

The style of stairways is constantly being explored by designers and architects, as they experiment with different ways of connecting the floors of various types of home. Among the most ancient of the possible designs is the climbing pole, followed by the ladder, and eventually the solid, stepped ramp. The permutations we see today are a testament to our endless fascination for this pivotal building element.

When choosing a stair for a new home, conversion, or extension it is worthwhile considering all the options. Probably least in favour for domestic interiors is the solid, stepped construction — a monumental block usually of stone or concrete. Where the preference is for something lighter, there is the flying stair. Here, apart from aesthetics, the overriding consideration is whether walls are strong enough to support a structure that will be cantilevered. In many contemporary examples, a steel framework is first inset into the wall and treads, usually made of wood or stone, are then fitted to the ascending supports, which protrude from the wall.

Further options include flights of stairs climbing up a central beam that is fixed to upper and lower levels, or designs based on a pair of strings (the long rails at either side of the stair), which are also fixed top and bottom. And then there is the spiral or helical, which winds up through a space, either fixed to the walls of a cylindrical case or hung around a central supporting post.

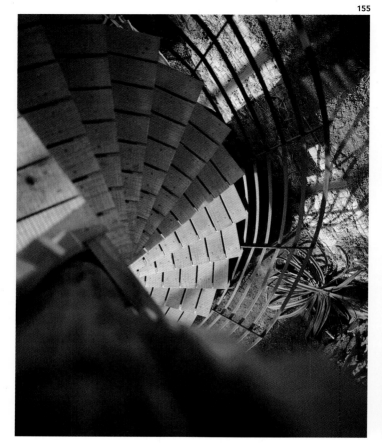

155

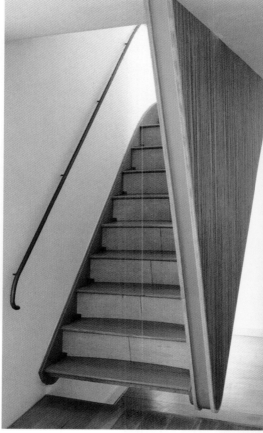

← The raw quality of unfinished wood strikes a lively note with this metal-framed spiral stair by Nash Architects. The whole flight has an open quality that is enhanced by the spaces between the timber sections of each tread, and between the narrow metal bands making up the handrail.

156

↑ The idea of skyhooks was the inspiration for this suspended stair in the home of architect Catherine du Toit and Peter Thomas, of 51% Studios. Its striking design incorporates a collection of materials — oak treads, plywood risers, corner wedges in recycled mahogany — and the whole is wrapped in a stripy veneer of zebrano wood.

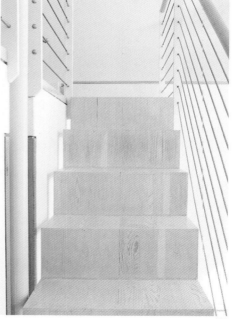

→ The detailing of finish is so precise in this flight of stairs that the steps appear almost to be made of folded wood. The simple pale wood has been pulled slightly free of the wall on the left, which allows an exciting slice of light to appear at the side. The balustrade is made of lengths of metal cable.

157

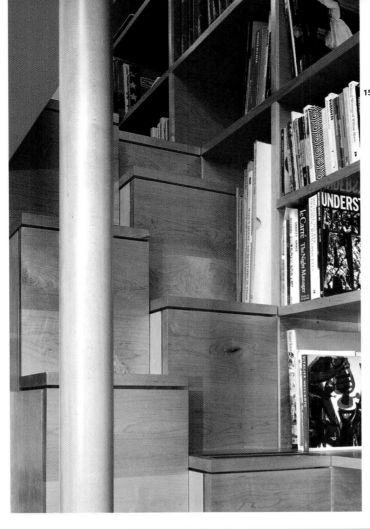

158

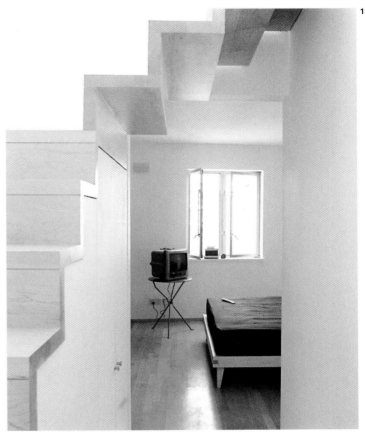

159

← The art-historian and cartoonist owner of this house commissioned an extension to provide extra space for his expanding office, and also a guest bedroom and bathroom. The design, by Freeland Rees Roberts, incorporates a library with this unusual space-saving stair rising to the office above.

→ This stunningly beautiful dog-leg style stone stair is a sculptural addition to the space. The first part of the flight is solid, but when it turns the corner the stair is revealed as a construct on of just treads and risers.

→ Inset into the treads of these unusual library stairs (see also picture 158) are strips of black carborundum – a compound of carbon and silicon. This material has abrasive qualities, and has been used here to add extra grip to the maple-wood stair treads.

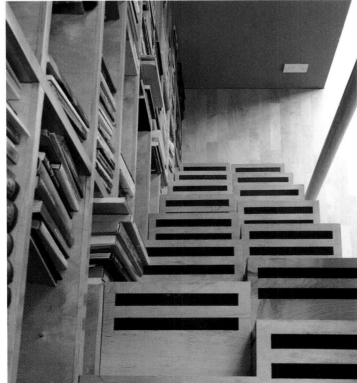

160

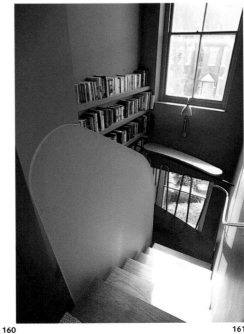

← Stairs are often scene stealers, and in this project, by architect Birds Portchmouth Russum, the timber flight of steps is utterly unmissable. Particularly appealing features include the imaginative rounded glass balustrades, the built-in library, and of course the striking cobalt-blue colour of the paintwork.

161

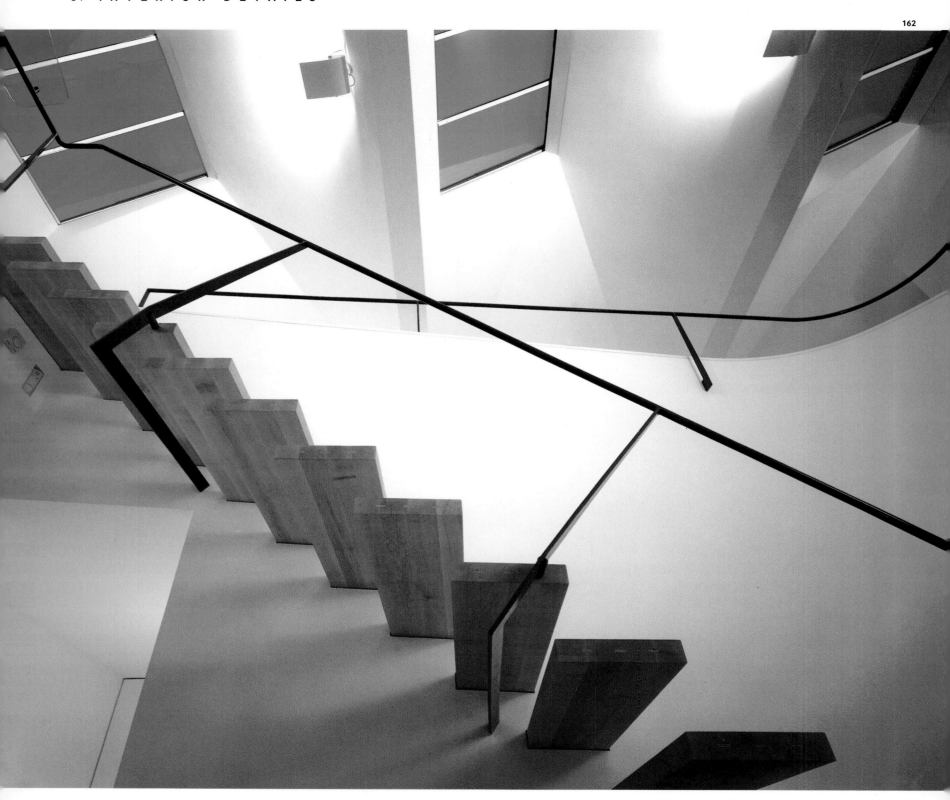

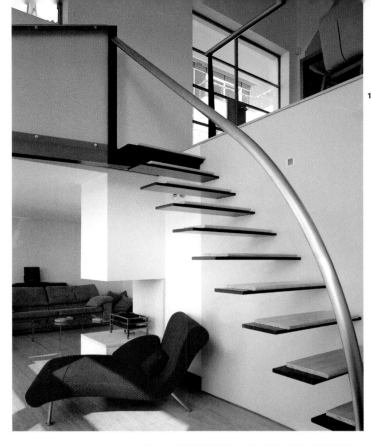

163

164

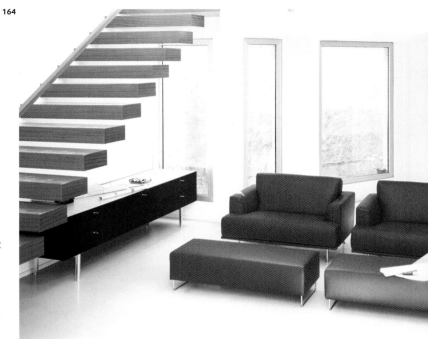

← An astonishingly light and minimal stairway has been created in this loft-style space by Julian Arenot Associates. The thin treads appear to have been pushed into the wall and then hover in space. Acting as a frame is the elegant hoop of steel handrail.

← The openness and lightness of this space quite take the breath away. For this penthouse apartment in a remodelled warehouse, architect Rick Mather has designed a timber stair with solid-maple treads cartilevered from the wall. To this he has added the slenderest of metal handrails. Inside the wall, the treads are held in a sturdy framework, but all we see is a stair that seems to float in space as it rises through the space toward the upper level.

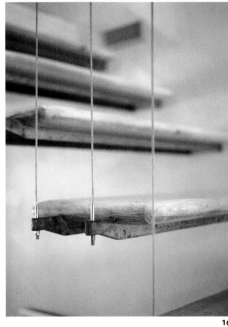

165

↑ A suspended stair made using simple, round-edged, timber treads set into metal cradles, which are then hung on steel tension wires, results in a stairway that is reduced not only to the minimum of materials, but also to the minimum of visual intrusion.

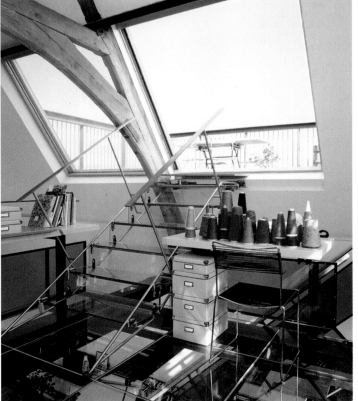

↑ Against an almost entirely neutral backdrop, this dramatic flight of stairs consists of chunky timber treads cantilevered from the wall. As a perfect complement, the scheme also features stunning red leather chairs and ottomans by Cassina.

← Architecture practice Brookes Stacey Randall has a reputation as an innovator in the use of glass. Here, a glass and steel stair rises from a mezzanine work-space to the roof terrace, reached through a sliding door-cum-window. For extra zest, the architect also used glass panels, fitted into a metal grid frame, for the floor of the work area.

166

materials for stairs

The range of materials used to construct a stair is now almost limitless, ranging from the solid and heavy old faithfuls, such as stone, concrete, and steel, to the more ethereal glass, aluminium, and resin. Your choice of material depends on many factors, not least of which are budget, function, location, and taste.

Climbing through the upper floors of a building, a heavy cast-concrete flight might be inappropriate or even dangerous. However, in the lower floor area, a similar design in stone or concrete could look incredibly impressive — almost adding ballast to the entire building. Yet stone can still be used to make a reasonably lightweight structure.

Steel is a favourite material where more contemporary-looking stair frames are desired. It can be light and incredibly strong, and it is often used in combination with another material for the treads — most often timber or glass. Of course, the timber stair has never been without its fans. Such is the versatility of this material that it can be used either in a solid monumental form or as a lightweight piece of construction.

And finally there is the glass stair. Although this material can look utterly beautiful, for anyone on a modest budget it is likely to be way out of reach.

→ The design challenge of these stairs, by architect Jonathan Woolf and engineer Bob Barton, was to make them as slender as possible so not to block light from a nearby window. The treads are made of thin slabs of cast aluminium, and the frame is in mild steel sprayed to give it a matt finish.

↓ From its solid cast-concrete base, this dog-leg stair turns the corner and is transformed, continuing its climb through space as a lighter, open-tread design with timber treads supported on a central steel beam. The handrail is flat steel, which continues at the stair top as the balustrade.

167

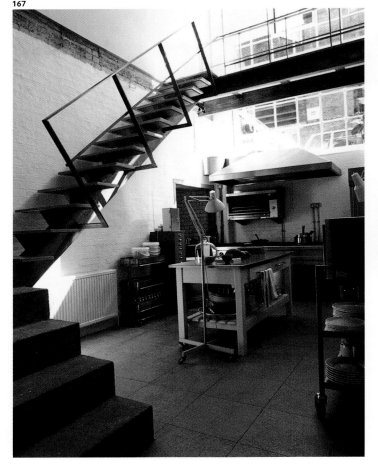

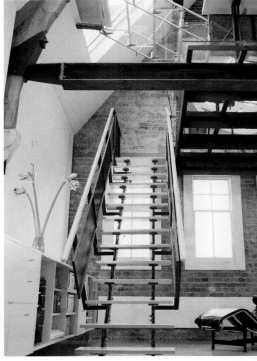

↑ In this conversion project, architect Brookes Stacey Randall wanted to retain as much light as possible. To keep sunlight cascading from rooflights into the living area below, a mezzanine with a glass floor was created, reached by a flight of open-tread stairs made of steel and wood.

170

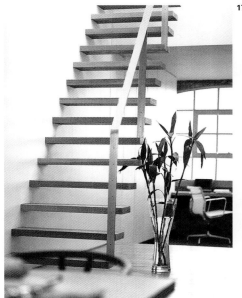

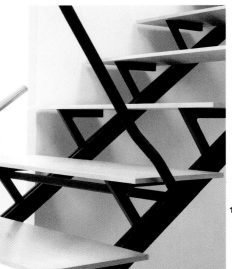

→ Between the dining area and office, this open-tread stair has been inserted to reach the sleeping area of the apartment. In this project by Simon Conder, the stair is built with slabs of oak for the treads, cantilevered from the wall and still retaining some of their springiness. The handrail is stainless steel.

169

→ A beautifully finished, black metal spiral stair, by designer Vincent Mazzucci, swirls upward from a black slate floor. With the first step suspended above the floor, the stair appears to leap into space.

↓ There are times when a small flourish makes a huge difference. The change in level between these two floors could have been bridged by steps that were quiet and functional, but instead architect Pip Horne decided to celebrate the rise and fall by inserting a sweep of three shallow steps in cast concrete.

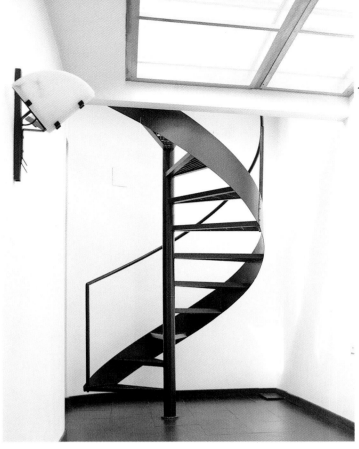

171

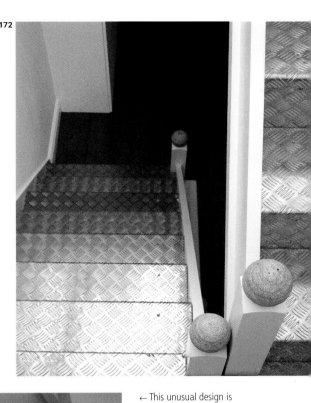

172

→ Providing interest and texture to what might have been a rather plain and traditional dog-leg staircase, the designer has wrapped the steps in industrial-style ridged aluminium sheeting. To add to the quirkiness, the newel posts are topped with balls of grey stone.

← This unusual design is an all-in-one, cast concrete-stair, which rises from the kitchen to provide access to a mezzanine level. The stylish yet functional handrail is made from a single band of steel.

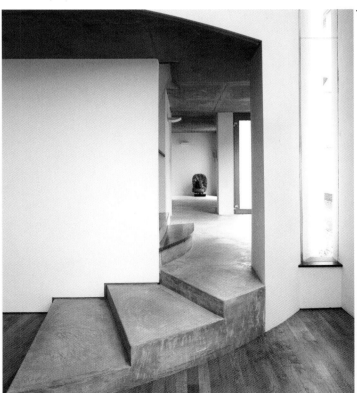

173

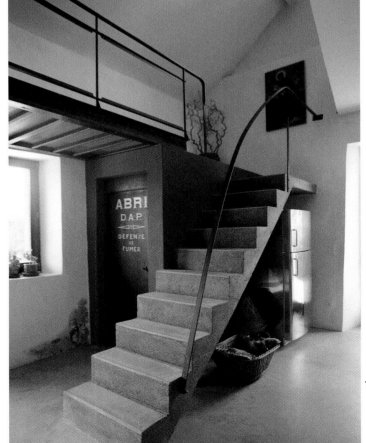

174

175

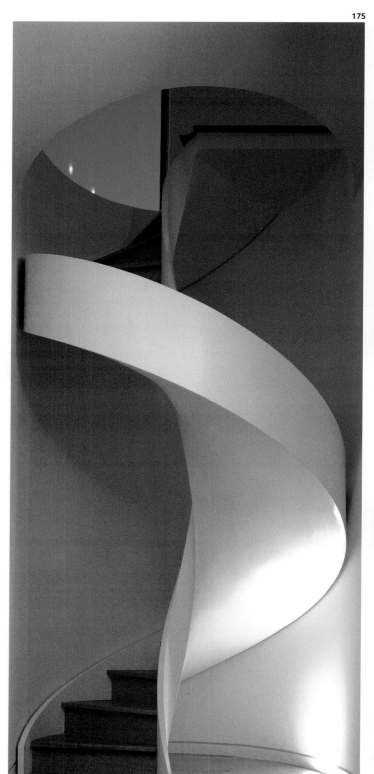

176

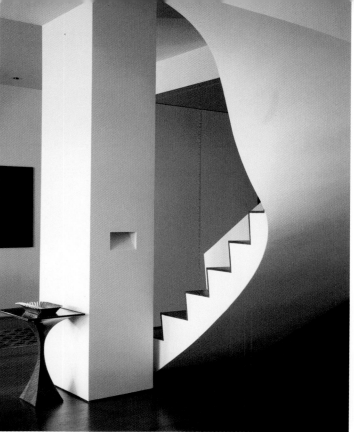

← Seeming almost to defy gravity, this sculptural stairway, by architect Tsao McKown, wraps itself around the chunky angular column and then climbs from the sheer timber floor to the space above.

↓ A spiral stair, by architect Ian Chee, climbs plant-like from its timber platform against the backdrop of a creamy, stone-lined wall. The timber of the living room floor is picked up in the stair design and inset into the triangular metal trays forming the treads.

← Looking like a free-flowing length of twisted ribbon, this white case, which was designed by Aluisw Marsoni, sinuously wraps itself around its timber stairs. The well-considered, floor-recessed uplighting shows off the beautiful curved sweep of open stair to best possible advantage, creating interesting pockets of bright highlight in the shadowy well.

178

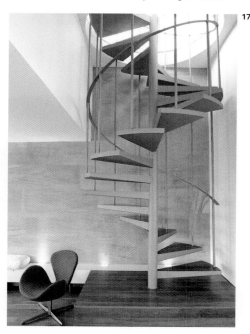

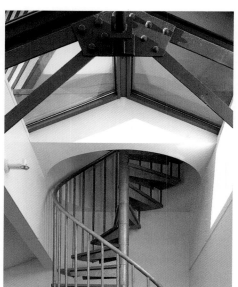

177

← An unusual mixture of galvanized metal and timber treads has been combined in this spiral stair, designed by architect Fletcher Priest. The choice of what are essentially industrial materials matches the chunky bolted steel beams supporting the roof.

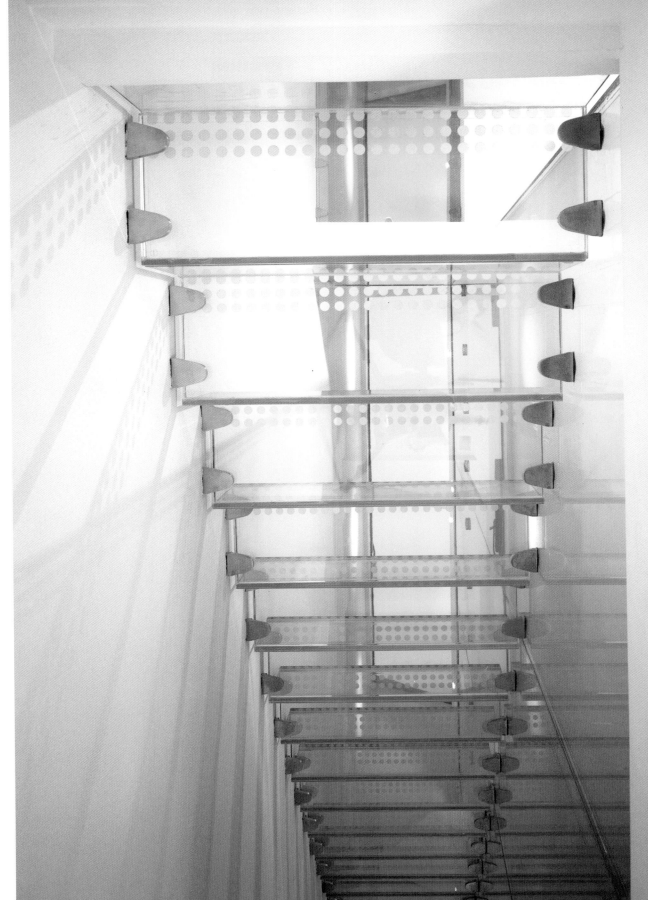

→ In his remodelling of this period town house, architect Alan Power created a light-filled interior for his clients. One key element was this glass stair, suspended between the wall and a floor-to-ceiling, horizontal, toughened-glass panel. Light falls through the entire space, after half the roof was removed and replaced with glass spanning from the front to the back of the building.

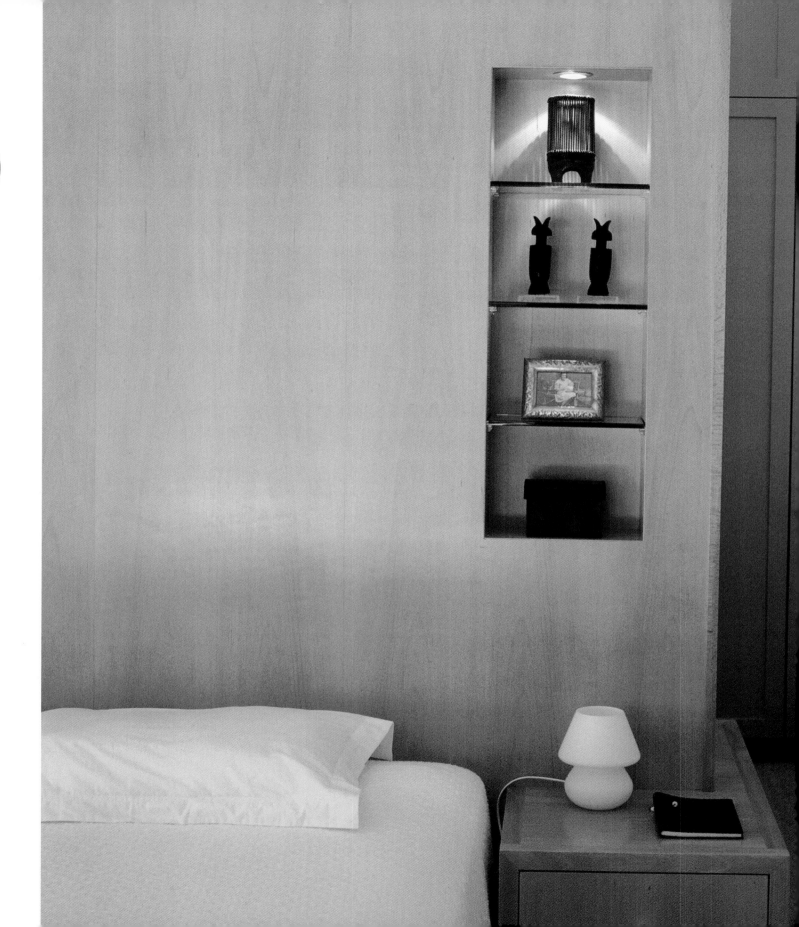

storage

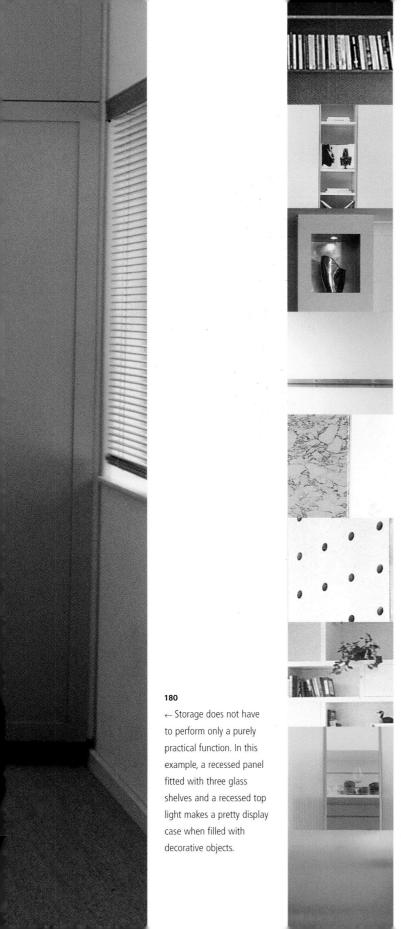

When it comes to considering storage options for the home, there is a universal law that says no matter how much storage space you have, it never seems to be enough. Quite simply, the root of the problem is that — unless you are a dedicated and ruthless minimalist — you are likely to own vast amounts of possessions.

Anybody who has moved home recently will certainly remember the surprise experienced when it comes to packing up. It hardly seems possible that the contents of a kitchen or bedroom can fill literally dozens of crates and various cardboard boxes. It is not surprising, then, that in recent years the skill of space organization has become a design discipline in its own right. There are now many companies that are dedicated solely to designing and manufacturing storage solutions, ranging from the well-ordered wardrobe to the home office built into a converted attic. And along with these storage experts, architects and designers share the same goal — that of building in maximum capacity with maximum efficiency. As we all know from experience, a well-organized space contributes to a well-organized life.

However, storage is not just about order — it is also about display, decoration, a way of expressing your personality, and making a statement about who you are. So as well as making storage efficient and practical, it is also crucial to incorporate fixtures and fittings that look good.

choosing a style

The perennial dilemma in choosing any form of storage system is whether to opt for built-in or free-standing units. Often the decision is based on matters of taste and space. As a general rule, built-in shelving and closets tend to make better use of space than free-standing units.

Just like a fitted kitchen, a modular system should be able to squeeze into the most awkward corners, while also providing a neat solution in larger rooms. Built-in units can be tailor-made for the room and to fit your exact requirements, or alternatively you can buy them off the peg.

The dozens of styles of systems on the market range from traditional-looking wood finishes to the most striking steel and glass units. The best advice when choosing a system is not to find one that looks good just for the here and now, but instead search for something that will continue to be in production for years should you need to expand it or make repairs.

Free-standing units offer a degree of flexibility that is simply not achievable with built-in types. The options include bookcases, room dividers, chests of drawers, and so on, all of which can be moved quickly and easily around the room and from home to home. There are also plenty of modern free-standing units on wheels, including bookshelves, room dividers, and display shelving. Wheel one of these into position to create a dividing screen, and then move it to one side whenever you want to enjoy open-plan space.

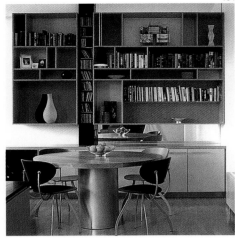

↑ This stunning collection of built-in shelving and cabinets was designed as part of an apartment project by architect Arthur Colin, and built by cabinetmaker Nicholas Dyson. The shelving is made using ply, the edges of which have been kept unpainted to show their laminated construction.

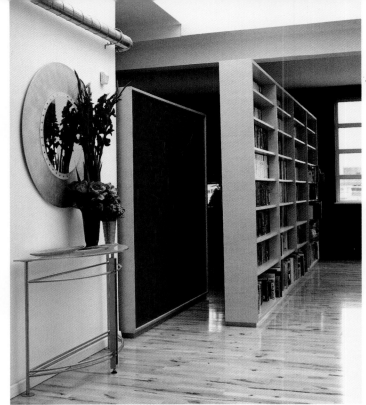

↑ This free-standing shelving unit does double duty as display shelving and room divider. It faces into the living area of the apartment, and behind a red-painted screen has been positioned to create a passageway leading to the bedroom beyond. Neither the shelving unit nor the screen reaches the ceiling, and so they define the space without encroaching on the feeling of openness.

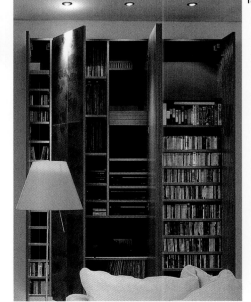

↑ This entire wall has been fitted with tall, slim, white, flush-faced wardrobe units, called Atlante by EmmeBi, to provide masses of storage space. The doors here are the "clip" variety, which are hinged; they are also available in a sliding version.

→ Designed by Fiona McLean, of McLean Quinlan Architects, this beautifully detailed music cabinet fits into a wall recess and accommodates both equipment and recordings, from CDs to vinyl. There is even built-in ventilation to prevent equipment over-heating. The flush-surface doors are finished in a startling burr oak veneer.

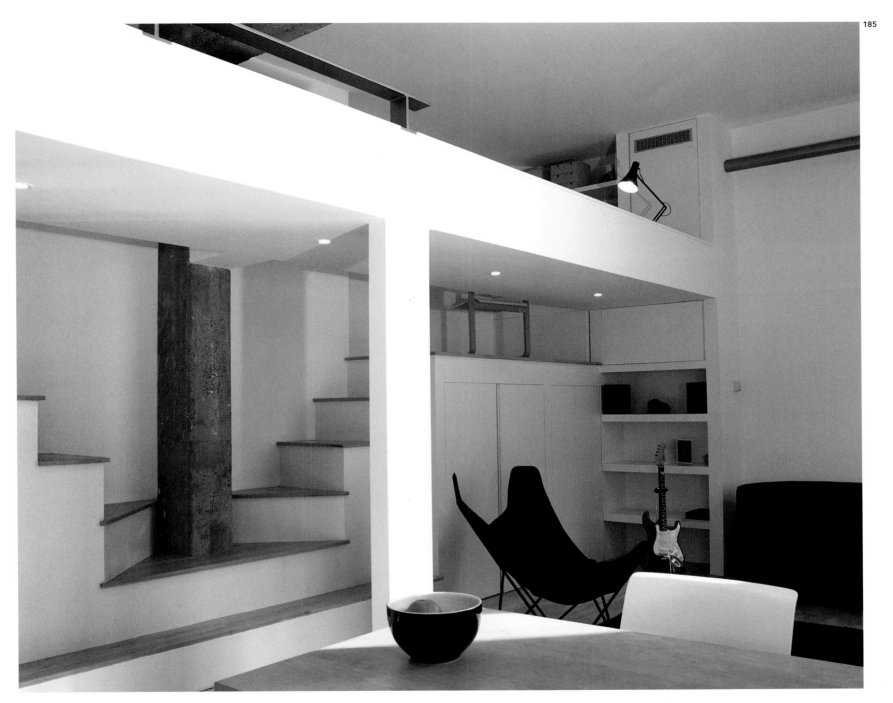

↑ To maintain the clean, uncluttered lines of contemporary living spaces, generous storage area is essential. Here, The Douglas Stephen Partnership has built in a series of shelves and cupboards, providing plenty of space both to display and to conceal possessions.

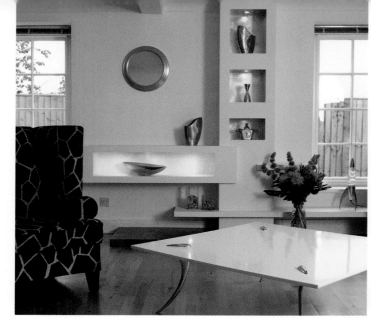

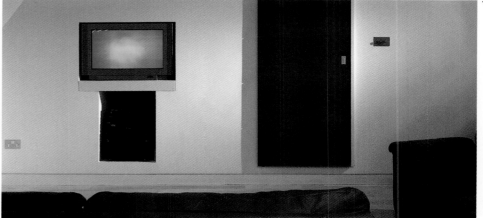

↑ Storage units can be made to look as beautiful as the objects they display, and here the designer has shown real panache in an interior refit that features elegant, interconnecting vertical and horizontal showcase units with integral display lighting.

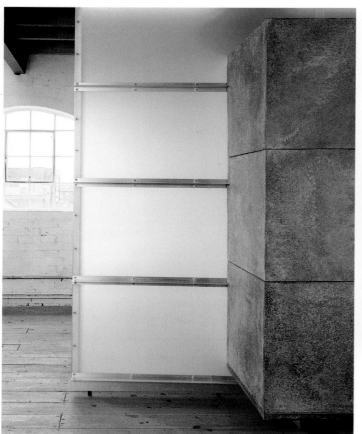

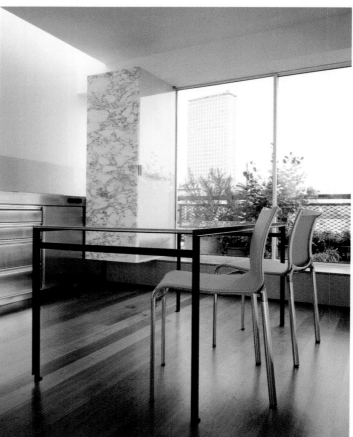

↑ This is a tidy solution where floor space is in short supply, or where an uncluttered look is the desired effect. Sanya Polescuk Architects has pushed the TV and music system back into recesses built into the wall.

← Because space was at a premium in this city-centre apartment, the kitchen was kept to a minimum and architecture practice Procter Rihl devised an ingenious hanging cupboard, partly supported by the step beneath, to house both the refrigerator and the oven. The cupboard has a glass door and is faced in an unusually lively version of the Carrara marble called Arabescata.

← This lightweight screen wall of opal polycarbonate sheeting and aluminium incorporates a copper box that serves as a wardrobe. The apartment design is by architect Fraser Brown McKenna.

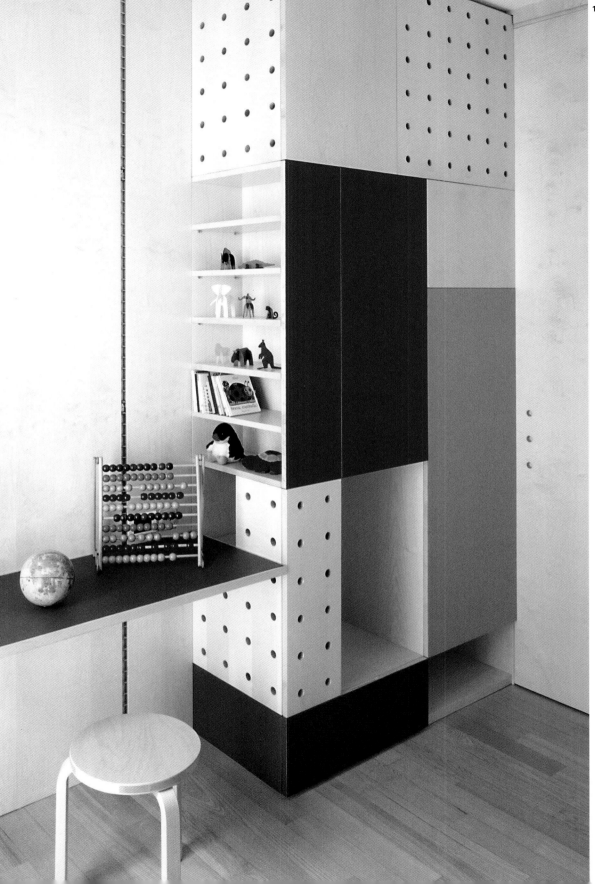

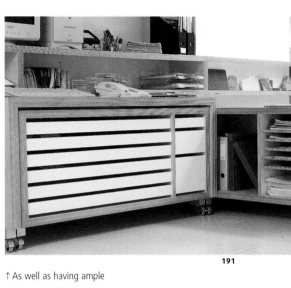

↑ As well as having ample storage space, it is also important to make sure that it is of the right type. This home office, for example, contains a variety of storage solutions to meet specific needs: shelving for bulky items, including the computer monitor and reference magazines; an area for stationery; space for files; boxes for storing samples; and a plan chest for storing large sheets of flat paper.

← The charming cubist store cupboard, shelving unit, and desktop in this children's room, by architect Marco Romanelli, was designed for the architect's own home in Milan. The floor-to-ceiling unit provides generous storage space for clothes, toys, and books. A practical detail is that the desktop can be raised as the child grows.

planning and usage

In setting out to plan and choose storage space, it is important to start by identifying the type of material to be stored – every last thing, right down to boxes of holiday snaps. Take decisions room by room – what are the basic essentials, what are the treasured extras, what can be stored elsewhere, and what can be dispensed with?

Start to draw up lists of items that are in everyday use, those things that are needed fairly regularly, and those that are too useful or precious to move out altogether. Build up a picture in your mind about how and where to accommodate all these various items.

Next, make an assessment about how much space your possessions will occupy – measure existing bookshelves, cupboards, wardrobe hanging rails, and so on, and, for the new scheme, make calculations that err on the generous side. It's likely that things will require more space than you imagine and that you will also need some empty space to expand into.

Now you can think about the range of storage options – do you need shelving and cupboard space, and approximately how much of each? And, finally, there are questions of style. Is your taste for a few well-chosen antiques, or perhaps something utterly contemporary, or a mixture of the two? This may be the moment to commission a designer or cabinetmaker to make something unusual and tailor-made for a specific space.

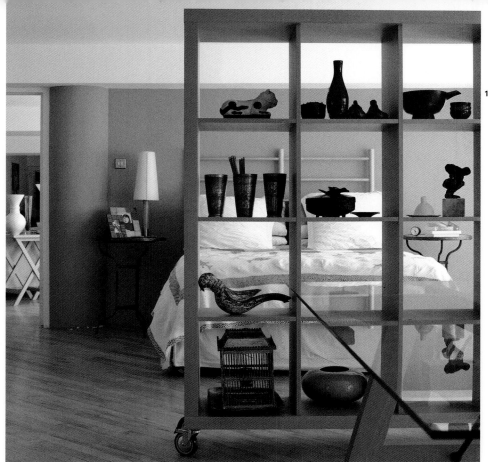

192

← Where it is desirable to keep light flowing through interior spaces, consider this style of open-plan shelving unit, which makes an excellent room divider and display case. It is fitted with wheels, making it easy to move to a new location.

↓ An entire wall of fitted cupboards and shelving provides lots of storage space in this child's room, part of a project by Barbara Weiss Architects. A mixture of open shelves and closed cupboards adds interest to the design and helps to break up the structure's impact on the room.

194

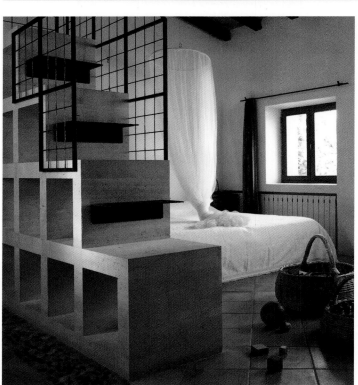

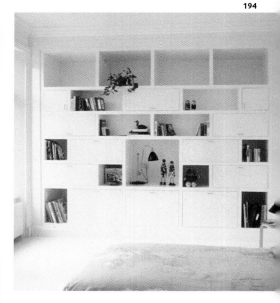

← Stone has been used in a monumental way here to create a stunning room divider, which doubles as a bookcase and trebles as a stairway to the floor above. The unit separates the bedroom from the living area in the Mallorcan family home of architect Astrid Lohss.

193

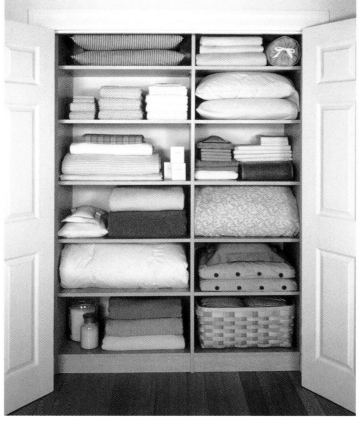

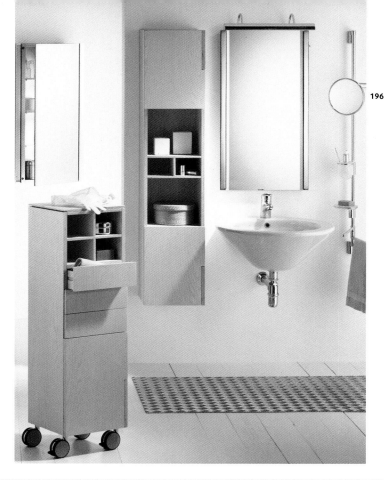

→ Ever since the bathroom became a haven of tranquillity, more attention has been paid to its furnishings and fittings. Here, designer Carlo Bartoli has produced a collection of free-standing and wall-hung units, called Luna, for the Italian manufacturer Colombo Design.

↑ Making the most of even the smallest storage spaces, the international company Californian Closets designs modular units that cater for all types of storage requirements. These include tools in a garage, andwardrobes in the bedroom, as well as this traditional linen cupboard.

→ A modular fitted wardrobe system called Rimadesio has been built into this space. The uprights for the U-shaped design are fixed between the floor and ceiling, and the shelves, are then hung onto this frame. For extra flexibility, the drawer units are mounted on wheels.

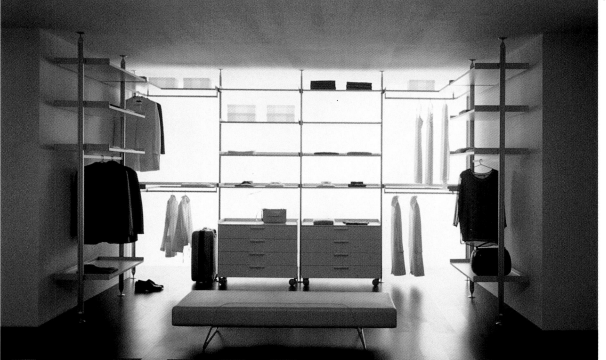

198

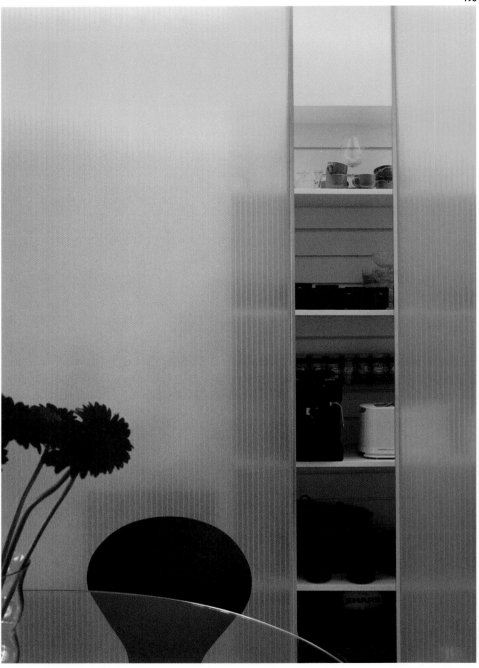

↑ While it is routine to have a light inside the refrigerator, it is rare to find them fitted in cupboards and cabinets. Here, the architect Stickland Coombe has incorporated lighting inside this storage wall. The shelving is fitted behind sliding doors made of Triwall polycarbonate sheeting.

199

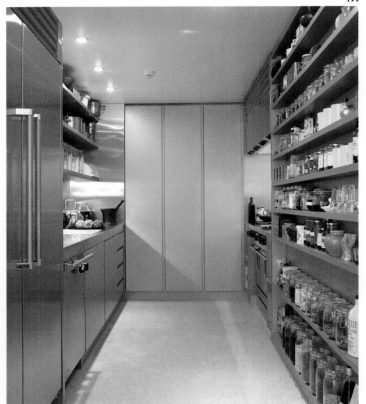

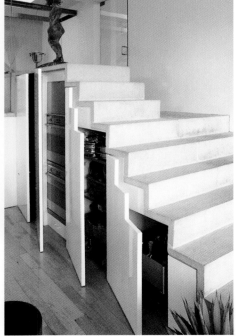

200

↑ This galley kitchen is lined entirely with stainless steel, which has also been used to make the storage units and shelving. Although room dimensions are tight, there are plenty of cabinets as well as space above the sink for pans. Meanwhile, the shallow, open shelving provides a huge amount of display space for food storage.

← In small homes, no corner can be wasted. Here, even the space under the stairs provides valuable storage, housing the oven, pots and pans, baskets, and other miscellanea.

↓ One of the traditional problems most people encounter when it comes to kitchen storage is how to accommodate all those small but essential items. In this detail of a contemporary-style project, by Fulham Kitchens, the problem of storing herbs, spices, and condiments has been solved by incorporating pull-out vertical drawers.

201

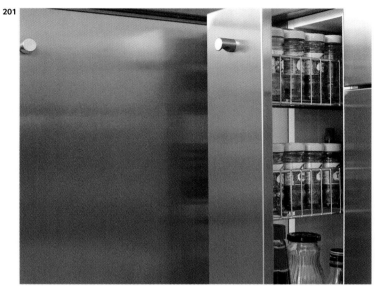

202

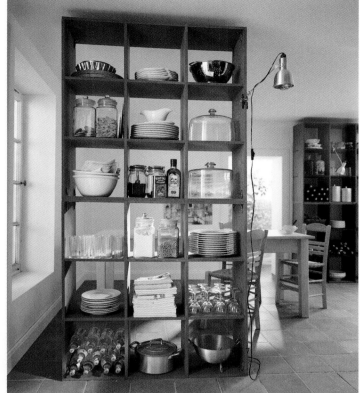

← In an unfitted kitchen, one option for storage is to make a decorative feature of the objects themselves. This modular, open-plan shelving called Brigitte is made by the German company Octopus.

203

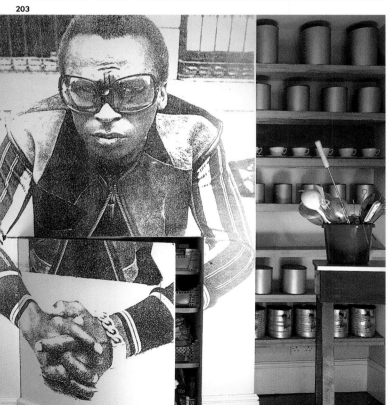

← This a complete departure from the sleek, high-tech kitchen. The room is more informal, with open shelving for displaying kitchen objects. Where the fireplace used to be, a huge black-and-white photocopied portrait adorns a useful storage cupboard for household cleaning materials.

→ To make the most of those tiny left-over spaces that are inevitable in any fitted kitchen, Fulham Kitchens has devised a number of units that turn even the smallest gaps into invaluable extra storage.

204

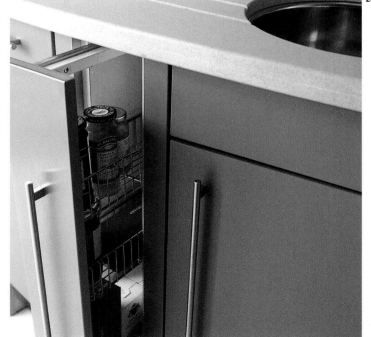

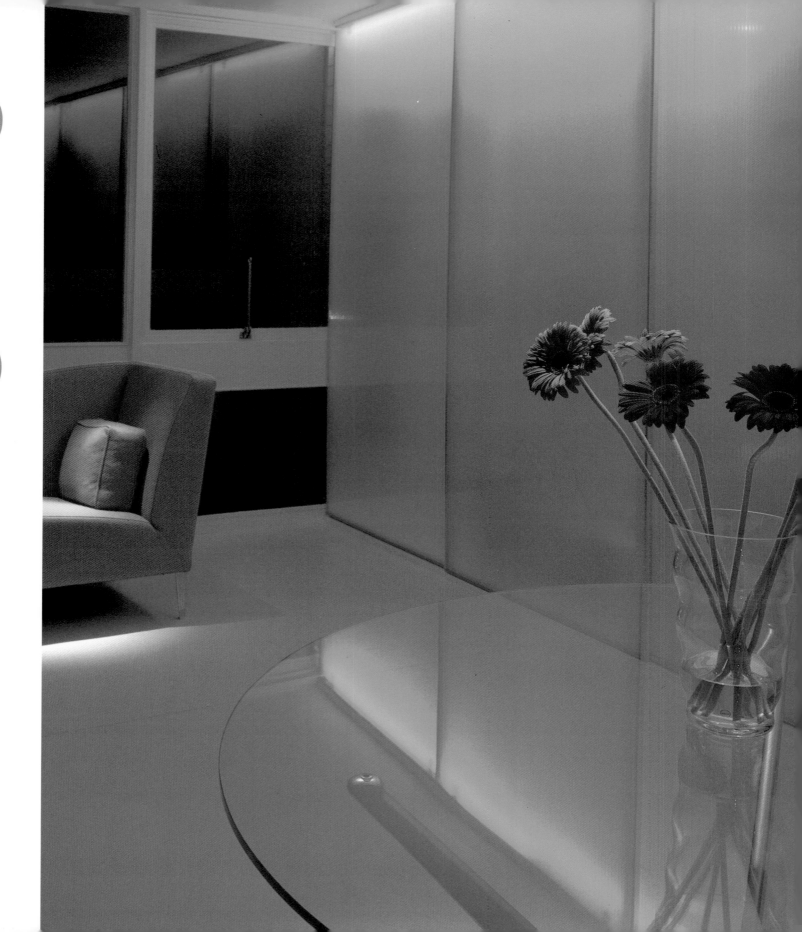

lighting

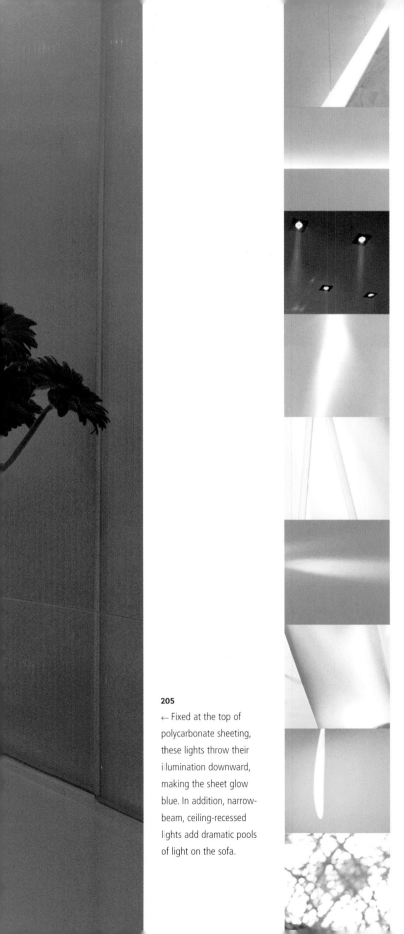

205
← Fixed at the top of polycarbonate sheeting, these lights throw their illumination downward, making the sheet glow blue. In addition, narrow-beam, ceiling-recessed lights add dramatic pools of light on the sofa.

Light is a vital component in the interiors of our homes; it gives us the means by which we can see and enjoy indoor spaces as a series of shapes, colours, and textures. In addition, it sets the tone and atmosphere. Of course, sunlight provides one of the most welcome and comfortable forms of illumination indoors, but artificial lighting must be installed as a supplement for use at night and for those occasions during the day when natural light levels are low. Turning on an electric light bulb is the simplest way of filling a space with a pool of light – the effect, however, is likely to be uninspiring. The application of this precious yet ubiquitous element in such a way as to make a room comfortable and inviting can be a difficult design skill to master.

One way to understand how to manipulate light, particularly the artificial variety, is to try to think how a painter might approach the subject. Imagine a lighting scheme as being multilayered, built up first of washes of background light, which might include a central pendant. Then, for more interest, add height and depth with wall lights, table lamps, and tall floor-standing lights. All the while, bear in mind that the quality, intensity, and spread of these sources of illumination will react with the room's colour scheme.

Next, for some real drama, add in the highlights – perhaps using spotlights to pick out architectural details or to focus on a painting or a piece of sculpture. Where beams of light are at their most intense on a subject, there, at the edges, we will also find the densest shadows to give form and underline the dramatic tension. When planning a scheme, take into account that darkness and shadow are just as important as light for adding contrast, excitement, and mystery.

lighting requirements

When setting out to plan a lighting design scheme, there are two key steps in assessing the illumination needs of any room. The first is to take account of the size and shape of the space. As a rule, the larger the room, the more light sources you will need to create an even lightfall, supplemented by pools of light for dramatic touches. If the room has very high or low ceilings, take this into account too as lighting can be used to help shape the space.

The colour and texture of the decor and furnishings play their part as well. To take extreme examples, a contemporary white-painted room with pale-coloured furniture will require different lighting from a more heavily decorated space with dark-wood furniture and richly coloured cloth or leather upholstery.

The second main point is to think about is how the space is to be used and what type of mood you want the lighting to create. Natural illumination will always have to be supplemented by artificial lighting on dull days or dark winter mornings and evenings, but there may also be areas that require specific task lighting – areas where you may be involved in activities such as cooking, reading, sewing, or working at a computer, for example.

To provide the flexibility to change the mood of a room, from bright and upbeat to something more restful, try introducing two main lighting circuits – one to cater for general ambient light and the other for supplementary lamps. Dimmer switches are ideal ways of varying the intensity of illumination and fine tuning the effect.

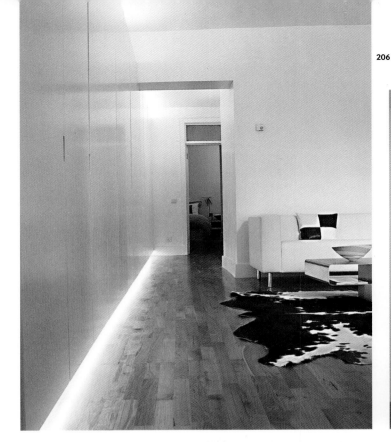

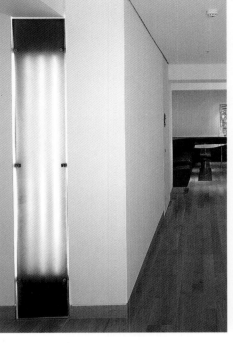

↑ One entire wall in this apartment has been lined with satin-white, flush-finish closets, fitted top and bottom with tube lighting. The lighting design introduces an interesting effect and, intriguingly, makes the closets seem disconnected from the floor.

→ This is a simple yet stunning wall light called Riga, designed by Antonio Citterio and Oliver Low for Italian manufacturer Flos. The fitting incorporates a new-generation fluorescent tube sitting behind a long aluminium baffle – in an anodized natural or painted finish – which can be tilted to change the direction of the light.

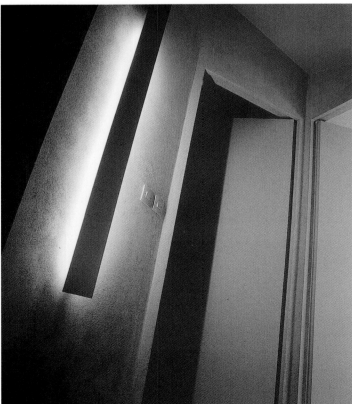

↑ Lighting doubles as an artwork in this apartment, by architecture practice Wells Mackereth. The fluorescent tube lighting has been recessed into the wall and faced with a pink and violet translucent cover. Positioned in the entrance hall, the glowing column of light makes an arresting feature.

209

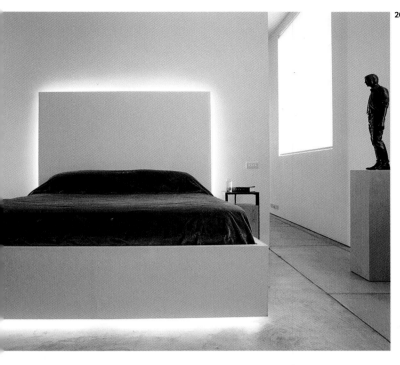

210

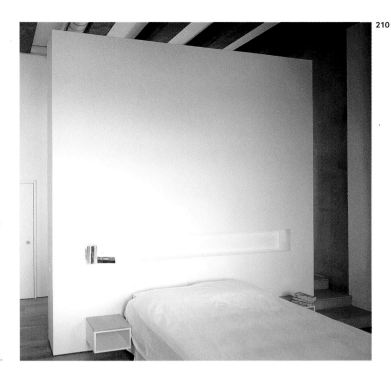

→ In this apartment, by architect Seth Stein, reading light is cleverly supplied by a long lightbox arrangement set into the headboard-cum-wall behind the bed. Lights have been set into the top of this recessed shelf, and placed behind a baffle in order to prevent light glaring back from the page.

↑ The bed takes centre stage here, floating on a raft of crisp white light in a serene white space. The scheme features light sources hidden out of view behind the headboard and around the base of the bed.

→ An ethereal quality of light pervades this bedroom, designed by architect John Pawson. The light sources are hidden, so only the warm, glowing quality of the illumination is visible. One set of lights has been placed behind the headboard, while others have been fitted at the top edge of the room, by the window, where a slot has been made in the ceiling to accommodate them.

211

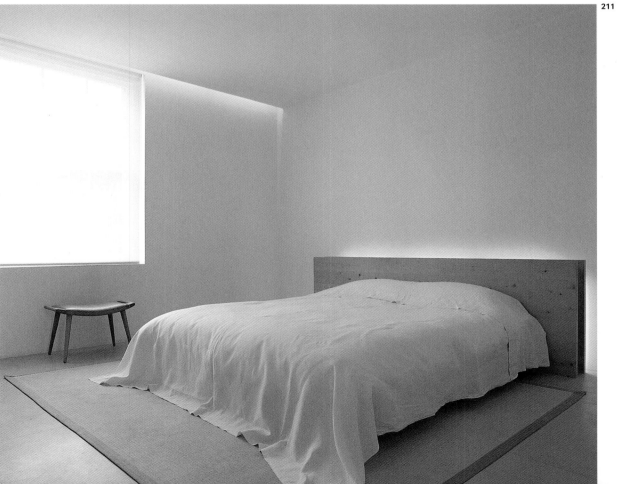

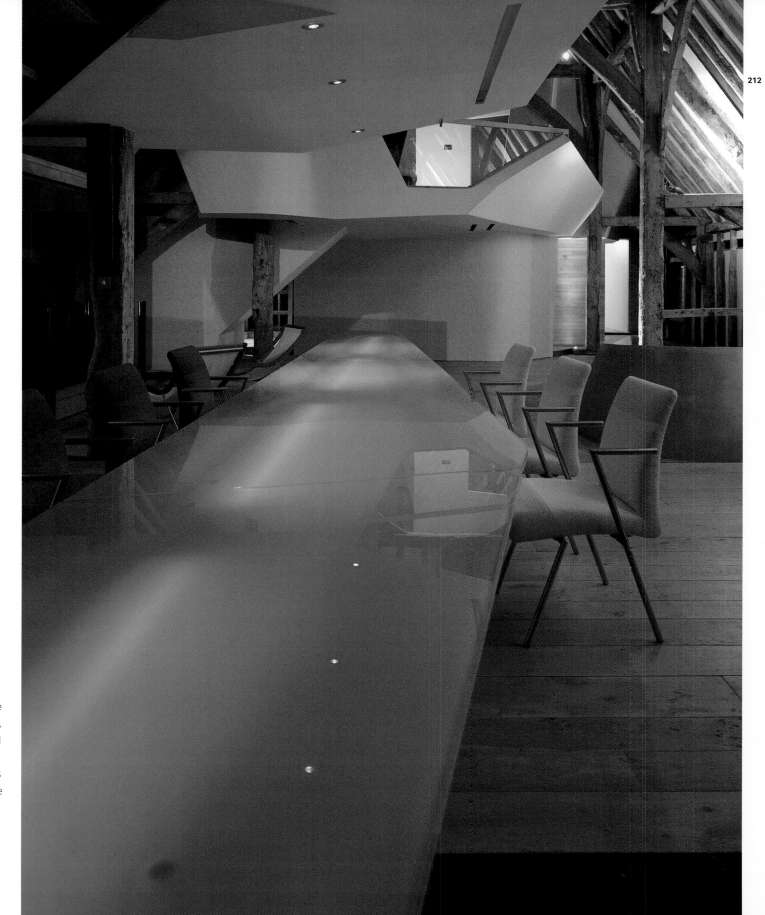

→ This lighting scheme enhances the drama of a highly unusual space inside a converted barn. The long, asymmetrical, glass-topped table features tubes of lighting beneath. Sparkle is added from above by a line of low-voltage halogen lamps in a recess built into the suspended ceiling.

213

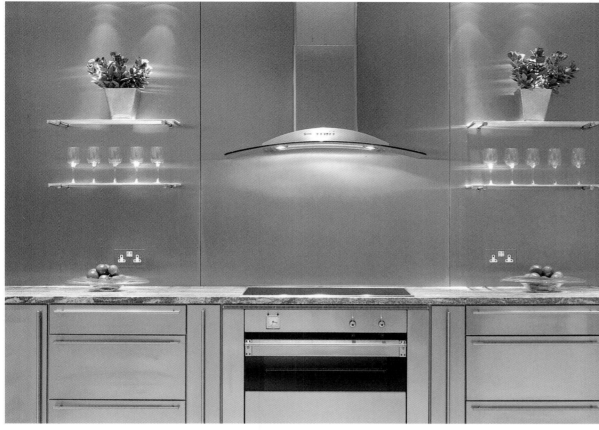

← A stainless-steel-clad kitchen is shown to best effect with an accomplished display by specialist company Lighting Design International. In the middle, the Neff extractor hood incorporates a pair of small bright lamps, and around the circumference of the room are ceiling-recessed, directional low-voltage halogen lamps. Those above the shelves highlight the flowers and glassware.

214

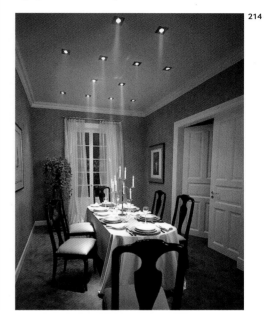

→ A pair of ceiling-recessed, low-voltage halogen lamps fitted into the top of this shower cubicle provides an exciting crisp light, which is reflected in the cobalt-blue mosaic tiles. Electrical safety dictates that fully enclosed lamp units must be specified for damp areas such as kitchens and bathrooms.

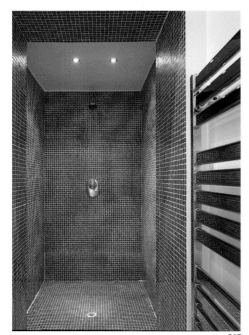

215

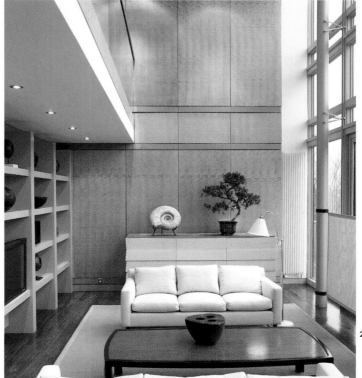

↑ A constellation of halogen lamps in the ceiling adds magic to this traditional-style dining room. Halogen lighting was designed for adding zest to store window displays, and it performs a similar role in this environment.

← Recessed halogen lamps, powerful downlighters at the top of the double-height space, a small light fitting behind the bonsai tree, and a floor-standing reading lamp by the sofa offer great flexibility and the chance to conjure a variety of lighting moods.

216

→ This unusual bedroom design, in a project by architect Aukett Tytherleigh, features a bed enclosed with long drapes that can be pulled back to reveal great cityscape views. Lighting includes ceiling-recessed lamps in the main area, a lowered ceiling off-centre over the bed with additional recessed lights, and a pair of wall-fixed reading lamps.

→ Lighting fixed low down is unusual and eye catching. In this room, a series of low-voltage halogen lamps, with square steel and glass fascias, have been fitted into the timber floor, where they cast their light upward beside perforated steel stair treads.

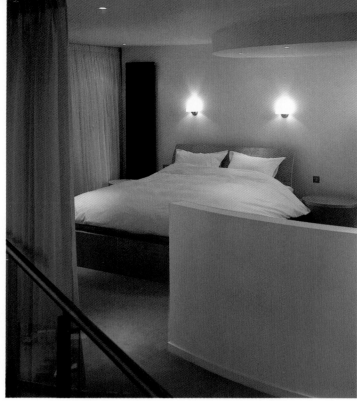

217

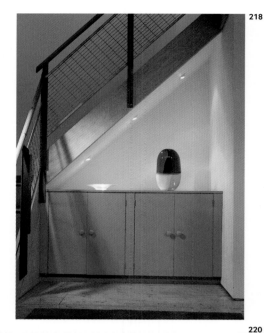

218

→ Even a small area under a stair can be given extra interest with a well-considered lighting scheme. This trio of small, recessed, directional light fittings illuminates the decorative glass objects to produce a theatrical display area.

220

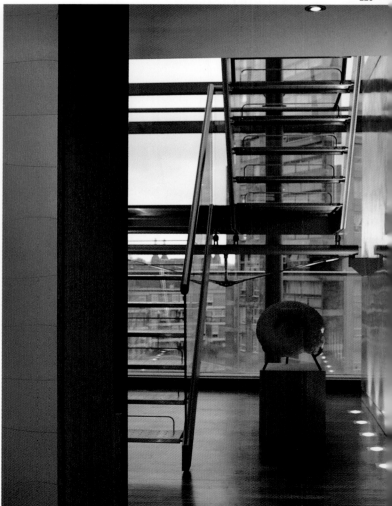

219

→ In this view of the floor-inset halogen lamps (see also pic 219), you can see them in their full room setting, where it is possible to appreciate the stunning effect created as they uplight the wall and stairway.

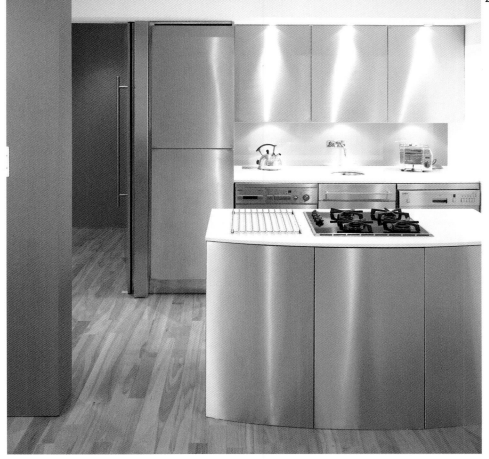

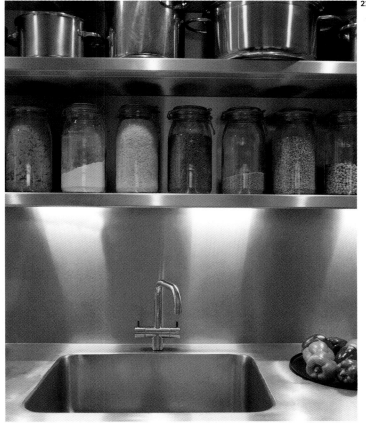

↑ The sheen of brushed stainless steel has been given even greater lustre in this scheme, by Anelius Design. The three-panel rhythm of the wall cabinets and island unit is underscored by the lighting. The cabinets have three low-voltage baffled lamps beneath to cast a good, strong working light onto the counter top, while an additional set of three lamps, fitted above the cabinet doors, throws a beam of illumination down each fascia.

→ Just a single unusual lighting element can add a real focal point to an interior. In this home, large slots have been cut into the floor to make glass-topped troughs to accommodate spotlight uplighters.

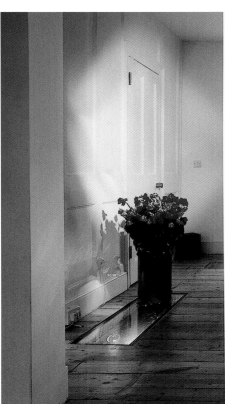

↑ The ambient lighting in this kitchen has been boosted by the addition of tiny light sources fitted behind the lower shelf. Though only small, these lights provide useful shadow-free illumination just where it is needed — on the worktop and sink.

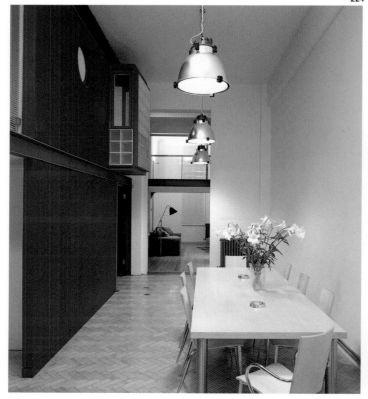

224

↓ This delicate track lighting system creates a delightful yet very practical kitchen lighting scheme. The track has been installed close to the edge of the room so that the low-voltage halogen lamps can cast their light where it is most useful – on the worktops and the hob.

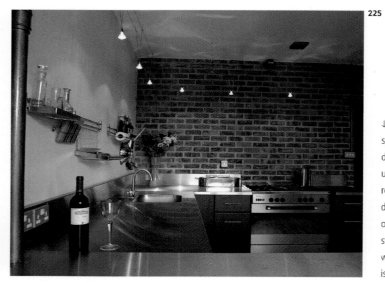

225

↓ This vast open-plan living space is divided into distinct zones. The kitchen, under the great sloping roof, is marked out by the distinctive lighting – pairs of industrial-style lamps on stems suspended over the work islands. The architect is Kuth/Ranieri.

↑ In this dining area the architect, Buckley Gray, has taken advantage of the very high ceilings and added three industrial-style aluminium pendant lamps.

→ Making a wonderful contemporary interpretation of the chandelier is this raft of tempered glass studded with lights. The power supply passes through the conductive paint tracks, and the fitting comes with a remote control that enables each lamp to be adjusted individually. The design, called Lastra, is by Antonio Citterio and Oliver Low for Italian manufacturer Flos.

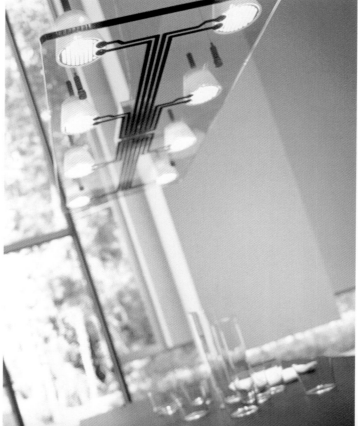

226

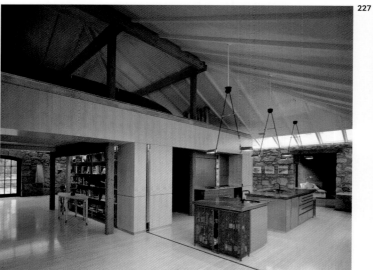

227

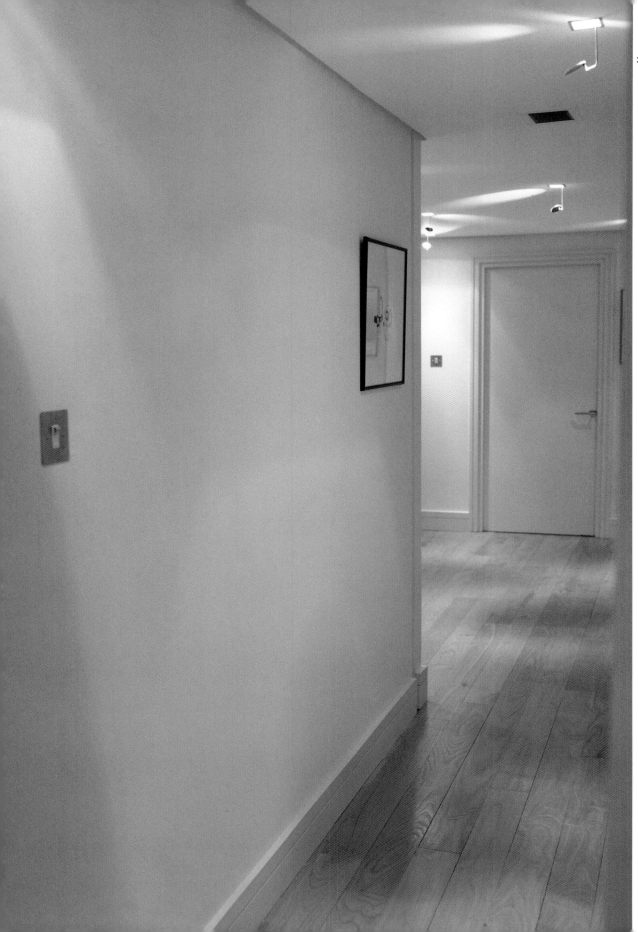

light sources

The tungsten light bulb is the most common artificial light source. For the first century of it remained virtually unchallenged, but in the past few decades many different types of lamp have been developed for the domestic market.

To make the most of the lights on offer, it is useful to have a working knowledge of the main types. The ubiquitous tungsten bulb is based on a filament in a glass dome that glows when charged with electricity, it comes in a variety of styles, including tubes.

The most significant competitor on the domestic lighting scene is halogen, which is available in low- and mains-voltage varieties. This source was originally used for store window displays, where its crisp, white, sparkling illumination is ideal. As well as clear illumination, these lights also benefit from being small and powerful. On the down side, however, the low-voltage types are difficult to fit into older properties without plasterboard ceilings, they require a hefty transformer, and they are still relatively expensive.

The next major option is fluorescents, which most people think of as bleak unattractive tubes flickering in the kitchen or garage. However, new-generation fluorescents are not only kinder on the eye but are also incredibly energy efficient.

← Attractive and very unusual ceiling lights have been installed in this apartment. Each lamp fitting is recessed into the ceiling, but the beam of light is then bounced across the surface plane by pink and blue reflectors suspended on stems just below the lamps.

light fittings

Artificial lighting can be used not just to shape the mood of an interior, but also to help shape the space itself. In response to growing interest in the potential that good lighting has to offer, designers and manufacturers are now producing fittings to suit every purpose.

The main categories of lighting unit to select from have self-explanatory titles. They include: uplighters — wall-mounted lights or free-standing units, such as standard lamps, that are designed to cast their light upward; downlighters — ceiling-recessed lamps, pendants, and track lighting, which shed light downward; spotlights — lamps with a narrow beam of light, which can be focused up or down on a room feature or object; and task lights — work lamps, such as the classic Anglepoise, which sit on a desk to provide an intense, directed light. In addition to these, there are also decorative lights, ranging from chains of tiny, colourful fairy lights to a multitude of different designs of table lamps.

With these basic lighting tools, it is possible to manipulate our perception of space. For example, if a room is already tall but you want to accentuate its height further, then install uplighters to wash the ceilings with light. However, if you want to lower the apparent height of a high ceiling, add pendant lamps to cast their light downward. Meanwhile, in rooms with low ceilings it is best to avoid pendant lights. To make the space appear taller, keep furniture and pictures at a fairly low level and then wash the walls and ceiling with the illumination from uplighters.

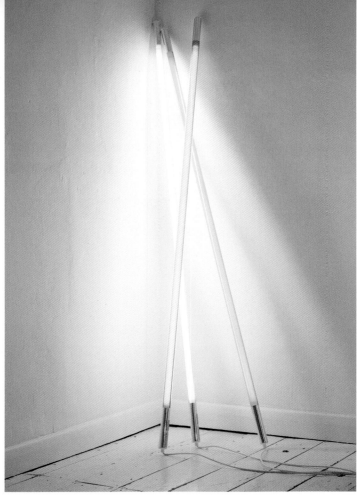

↓ This creation is called the Chromawall, by Jeremy Lord. Here art meets lighting design: this installation of different-coloured, gently pulsating light panels can be constructed to cover an entire wall.

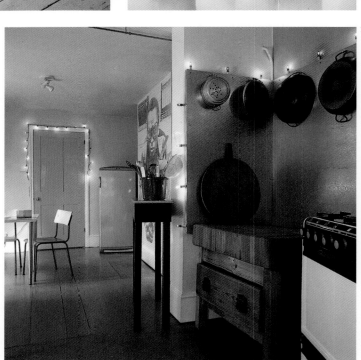

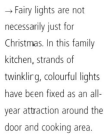

↑ Free-standing coloured light tubes, here in pastel hues, make a striking and unusual pool of corner light. The lights can be used in any combination and moved around the space at will to suit your changing moods.

→ Fairy lights are not necessarily just for Christmas. In this family kitchen, strands of twinkling, colourful lights have been fixed as an all-year attraction around the door and cooking area.

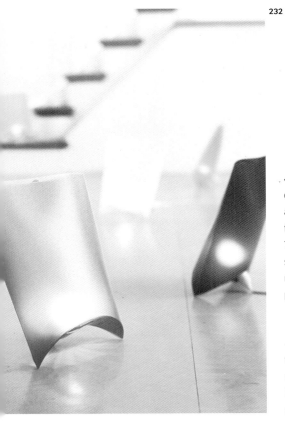

232

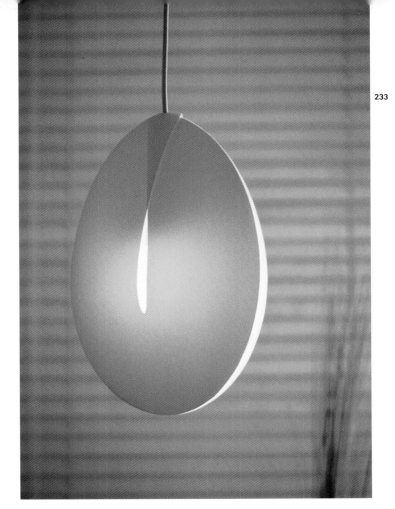

233

← Bags of Light, by the designers at Black + Blum, are made using translucent folded polypropylene. This extremely appealing soft lighting effect is reminiscent of Chinese paper lanterns.

→ This understated yet very satisfying oval shape, called Seed, is a pendant lamp from the designers at Black + Blum.

→ Lamps with paper or fabric shades produce a soft, diffused quality of illumination. These two small, free-standing lamps are designed to glow with rich, saturated colour to conjure a particular mood, rather than to provide lots of practical illumination.

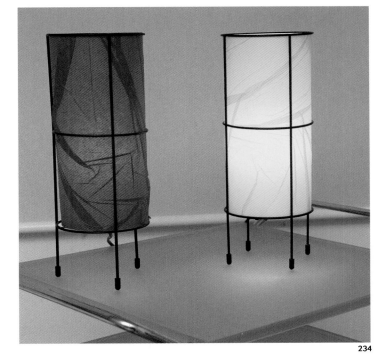

↓ This trio of pendant lamps, called Arrow, is by the designer Lindsey Bloxham. The lamps are made using hand-dyed laminated silk – a material similar to parchment in its effect – which is then folded, origami-like, into shape.

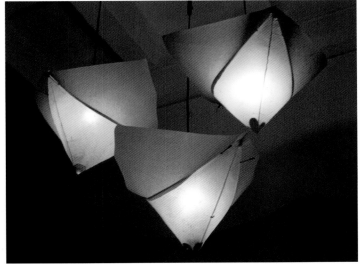

234

235

236

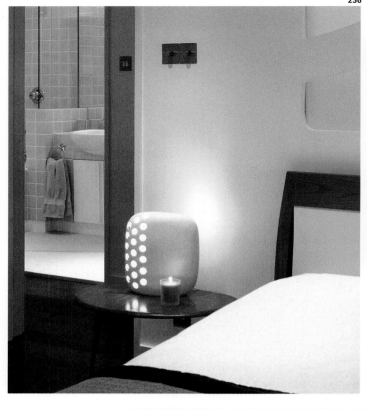

237

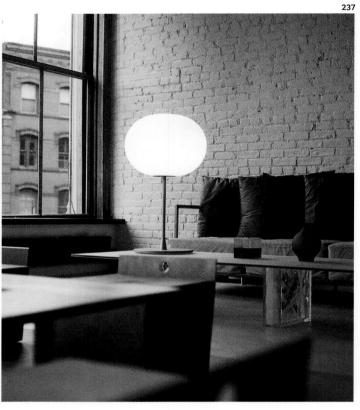

← As part of the Glo-Ball series, by designer Jasper Morrison and produced by the Italian company Flos, this satisfying, slightly squashed globe is available as a table lamp, a long-stemmed floor-standing lamp, and as a ceiling light.

↓ With its spindly arms and legs, the Climbing Light, designed by Black + Blum, has instant appeal while also succeeding in being a fairly practical light source. Its crown-silvered light bulb controls the throw of light, directing it downward and sideways, and thus making it useful as a task light for reading. The on/off switch is also easily accessible from the bed.

↑ The combination of a scented candle and the subdued illumination from a soft, pebble-shaped lamp has a calming and serene effect in this bedroom.

→ Irresistible and easy on the eye, and appropriately called Nest, these balls of softly glowing light are the creation of Tocs Design. They are made using pure cotton twine and are available either as floor-standing lamps or in a version that can be suspended from the ceiling or any other convenient surface.

239

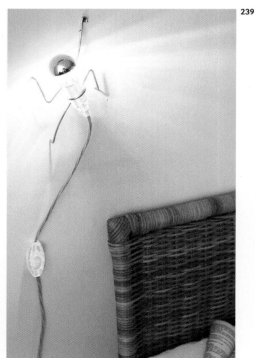

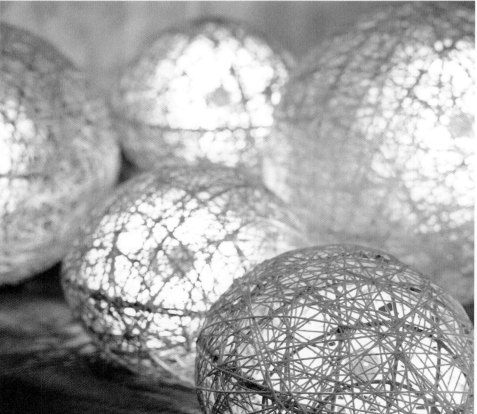

238

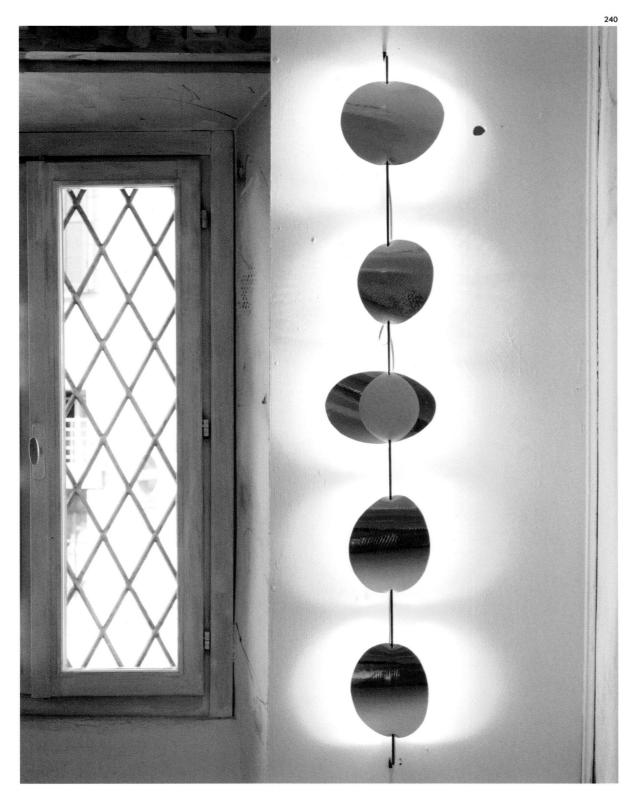

240

lamps

Along with its obvious and prosaic function of providing illumination, artificial lighting can also add poetry to a space. Lamps and light fittings work hard — not just throwing out their glowing halo of light but also as decorative features in their own right. And even in the simplest of spaces, one glorious light fitting can add that special something — a real touch of magic.

In recent years, countless independent design studios have become established with the sole aim of providing the market with stunning, sometimes highly idiosyncratic, lamps. But in order to gain some impression of how they might look in their intended setting, always make sure you see them switched on before making a decision about which to buy.

Many showrooms are now fitted out as domestic room settings and, although there will be obvious shortcomings, this at least makes it easier to assess how the lamp might work in your own home. Instead of opting for the safer more staid designs, consider lamps or fittings that have a real presence. One or two unusual pieces of lighting design can have the impact of a work of art. And don't just limit your palette to white light — coloured bulbs and fittings can add focal points of interest and warm up neglected corners.

← This unusual light fitting, by designer Gaston Martioorena, comprises a slender metal stem that is fixed to the wall. Onto this are fixed six lamps behind curved foil shades. The lightfall is focused on the wall, but it then spreads outward to create a beautiful string of soft, reflected light.

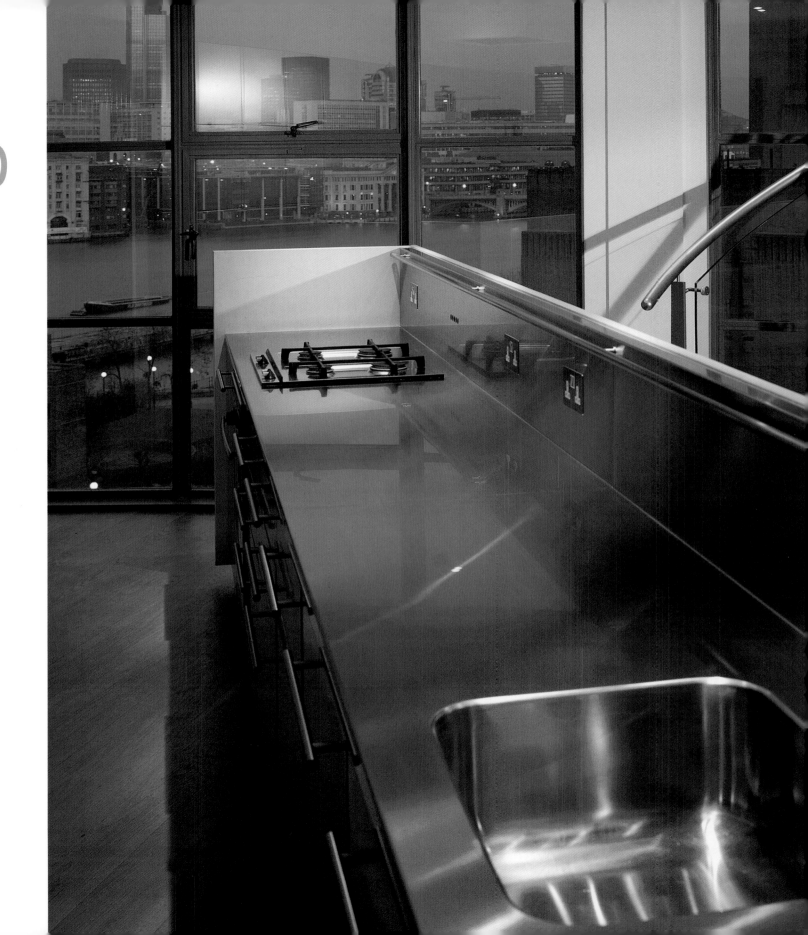

fittings

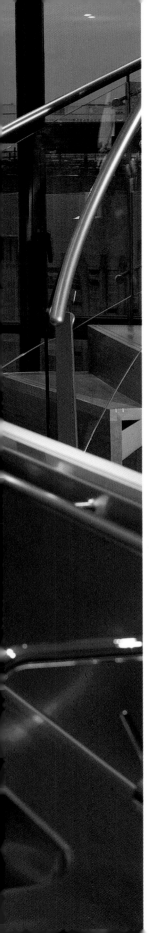

← The beauty is in the detail with so many contemporary interiors. In this apartment, by Auckett Tytherleigh, the design touches that really count include the seamless stainless-steel worktop with built-in sink.

With the main surface finishes and built-in elements of your home's interior covered in earlier chapters of the book, you can now turn your attention to the realm of fittings. It is here, in the detailing, that it is possible to add some real highlights – and often at only a little extra expense. Inside those beautiful empty spaces, you can begin to plan the exciting details, from kitchens and bathrooms right through to heating and handles.

Against the backdrop you have created, it is time to set the scene by considering the styles and materials of the finishing touches. You need to consider, for example, whether the overall effect is to be sheer and minimal, or do you envisage big, eye-catching splashes of colour and intriguing textures? Whatever finish you choose, will it vary between spaces or stay the same throughout the whole home? You could perhaps choose to create a living room that is simple in design and pale in colour, while opting for a bedroom that is charged with colour, with wild radiators in the shape of huge potted plants.

As in all other aspects of design and planning, budget is always a major consideration. If you are contemplating commissioning work or having items or materials especially imported, then you can expect to pay considerably more than you would for items selected off the shelf. But bear in mind that although finding just the right item will take time and patience, any extra effort spent at this stage will be rewarded many times over when the interior is complete – and you know the job is well done.

kitchens

It is almost impossible to believe that little more than a century ago, the kitchen was either out of bounds to all but staff or else was hidden in a basement or somewhere at the back of the house. Today, in its centre-stage position, the kitchen has been reborn as the beating heart of most homes.

When it comes to designing and fitting out the kitchen, the primary concern is that it must work as a highly functional space. In addition, however, in many homes it must also be capable of transforming occasionally into a dining space for formal entertaining.

There are two basic styles of kitchen: fitted or unfitted. There is also a hybrid of these two styles, which could be called semi-fitted. The fitted version is a perennial favourite, and this popularity is based on the fact that it is extremely practical, with rows of box units configured to provide as much storage space as possible.

The unfitted version – these days almost always seen in an industrial style with a predominant use of stainless steel – has the advantage of greater flexibility. It is a loose-fit idea composed of free-standing cabinets, units, and shelves, but even here the sink and cooker must still be fixed in place.

Finally, a recent newcomer to the kitchen scene is the all-in-one unit. These neat solutions are single units featuring a refrigerator, oven, hob, sink, and storage. They are ideal for any house or apartment where cooking is not a favourite pastime or where space is at a premium.

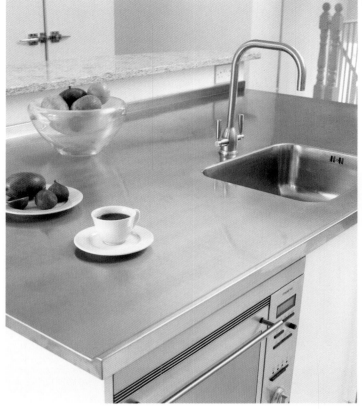

242

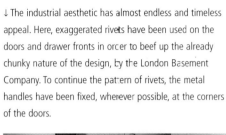

↓ The industrial aesthetic has almost endless and timeless appeal. Here, exaggerated rivets have been used on the doors and drawer fronts in order to beef up the already chunky nature of the design, by the London Basement Company. To continue the pattern of rivets, the metal handles have been fixed, wherever possible, at the corners of the doors.

243

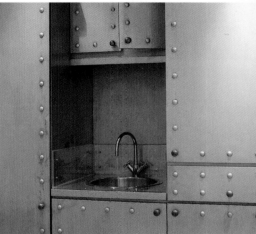

↑ The use of stainless steel means that this large area of worktop and sink can be formed in one continuous piece of material. It is very hardwearing and quick and easy to wipe clean, and it has no joins to trap food.

→ Ideal for small homes or for occasional cooking is this stainless-steel kitchen called Steel, from the Quantum 2K range of kitchen specialist Space Savers. It is built as one unit, with oven, hob, sink, fridge, dishwasher or washing machine, extractor hood, and storage space.

244

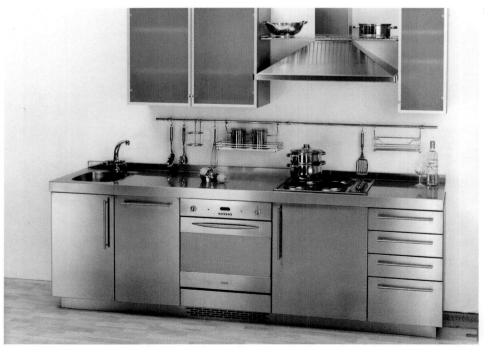

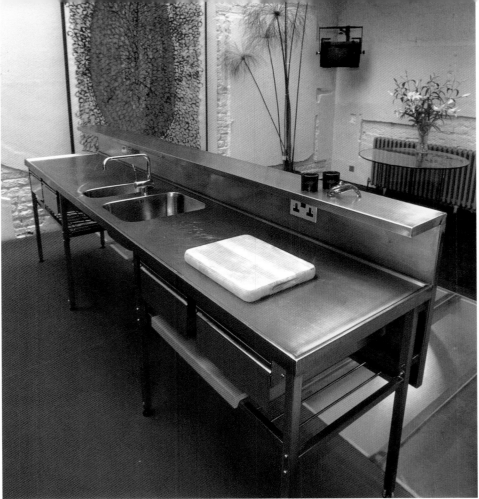

↓ This very compact design, described as a sink-workcentre, is produced by the manufacturer Franke. The unit, which incorporates a sink and draining area that doubles as a worktop for small-scale food preparation, could be the ideal solution for a studio apartment or a holiday home, where light meals and snacks are more likely to be the order of the day than full-blown entertaining.

246

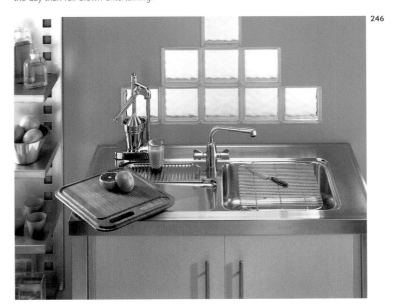

248

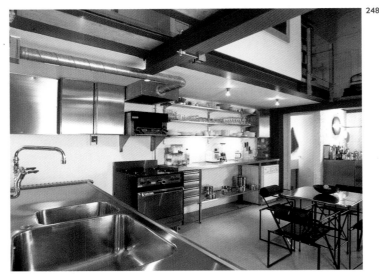

↑ Domestic versions of professional-style multi-purpose units such as this are now readily available. Along with a cooker, it is all you need in a basic kitchen. Particularly good design details include the large upstand and shelf top, and built-in electrical sockets.

→ This design, which borrows from the large-scale units of an industrial kitchen, also incorporates a domestic touch – the use of wood for the legs and frames. To show what is inside, the wall cupboard doors are faced with glass.

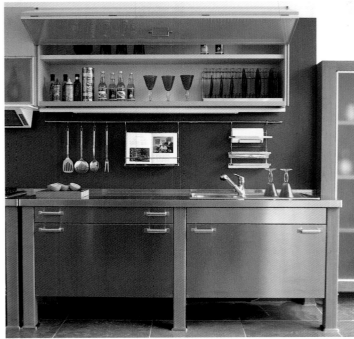

247

↑ This design takes the professional kitchen look to the limits – take away the table and chairs and it is virtually impossible to tell whether this is a restaurant or home setting.

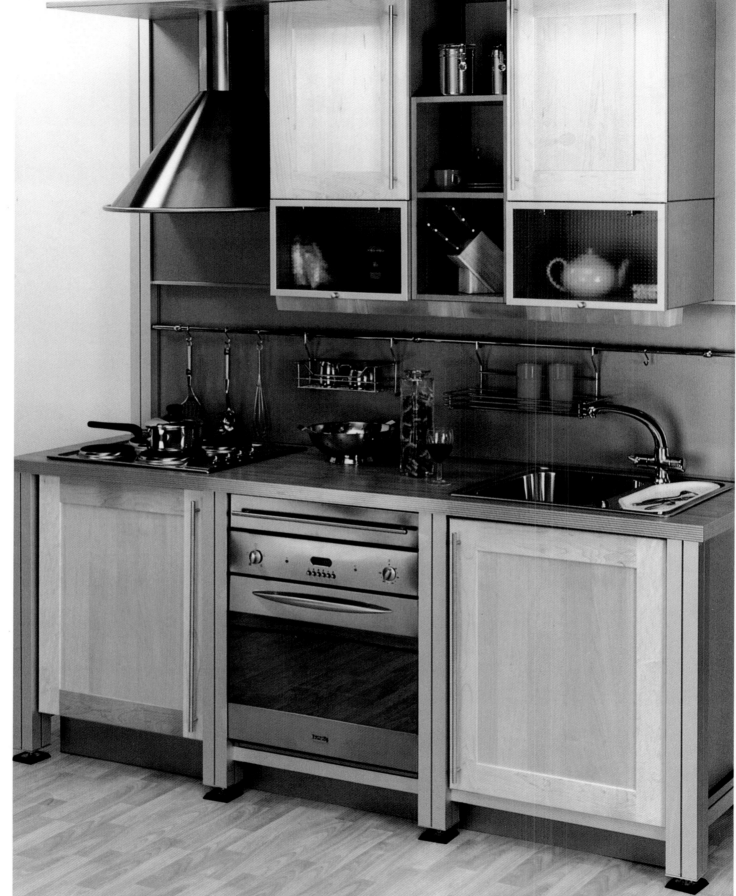

→ This is as neat as it gets. The all-in-one unit, called Quantum Studio, is an entirely self-contained and thoughtfully designed minimal, free-standing kitchen unit in metal and blond wood. Although small, it incorporates a hob with extractor hood, oven, sink, and storage space, including cunningly mounted cutlery drawers beneath the wall units. It is part of the Quantum 2K range, which is available from kitchen company Space Savers.

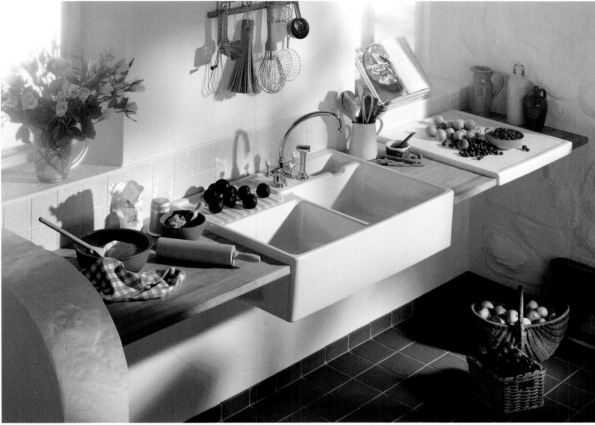

250

← For a rustic style of kitchen with all the convenience of modern design, this deep, white ceramic Belfast style sink is difficult to beat. Unusually, this contemporary unit is divided into three different-sized bowls. In addition to the sink, there is also a ceramic worktop, which is ideal for cooking jobs that require a cool surface, such as rolling pastry. Both items are by Franke.

251

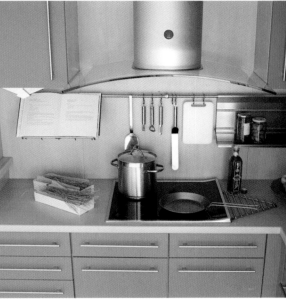

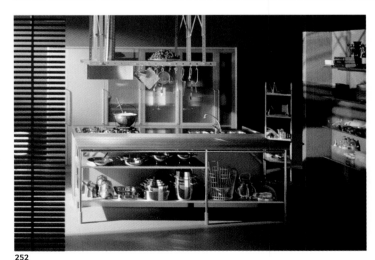

252

↑ This suite of fittings, by Antonia Astori for Driade, provides a central work station with hob and sink set into a stainless-steel worktop, as well as a wood counter top. Behind this unit are cabinets with frosted glass doors.

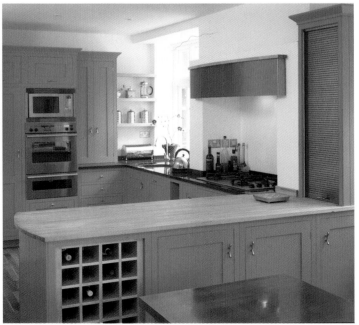

↑ The very versatile hanging rail in this kitchen design, by Fulham Kitchens, not only holds cooking utensils, but also provides a sensible place for a recipe book rest and a shelf for seasonings.

← This fitted kitchen includes design details such as a maple veneer wine rack and round-ended work counter, as well as a built-in oven, grill, and microwave. Because there was little space for wall cupboards, Roundhouse Design built two small units that sit on the worktops, which are of granite and beech.

253

Now that the kitchen has taken such pride of place in the home, it warrants being treated with the respect due to one of the most important spaces in our lives. After all, this is where most of us spend most of our time when we are at home. It is also likely to be the place where we entertain friends. Thus there is every reason to lavish more than a little attention on it.

When you are first planning a kitchen, take account of how the room might be used. Don't feel pressurized into lining the entire space with cupboards — reduce the units and fittings to the bare minimum if you don't plan to cook regularly or lavishly. And build in space for a big table if you like having friends around. If, however, there is more than one keen cook in your family, then incorporate lots of extra worktop space.

Don't feel inhibited when it comes to choosing colours for the kitchen. If you want a pink and purple space, then go ahead and have it. When it comes to the choice of materials, you will need to build a space that is both practical and beautiful — timber or steel-fronted cabinets are easy to clean, for example, and they are also robust enough to cope with plenty of knocks. For counters, think about stone, slate, and timber, or perhaps man-made materials such as Corian. All natural materials need to be thoroughly sealed, and just about every worktop option is expensive — apart from the laminate counters sold at every home-build outlet. And floors need to be durable — a pale limestone floor will look exquisite when first laid, but it could quickly lose its appeal as it picks up every mark and stain.

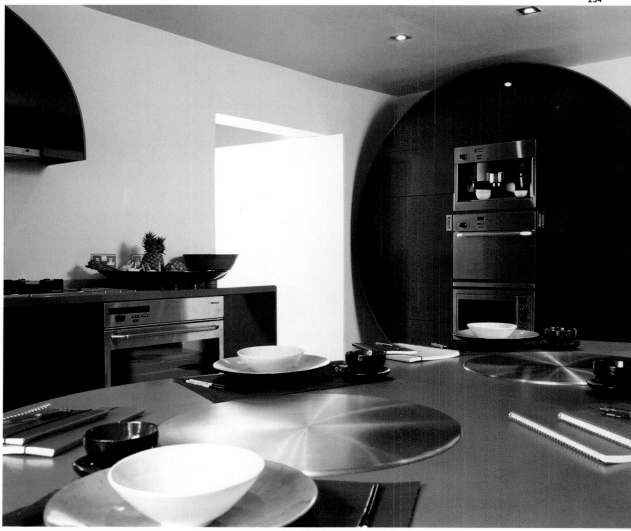

254

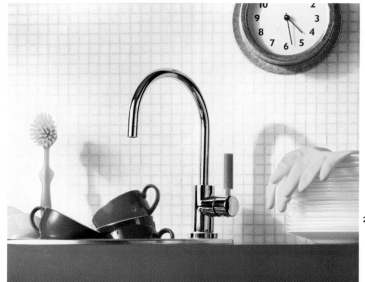

255

← The Tara Classic mixer tap has a simple and stylish arched neck and single-lever mixer. It is designed by Sieger Design for manufacturer Dornbracht.

↑ This project, by designers Wayne and Geraldine Hemingway, features large amounts of surface material Corian in Sage and Adobe colours. The Sage finish is used as a thermoformed cladding around the wall unit, and the Adobe finish, with its heat-resistant properties, forms the table top with inset stainless-steel cooking plates.

256

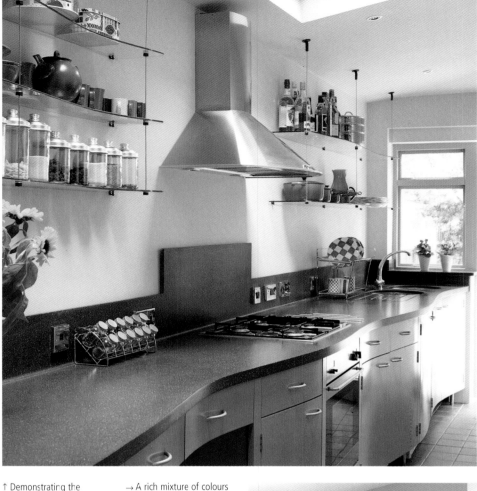

257

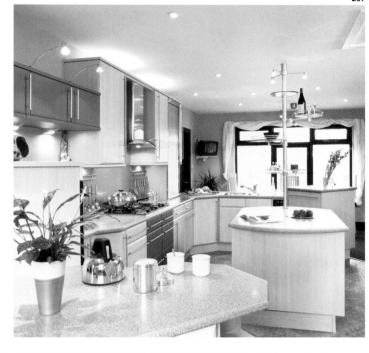

↑ Demonstrating the versatility of Corian, an acrylic resin mixed with natural minerals, this kitchen design by Trevor Baker incorporates a sensuous, wave-shaped worktop and cabinets.

→ A rich mixture of colours and textures is to be found in this contemporary Shaker-style fitted kitchen, by Roundhouse Design. The scheme features doors in Mediterranean blue, walls in olive green, and – close to the cooking area – cherry-wood doors and chunky shelving. The worktops are a combination of black Italian slate and solid cherry. The fridge-freezer is stainless steel and made by Siemens, while the free-standing oven is by Smeg.

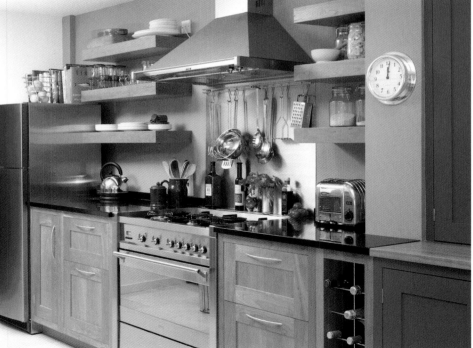

↑ This unusual kitchen design composed of different work islands has been given highly durable, heat- and stain-resistant solid work surfaces made of Corian. The shaped, grey-flecked, light-coloured worktops are in a finish called Mont Blanc. The choice of different work areas is a great bonus when there is more than one cook to accommodate.

258

259

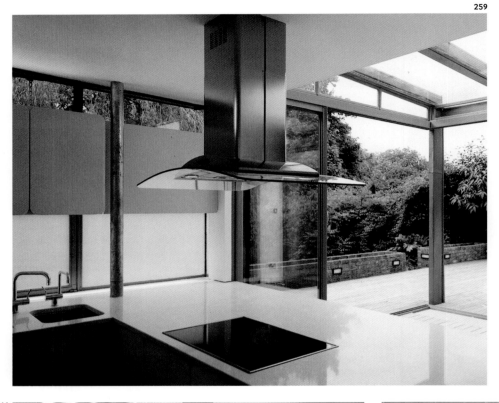

260

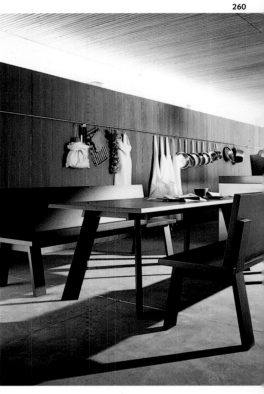

← This kitchen, by Littman Goddard Hogarth Architects, is wrapped around with glazing, including the horizontal strips above and below the wall cabinets. The worktop is believed to be the largest piece of Caesar stone ever quarried in one piece.

→ With powerful references to the traditional farmhouse kitchen, this design collection, Nemus from Bulthaup, features dark timber throughout. It is built in oak in three colours – grey, dark brown, and black-brown. Cushions to cover the bench seats are also available.

261

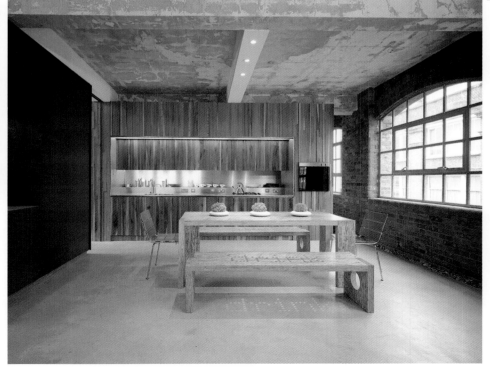

262

↑ Mixed with rich-coloured wood furniture is a versatile, unfitted, semi-industrial-style kitchen with free-standing refrigerator and cabinets, The fixed sink unit and matching cooker, and work counter trolleys on wheels are by Bulthaup.

→ The softening effect of natural timber has been introduced into this former industrial building to take the hard edges off the large areas of concrete and brick. The fitted kitchen is faced with a highly unusual African walnut.

→ The design crossover between domestic interior, professional kitchen, and office is fascinating. In this kitchen, by designer and manufacturer Bulthaup, the clean-cut, industrialized styling produces a distinctly multifunctional space.

↓ This open-plan kitchen and dining area, called Malva, by Antonia Astori for Driade, features a linear design of stainless-steel units. Interesting touches include the projected clock and, on the wall, a Maestrale extractor hood, and a Plug-in-kit hanging bar. The floor is finished in large sheet-metal tiles.

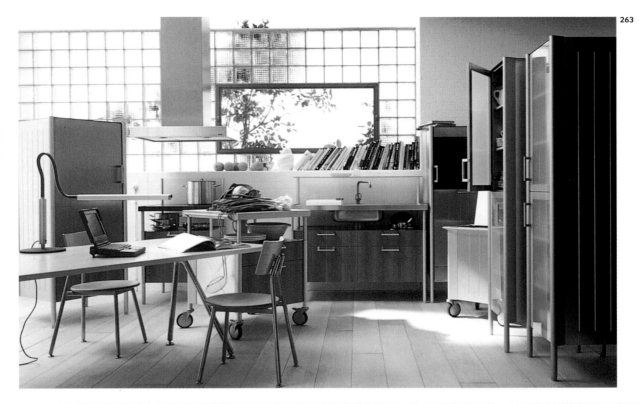

263

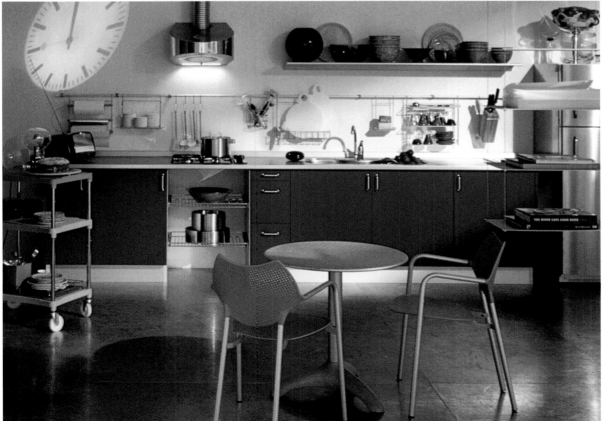

264

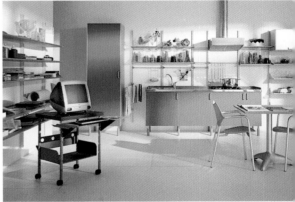

265

↑ Fitted units, called Verbena, here in a pale green finish, look chic with the stainless-steel modular shelving and accessories, all of which are produced by Driade. The loose-fit kitchen works well in this multifunctional living space.

Work counters are among the most important elements of the kitchen, and when it comes to details, this is the one you must get right.

One of the most frequently used and least glamorous of all counter tops is the laminate strip, commonly available in every home-build store. These tops might not always look as glorious as slate or marble, but they are incredibly good value and hardwearing. It is probably a good idea to avoid pure white, however, since this colour has a tendency to pick up stubborn tea and wine stains.

Of the other options, wood is extremely popular, but it is often difficult to care for. It looks great at first – before it picks up the inevitable knocks and stains. Of course, you may favour a worn-in look, in which case this material is a good choice. To minimize damage to a wood countertop, always cut and prepare food on a board, and use a matt-finish varnish or a preparation such as tung oil, which soaks into the wood and drys hard.

Concrete and stone are tough and durable, but always take advice from suppliers about how best to seal the surface – natural materials have different degrees of porosity, but most will absorb some liquids, especially oil.

Finally, there are artificial materials, such as Corian. This is made of resin and natural minerals, and although expensive is almost indestructible. It can be shaped, cut, and moulded into virtually any form.

→ This is a stunning continuous work surface in Rio Neblina honed slate. It incorporates two apertures, to accommodate two undercounter stainless-steel sinks, and tapered grooves for the draining areas. The slate was supplied by Kirkstone and the kitchen was designed by Samantha Sandberg.

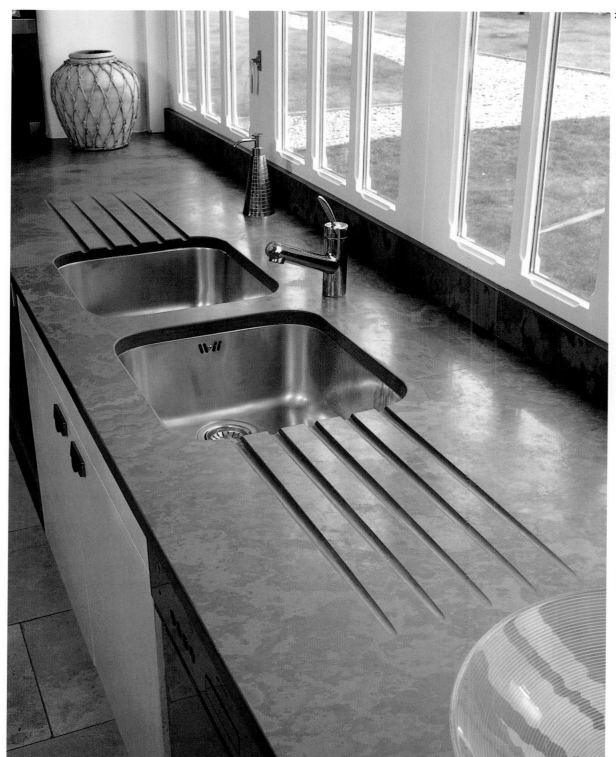

266

267

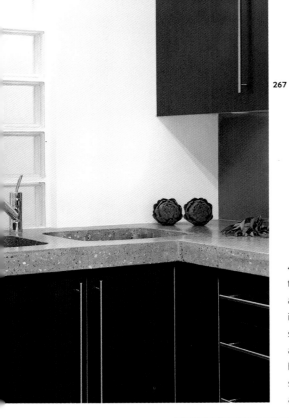

← Making a real statement, this unusually thick and attractive work counter is made of cast concrete speckled with coloured aggregate. The whole slab has been polished to a smooth finish to provide a rich, durable sheen.

268

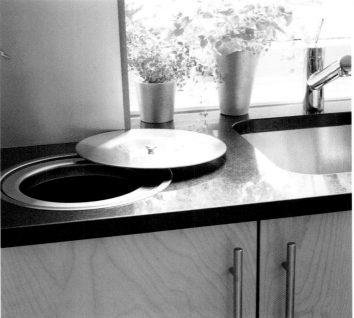

← In this modern-style kitchen, birchwood doors and long, stainless-steel handles contrast with the dark grey of the granite worktop. Appealing details added by the design company Fulham Kitchen, include the large top-loading waste-disposal unit, which has been set neatly into the counter top.

→ This pale blue kitchen has been finished with a mid-grey work surface called Sierra Oceanic, made from the tough, heat- and scratch-resistant material Corian. The white circular disk visible on the island unit is a chopping board, also made of Corian, which sits over a cylindrical cupboard.

270

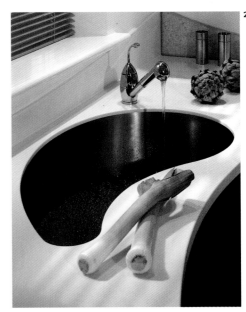

↑ This contemporary kitchen was designed to be in complete contrast to the Georgian-style home in which it is located. Unlike the formality of Georgian geometry and straight lines, the kitchen is a curvaceous and utterly sensual space. Details to note include this very appealing stainless-steel kidney-shaped sink, which has been inset into a shaped white Corian work surface.

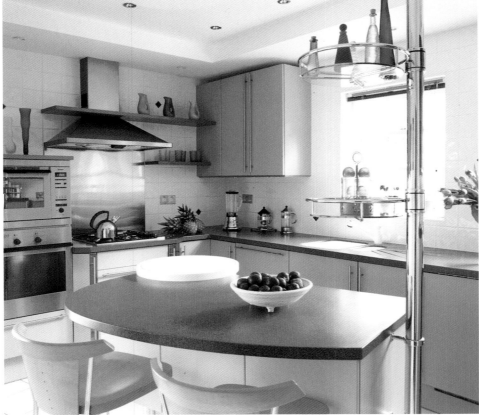

269

271

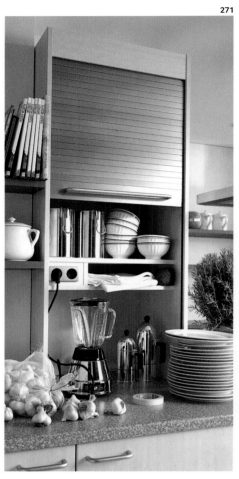

272

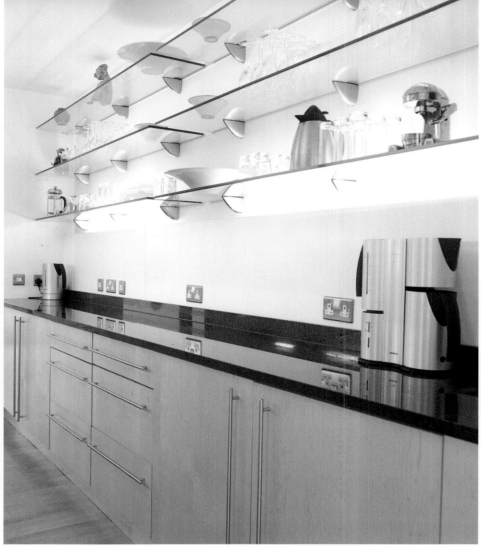

→ The slatted, tambour-door-fronted cupboard is a feature in this kitchen, by Poggen Pohl – as the door slides up, the contents, including an electrical socket and food blender, are revealed. Thus appliances can be readily accessible yet not permanently on display.

↓ In this kitchen of Italian chef and food purveyor Antonio Carluccio, the kitchen is clearly designed to be a convivial place. And storage is also important, with a central island unit featuring a cantilevered chopping area and a substantial rack above for stacking pots and pans.

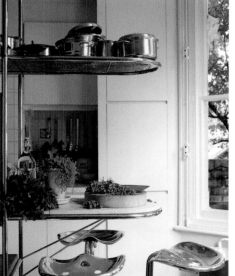

→ The top-loading dishwasher is a great idea for making the best possible use of awkward corners. This model is extremely compact and tucks away under the hinged work counter. It is available through small-kitchen specialist Space Savers.

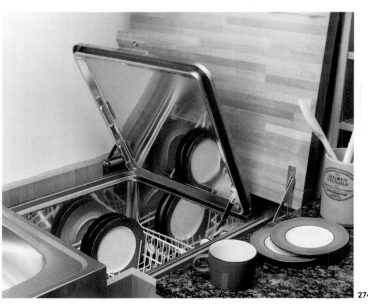

↑ This is an unusual storage system, using long shelves of glass held in place on aluminium supports. Under the lower shelf, long tube lamps cast their light up to make the glass glow. Glass shelving is a useful, low-impact alternative to wall cupboards, which tend to be a powerful visual intrusion. This shelving is fitted above a run of very shallow base-unit cupboards.

273

274

275

The kitchen is home to an extraordinary number and volume of possessions, from a range of electrical appliances to the bone china dinner service, and then on to awkward-shaped bowls and plates and a full battery of utensils. In order to accommodate this huge variety of items, storage is a crucial component in the story of kitchen fittings.

People generally divide into two different types — those who celebrate their collection of possessions and like to see them on show, and those who prefer everything hidden and out of sight. In designing storage appropriate to your needs, you must decide which type you are. Of course, fitted kitchens usually offer generous storage capacity in wall and floor units, but it is worth comparing this level of capacity with other forms of storage — for example, the old-fashioned, free-standing dresser. This single piece of furniture is able to hold a truly vast amount of kitchenware, and it has the advantage of combining closed-in cupboards with open display shelving.

Even if you favour fitted kitchens, it is still often a good idea to build in an area of open shelving for displaying some of your prized items. The addition of some openness provides a welcome break from the often rather overbearing impact that ranks of fitted wall cupboards have on a room.

← This elegant island unit is the hub of the kitchen, with everything close to hand. There is a generous work surface, but also glass shelving above for everyday items. Noteworthy details here include below-counter space for storing bulky items such as the fish kettle, and the hanging rail for cooking utensils, which makes these useful items easy to find when they are needed.

bathrooms

The bathroom has gained a new, elevated status. Once a purely functional space dedicated to the routines of washing and general hygiene, it has now become a haven, a separate world far removed from the stresses of family, work, and everyday life.

The impact of this changed perception can be seen in the amount of money and space we are prepared to lavish on this room. Many homes now incorporate bedrooms with en-suite bathrooms, or perhaps separate bathrooms for adults and children. With increasing frequency, spare bedrooms are being transformed into extra bathrooms; we are building on bathroom extensions and even converting cellars into additional bathrooms, which might also include a small home sauna or mini gym. Some of the more extreme examples of the bathroom being incorporated into living space can be seen where bedrooms and bathrooms have merged into one, to make an open-plan suite for rest and relaxation.

Not surprisingly, many of the most brilliant ideas are borrowed from hotel designers, where the luxuriousness of the bathroom has to match, or even exceed, that of the bedroom. Here, designers with lavish budgets are free to incorporate such treats as spa baths and Jacuzzis, as well as the best power showers. And to add a real sense of style, there are luxurious materials too — marble, ceramics, and glittering mosaic tiles for floors and walls, with glass, stainless steel, copper, or wood washbasins and baths.

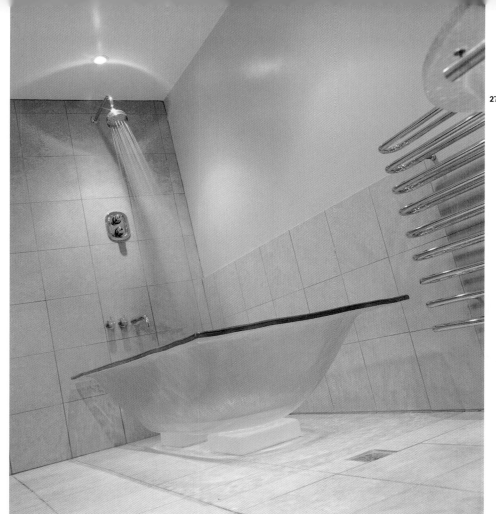

← The quest for transparency has now reached as far as the bathtub itself. After years of excitement created by glass washbasins, the solid, see-through glass tub has arrived. This comfortable-looking, cast-glass shape sits on base blocks, and its pale green colour has been picked up in the paint colour used on the wall.

↓ This modern, monastically minimal bathroom is by architect John Pawson. It features a rectangular, cream-coloured limestone basin and a limestone-tiled floor.

→ Snaking their way up this bathroom wall are two curvy, chrome-finish Cobratherm radiators, from Bisque. Their curvaceous, serpentine form is not only perfect for warming and drying towels, but also adds a sensuous, sculptural dimension to the bathroom. These radiators are available from Bisque in nine sizes and more than 1,600 colours.

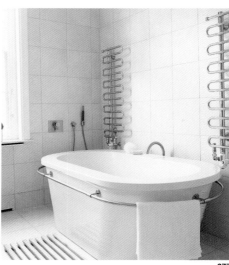

277

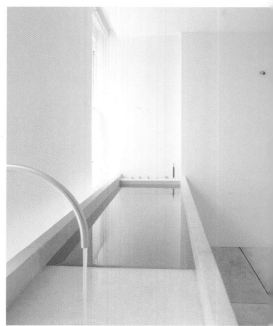

278

→ Taking centre stage in this impressive, monochrome bathroom is the aptly named Block bathtub, designed by Marten Claesson, Eerc Koivisto, and Ola Rune with Durat. This is a durable, stain-proof, heat-resistant, polyester-based material made with about fifty per cent recycled plastic. It is sold in plain or flecked colours, in sheet form, and can also be moulded to shape.

↓ Even in a fairly traditional setting, complete with wood-block floor and fireplace, this stainless-steel bath and washstand look quite stunning.

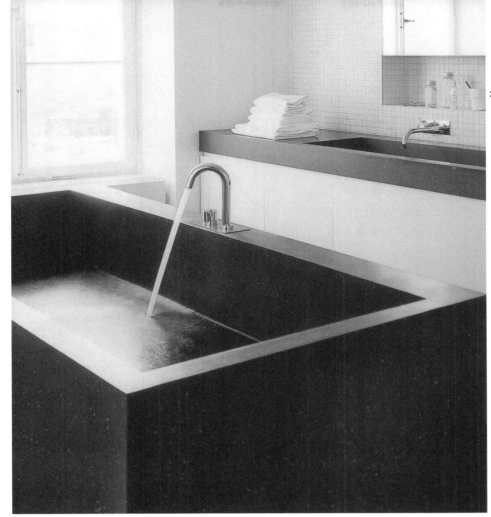

279

↓ Star of this bathroom, designed for a Berlin apartment by Jonathan Reed of Reed Creative Services, is the high-backed, doubled-ended, nineteenth-century polished-metal bath, which has been set on a shallow marble plinth. The bath is separated from the shower area by a screen wall composed of ribbed stone panels, and the floor is finished in hammered stone.

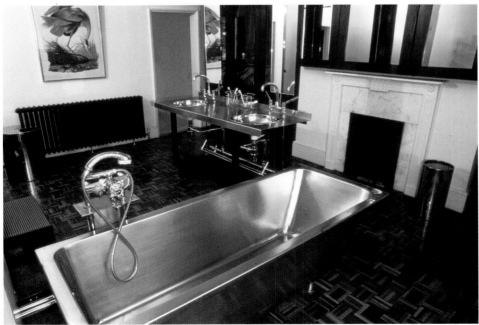

280

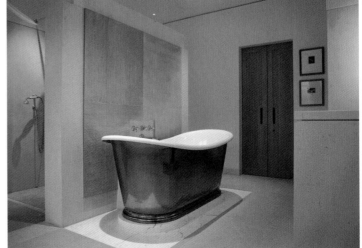

281

↓ Inspired by Japanese pared-down simplicity, this washbasin and bench are part of the Work in Progress bathroom range, designed by Giulio Cappellini and Roberto Palomba for Flaminia. The Aquagrande basin sits on an elemental wenge wood bench.

282

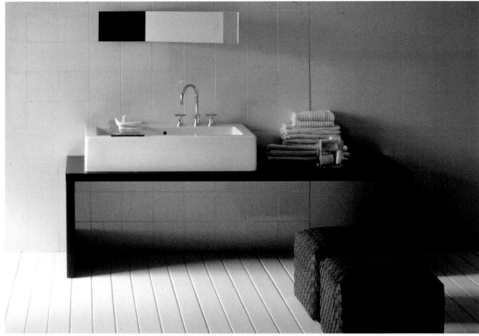

283

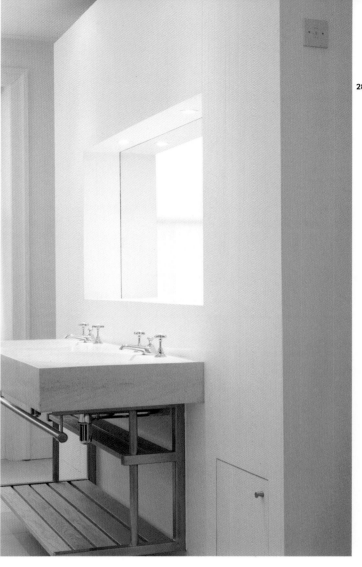

→ Architect Linda Morey Smith demonstrates the delightful impact created by the subtle introduction of colour into this white bathroom. The lively pattern of the blue and white marble counter is reminiscent of a stream of running water.

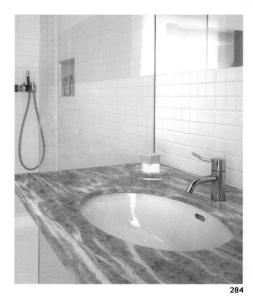

284

285

← For a haven of peace and calm, a combination of glass and ceramic is extremely soothing. In this project, by architect Stickland Coombe, the simple shapes and finishes are all that is required to make a beautiful space. The rectangular ceramic basin faces a huge panel of frameless mirror, and is washed in natural light from the skylight above. The shower is a simple glass box.

↑ In this project, by architecture practice Allford Hall Monaghan Morris, the double basin has been cut from a single slab of stone. In front of the basin unit — which was so heavy the floor had to be strengthened — a large mirror has been recessed into the wall, toplit by a pair of low-voltage halogen lamps. The wall, which stops short of the ceiling, divides the room from the shower area behind.

286

↓ The sparing use of wood in bathrooms can have a surprisingly powerful effect. In this white room, the deep, richly coloured hardwood counter adds a touch of luxury. It has been beautifully constructed with sheer-fronted built-in drawers, and is cantilevered from the wall – thus dispensing with the need for legs.

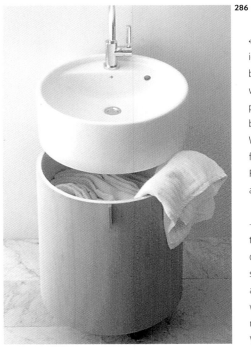

← In this space-saving idea, ideal for tiny bathrooms, a small washbasin sits above a pale beechwood laundry bin. They are part of the Work in Progress collection, from Italian manufacturer Flaminia, by Giulio Cappellini and Roberto Palomba.

→ Reminiscent of the traditional washstand, this design is based on a free-standing tiled unit featuring a large counter and stand, with a round white surface-mounted Loop basin by Villeroy & Boch.

287

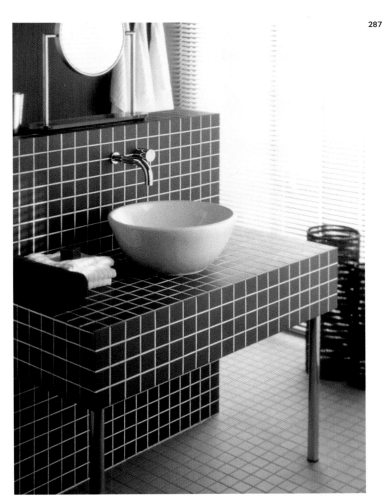

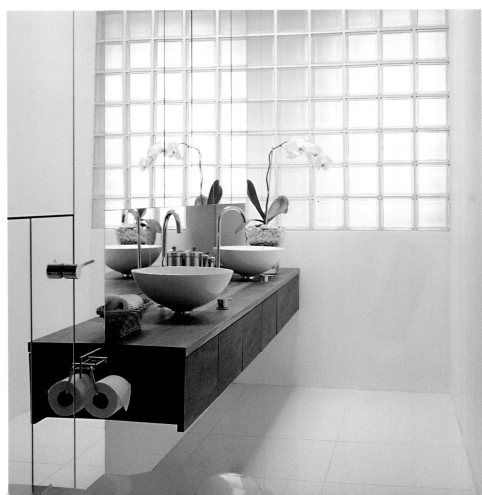

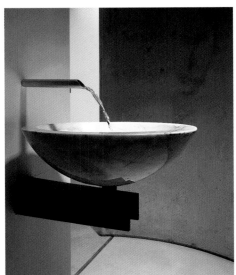

← Looking almost like an ancient water fountain, this grey and white marble bowl with its simple water spout is featured in a bathroom by architect Seth Stein.

288　　　　**289**

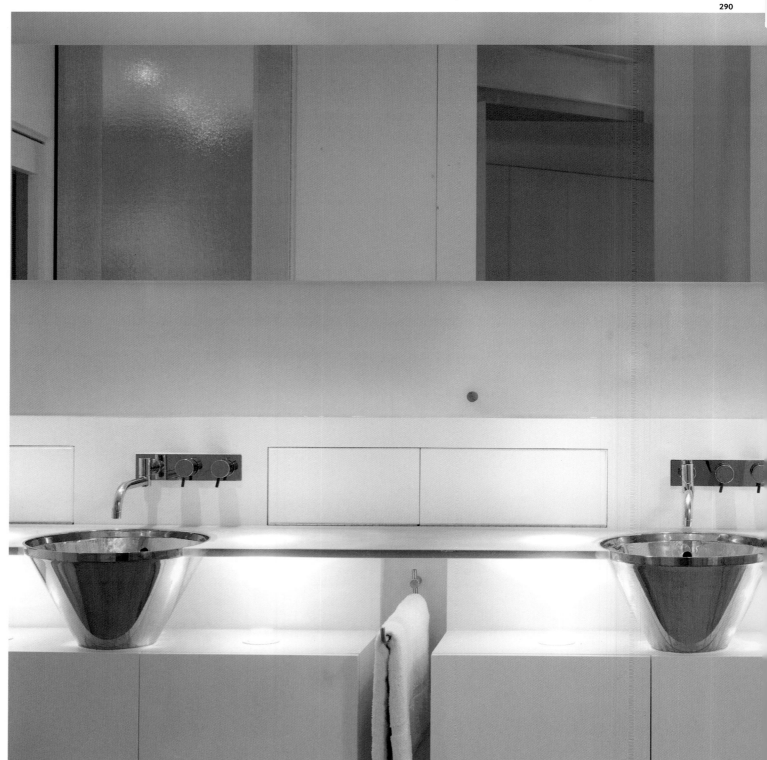

→ Subtle blues and greens combine with glass and stainless steel in this elegant contemporary bathroom by architect Rick Mather. The pair of conical stainless-steel washbasins sits on white, flat-fronted storage units. At their rims, the bowls are held in a sheet of clear glass. The lighting is particularly striking, with recessed fittings sunk into the unit tops, where they uplight the glass counter.

291

↓ This highly unusual contemporary washbasin combines white opaque silicon for the bowl and stainless steel for the frame. Although unusual, this elegant design – called Tension, from Cloakroom Solutions – is entirely practical in a bathroom or cloakroom.

292

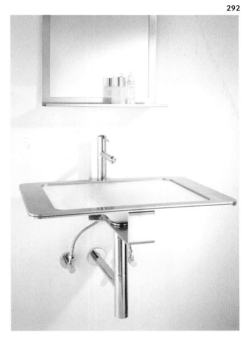

Shiny, reflective materials, such as glass and stainless steel, look wonderful in a bathroom. They work extremely well alongside water, creating reflections and adding shimmer and a splash of glitter and glamour. The growing choice of designs on offer demonstrates just how much we are attracted to them. It is a long way from the heavy, white ceramic and enamelled suites of the past.

These materials, which are relatively new arrivals in the bathroom, are extremely popular because they can be formed into delicate and unusual shapes. You no longer need a thick, solid basin resting on a pedestal or frame base. Metal and glass basins are readily hung from the wall, appearing free-standing, or they can be slotted into glass counter tops.

There are lots of aesthetic reasons to consider one of these unusual designs. However, be prepared for the down side – many of them are incredibly expensive, and both glass and stainless steel are very prone to watermarking. If you happen to live in an area with hard water – water with a high lime content – you can expect these beautiful items to require regular, if not constant, cleaning to remove the limescale splodges.

Hard water also plays havoc with taps, with the scale building up around every joint to disfigure the beauty of the designs. A partial solution is to add a water softener to your domestic water inlet. However, even if such a unit is extremely effective, just about any water supply will contain some mineral deposits, so be prepared to expend much elbow grease to keep these products looking their very best.

↑ This is bathroom design stripped to its most basic, with an open-bowl washbasin, simple tubular spout, and modern cross-head taps, all in stainless steel and fitted against a mirror. However, in order to keep everything looking so pure and perfect, all surfaces need regular cleaning to prevent water staining and the disfiguring build-up of limescale.

→ The detailing here is exquisite, with the lip of the stainless-steel basin sitting over a glass counter, which, as it meets the wall, is finished with a small bead of stainless steel. The bathroom is by Anne Hunter Interiors.

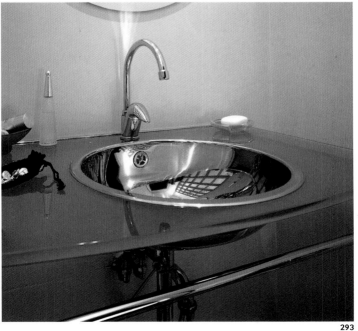

293

295

→ Harking back to an earlier era of luxury liners or railway carriages, this beautiful varnished cabinetwork, by Neil Blackwell, is a fine example of bathroom elegance. The sweep of wood counter finishes in a loop around a neat stainless-steel basin. It then continues vertically to make an upstand between the counter and mirror-fronted cabinets.

294

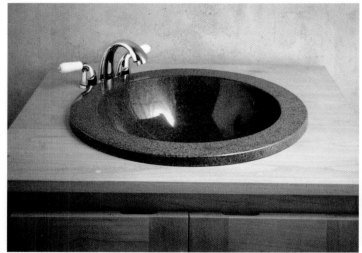

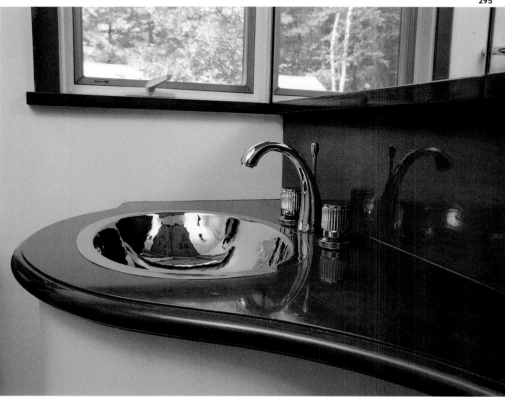

↑ A silky smooth blue granite bowl, also made in oval shapes, sits in the top of a small pale wood bathroom cupboard. These compact designs, from Bathrooms International, are ideal for en suite bathrooms or small cloakrooms.

→ This chunky handcrafted copper basin, from Bathrooms International, can stand either on a counter top or on a pedestal. It is also available with a rim, making it suitable for dropping into a counter top.

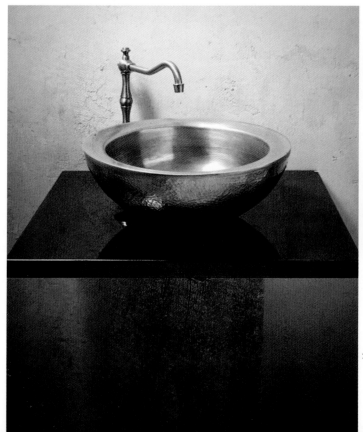

296

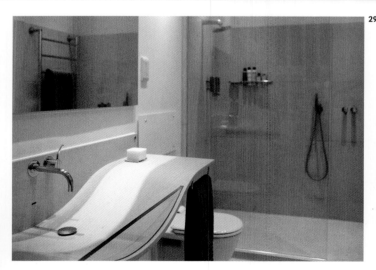

297

↑ Swooping down to the glass-fronted bowl below in a single piece from horizontal ledges at either side, this cream-coloured basin is an unusual bathroom feature.

298

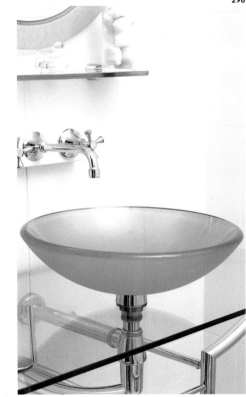

↓ Blue glass is particularly beautiful in a bathroom. This unusual basin is made of a single piece of cast glass, which moulds together a circular basin with a generous horizontal ledge on either side.

↑ In this bathroom, the pebble-smooth blue glass basin is called Blue Ice. It is shown with a glass-topped shelf unit, and both bowl and unit are by Avante Bathroom Products. The blue of the bowl is picked up in the mirror frame.

299

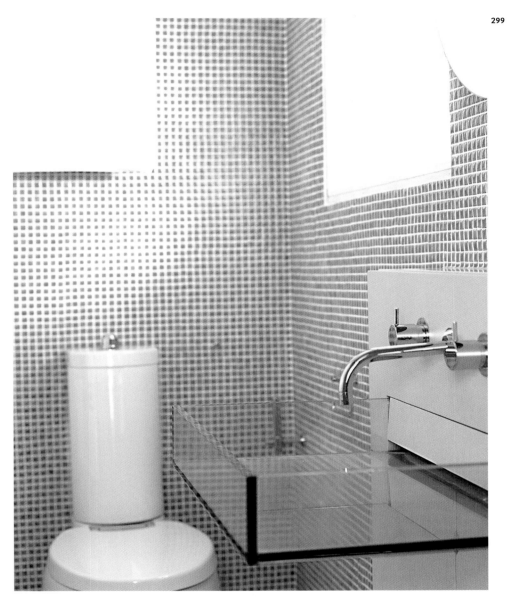

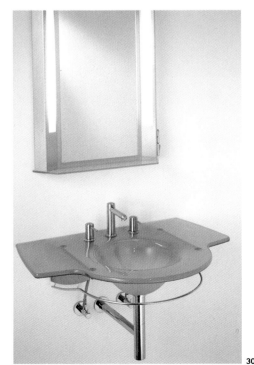

→ Water and glass make sympathetic companions, as may be seen here. This thick cast-glass bowl is asymmetrical and extremely tactile, making a pleasing contrast with the precision engineering of the tap.

300

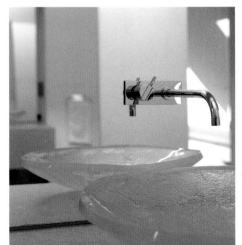

↑ An eye-catching WC and basin have been incorporated into this bathroom design. The circular WC, with its distinctive cylindrical water tank, is the Cesame Millennium WC; the highly unusual shallow cantilevered glass basin is called Agape. Both are from Original Bathrooms. The aqua-green mosaic tiling perfectly matches the colour of the thick glass of the basin.

301

302

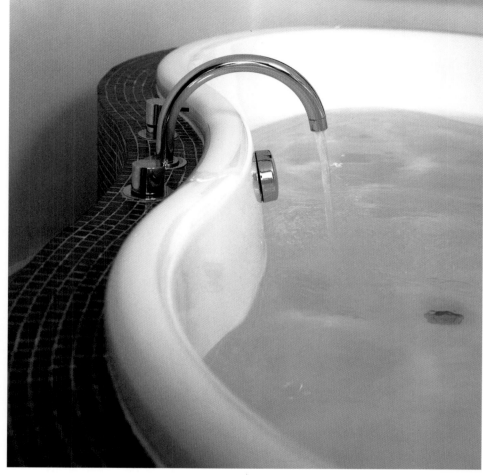

← A curvy, double-ended bath makes an eye catching feature in this bathroom, designed by architect Linda Morey Smith. To emphasise the unusual shape of the tub, mosaic tiling in a beautiful blue has been selected for use on the surround.

303

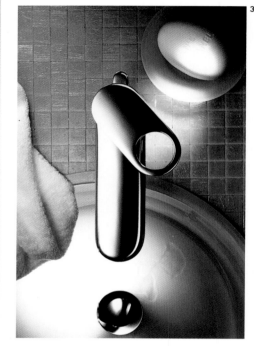

← An intriguing bird's-eye view of a tap and basin, which emphasizes the sculptural, almost abstract, shapes of modern bathroom fittings. This contemporary-style fitting, by specialist manufacturer Dornbracht, is part of the Domani series by Sieger Design. The handle fits comfortably into the palm of the hand, lifts up to control flow, and is moved from side to side to vary the temperature.

→ Producing an even sheet of water, the chrome-finish Niagara waterfall spout, available from Bathrooms International, turns tap water into a water feature. The spout can be used with traditional cross-head taps or high-tech levers, and it is available in both rim-mounted or wall-mounted versions. In addition, there is a curved version for round-end tubs.

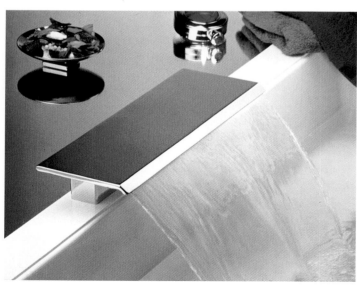

304

→ These wild, horn-shaped handles will add a splash of colour to any bathroom. They are available in crystal satin finishes called clear aqua, sapphire, and peach. They are available from Bathrooms International.

305

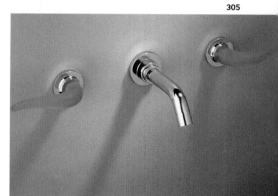

306

309

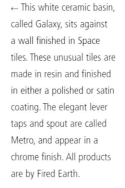

← This white ceramic basin, called Galaxy, sits against a wall finished in Space tiles. These unusual tiles are made in resin and finished in either a polished or satin coating. The elegant lever taps and spout are called Metro, and appear in a chrome finish. All products are by Fired Earth.

↓ This stunningly simple design is by Dieter Sieger for Dornbracht. The wall mounted fitting takes its inspiration from industrial-style taps, but has been adapted for domestic use. Called eMote, it is designed for use with sinks, and has touch-sensitive sensors to stop and start the water flow.

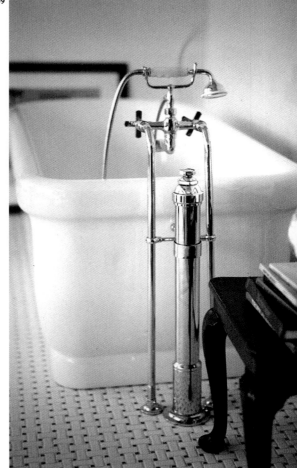

→ This unusual fitting is part of the Tara range, by Sieger Design for the manufacturer Dornbracht. It is a wall-mounted bridge mixer featuring distinctive angular cross-head taps. A thoughtful detail is the extensible spout, making it as practical as it is elegant.

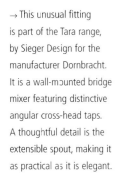

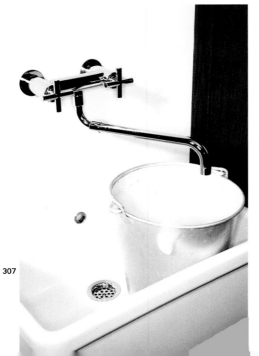

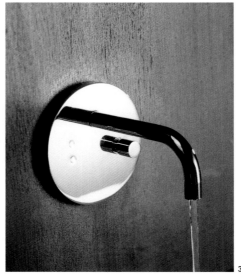

↑ There are some bathroom designs that remain perennially popular and so gain classic status. One such example is pictured here. By Michael Smith Town, and available from Bathrooms International, the deep, free-standing apron bath in Croquet White has a deck-mounted bath-shower mixer with risers. The unit is available in nickel, matt-nickel, and chrome finishes.

307

308

310

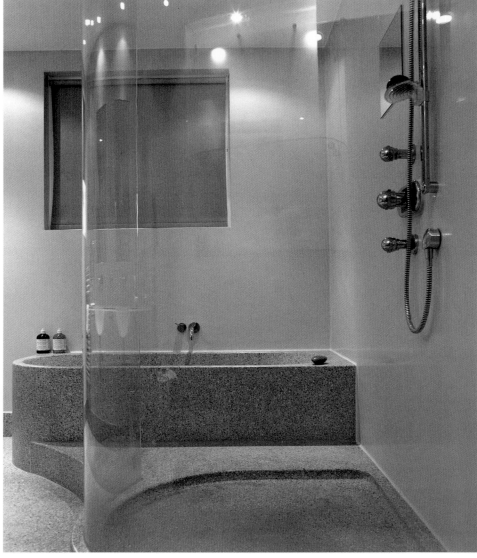

311

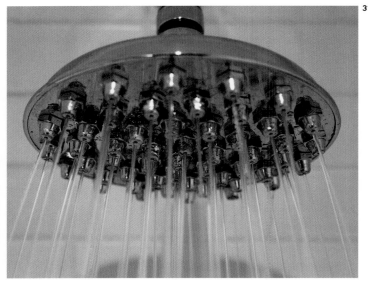

↑ Some ideas are just so good they refuse to date or to go out of fashion. One such example is this chrome-finished rose-style showerhead, which produces a truly exhilarating volume and pressure of water. Regular cleaning is essential in areas with hard water, however, to prevent a build-up of ugly limescale.

312

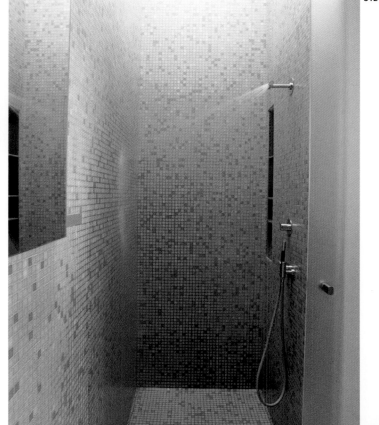

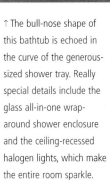

↑ The bull-nose shape of this bathtub is echoed in the curve of the generous-sized shower tray. Really special details include the glass all-in-one wrap-around shower enclosure and the ceiling-recessed halogen lights, which make the entire room sparkle.

→ A state-of-the-art shower has been installed in this cubicle, lined with mosaic tiles. The upper showerhead is a T-shaped bar protruding from the wall, while fixed on the wall lower down is another hose-style showerhead. Both fittings are by Vola.

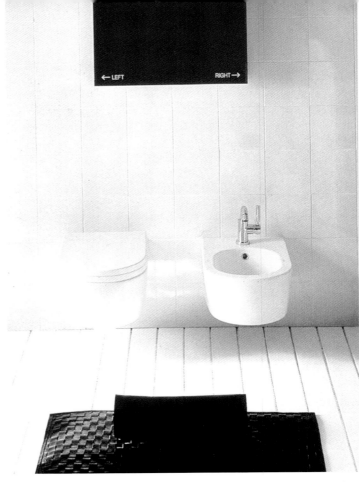

↓ Originally designed for use in settings such as public lavatories, factory cloakrooms, and prisons, stainless-steel bathroom accessories have now been brought into the home. The elegant design of this beautiful conical pan, with its clear plastic seat, looks completely at home in this bathroom finished with mosaic tiling.

314

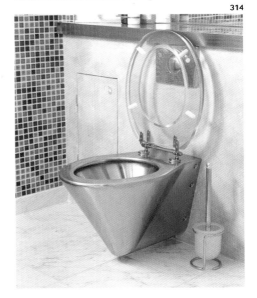

↑ The elegance of the best of Japanese design inspired the creation of this Link wall-hung WC and wall-hung bidet. They were created as part of the Work in Progress collection, by Giulio Cappellini and Roberto Palomba, for the company Flaminia.

→ Now that stainless steel is common in kitchens, it is also becoming popular in bathrooms. Here an entire range – basin, WC, and shower tray – is installed in a domestic bathroom, where the hard industrial edge of the products is softened by details such as the mosaic tiling.

In recent years, a huge amount of time and attention has been lavished on the design and development of stunning baths and washbasins. This, however, has left the WC and shower rather out of the picture. Now, though, it seems that their time has come.

Showers continue to gain in popularity. For a start, they use less water than a bath, and therefore have good environmental credentials. In addition, they take up less space than a bath, making them ideal for ensuite washrooms, and they are also quick and invigorating. And now that shower manufacturers are producing high-quality units that guarantee a powerful spray and controllable temperatures, attention is being turned to making attractive shower enclosures to house them. The old-style units with their wobbly doors and leaking seals are being replaced by much smarter and far more durable designs.

The lavatory, or WC, is the real Cinderella of the bathroom. In many homes it has been removed from the bathing space altogether, to sit in its own cubicle. Where there is room to do this, it makes good sense in a family home to help cope with the morning rush hour. Lavatory design has changed only slowly over the years, but interesting new models include wall-suspended pans – a feature that makes it extremely easy to clean the floors and keep them spotless. And, borrowing from industrial designs, the stainless-steel WC, with its stylish and easy-clean finish, is also becoming increasingly popular in the domestic setting.

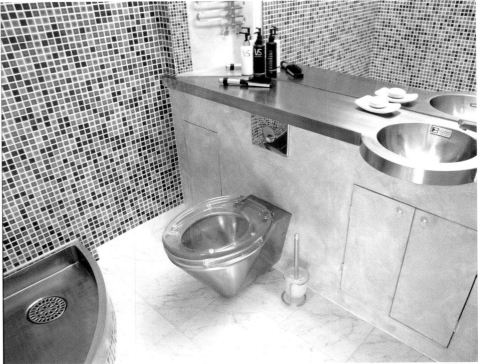

heating

In the majority of modern-style homes built during the second half of the twentieth century, the fireplace was considered to be an anachronism, a reminder of the dreary past when homes were heated with coal fires that left dirty smuts on walls and had grates that needed to be cleaned out and reblacked.

In the brave new world following the Second World War, central heating with radiators was the answer to everyone's desire for instant warmth and a comfortable, labour-free heating system. However, there was one element of the story that was totally overlooked – people like to see a fireplace, and enjoy the flicker of a moving flame. There is something way-back in our folk memory, a deep-rooted nostalgia, that suggests that the hearth is still the heart of the home.

Some of the first contemporary reworkings of the fireplace were created by architects in their designs for one-off homes. The hearth was treated almost as if it were a picture – because of central heating, the fire did not have to produce heat, so all that was required was a simple frame surrounding the moving image of the flame.

In more recent times, however, the idea of the fireplace has been developed and refined further, and now a number of companies are making modern-style fireplaces, some with artificial flames but also, surprisingly, plenty using solid fuel. The frames continue to be simple or even non-existent, and the fireplace itself is often lifted off the ground so that it can be seen all the better.

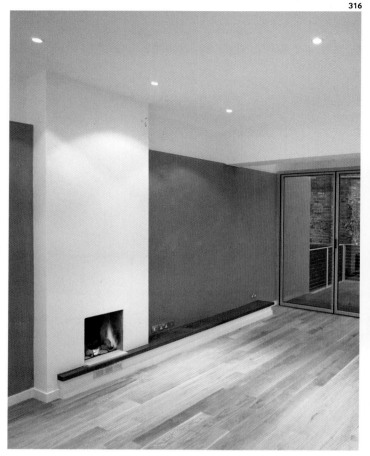

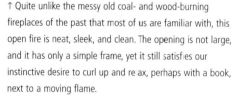

↑ Quite unlike the messy old coal- and wood-burning fireplaces of the past that most of us are familiar with, this open fire is neat, sleek, and clean. The opening is not large, and it has only a simple frame, yet it still satisfies our instinctive desire to curl up and relax, perhaps with a book, next to a moving flame.

↑ Despite all the advantages of central heating, we still yearn to see a living flame – whether or not it produces usable heat. Even in a contemporary interior such as this, by architect Buckley Gray, the fireplace and chimney breast remain the focal point of the room – it is even emphasized by being painted in a different colour.

→ Raised off the floor and set into a frameless recess, this is about as minimal as a fireplace can get.

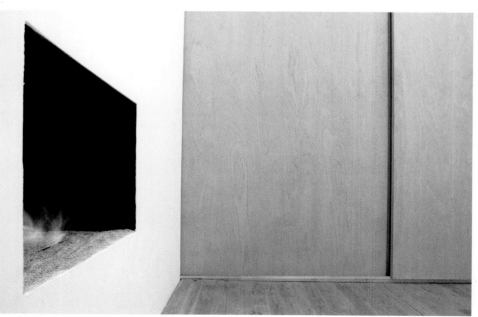

319

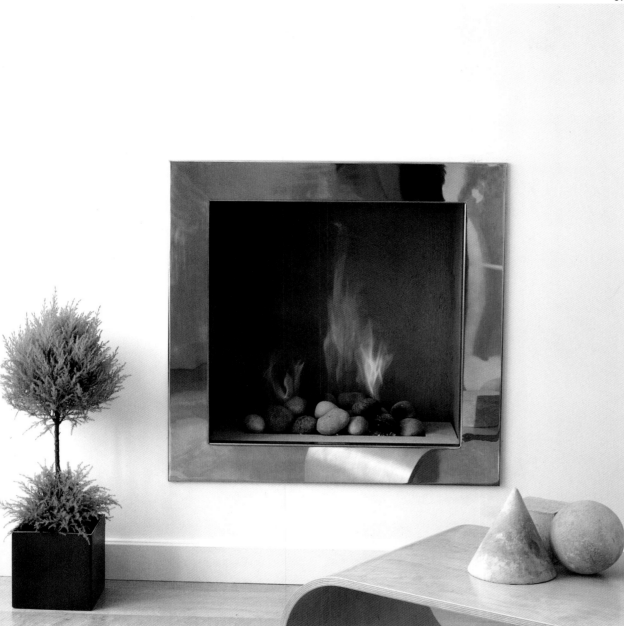

← When architect Henry Harrison realized how difficult it was to find modern-style fireplaces, he set up his own business — the Platonic Fireplace Company — to create new designs. This metal-framed unit, called Firescape, is inset into the wall, where it functions as a focus for the room. Here, the flames are shown licking around pebbles made from a material called fireclay — real stones would not be able to withstand the heat. For the ultimate in high-tech hearths, the height of the flames can be controlled using a remote handset.

320

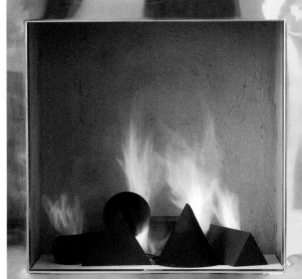

→ In this version of the Firescape fireplace, from the Platonic Fireplace Company (see picture 319), the realistic-looking pebbles have been replaced with intriguing geometric-shaped Geologs, again made in fireclay — a special material able to withstand high temperatures.

321

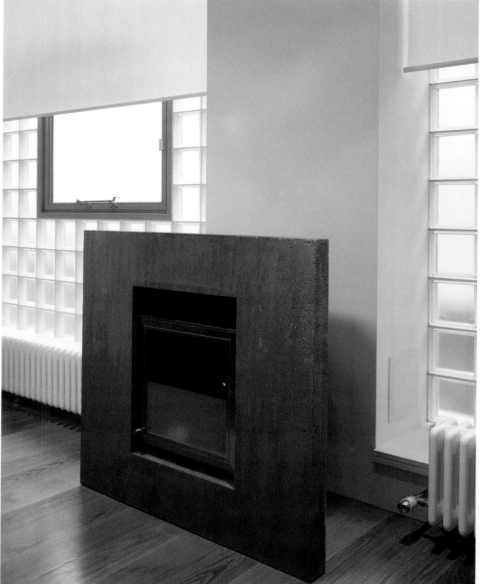

322

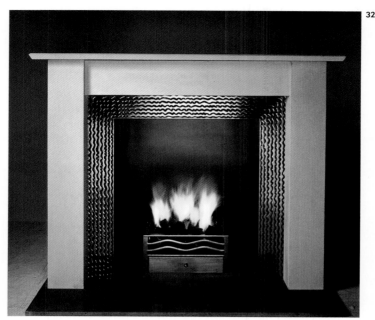

↑ Even the makers of the most traditional-style fireplaces have recognized the market's demand for a modern interpretation of the old designs. Here, Chesney's has produced a design called Murano, which features a honed-limestone surround, cast-iron ripple-effect slips (the metal inner frame), and a wave-pattern fire basket fitted with a gas-effect fire.

323

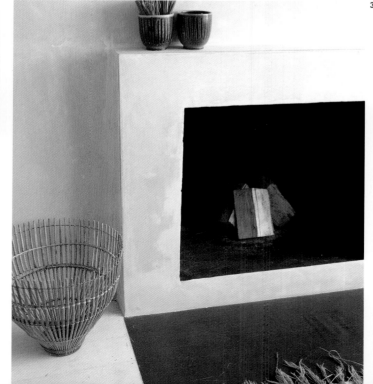

↑ Architecture practice Allford Hall Monaghan Morris created this concrete fireplace for a contemporary loft apartment. The frame, which has been pulled into the room, surrounds a coal-effect gas fire housed in a stainless-steel case.

→ Stancing just proud of the wall, this cast-plaster surround has been stripped to a basic rectangle. Designed by architecture practice Spencer Fung, the fireplace burns real fuel and features a black slate hearth set into the floor.

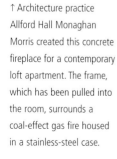

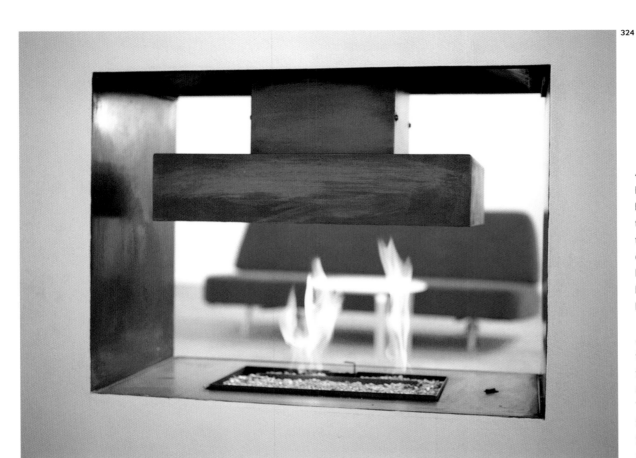

324

← This open-sided fireplace has been built into the wall between two rooms. As the flames rise through the grille below the chunky oblong steel extractor hood, this ingenious design becomes the focal point for both rooms.

↓ This streamlined, recessed fireplace becomes part of the abstract images that are on display in the room. The brushed stainless-steel finish of the frame of the fireplace is picked up and repeated in the skirting.

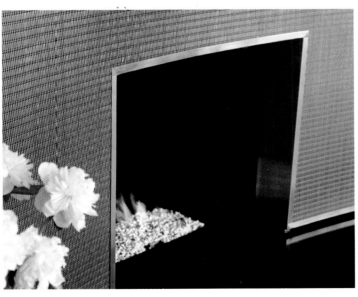

325

← This gas-burning fireplace, by architect Munkenbeck + Marshall, has been given a base of decorative white heat-proof granules. The plain opening is finished with a slender metal frame that has been set flush into a wall finished with a woven metal mesh.

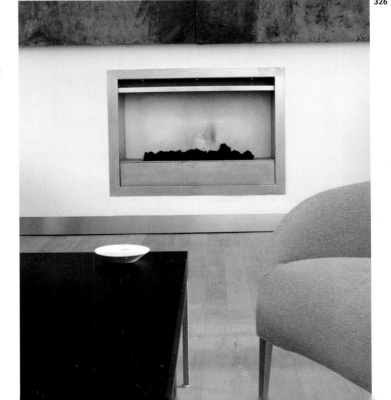

326

Such is our passion for fireplaces that we are, once again, prepared to put up with the mess and inconvenience of carrying and storing coal or logs and cleaning up the ash, just to have a solid-fuel fire. For many people, artificial gas and electric flame-effect fires, as good as they are, are no substitute for the real thing.

Despite the fact that our nostalgia for the hearth is so deep rooted, we are not entirely wedded to old-style fireplaces, and so this area of design has received a welcome fillip. The Scandinavian-style cast-iron wood-burning stove, for example, has enjoyed a tremendous revival, and it has the advantages of being highly fuel efficient while emitting a great amount of heat. The thick iron casing stays warm for hours after the flame is extinguished.

New designs for larger, incinerator-style stoves are also beginning to make an appearance, especially in homes designed by environment-aware architects. These stoves are designed to burn anything, from waste wood chips to whole logs. So efficient are they that they will heat an entire house as well as provide hot water for the family.

And finally, there are the exciting contemporary designs that are a true celebration of the hearth. As well as looking good in almost any interior setting – some are intriguingly suspended in space – these also generate generous amounts of heat.

→ There is no bolder way to make the fire a focus of the room than by setting it right in the middle of the space. This spherical steel design provides a fireplace with a huge capacity, and the warmth and flames can be enjoyed all the way around. Finished in a tough, heat-resistant, matt-black exterior, this unit, Mezzofocus, is by Diligence.

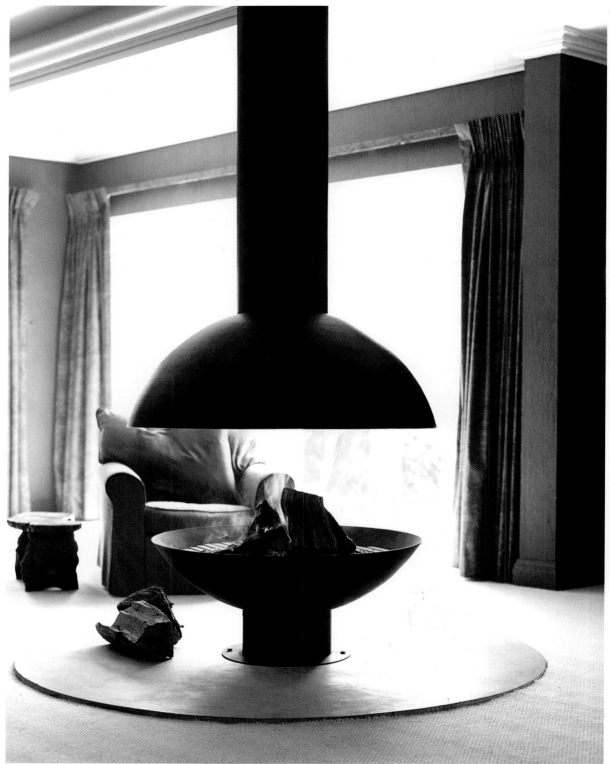

327

328

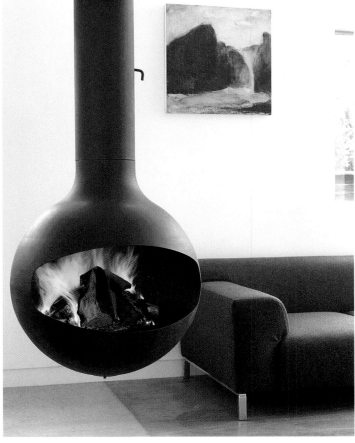

329

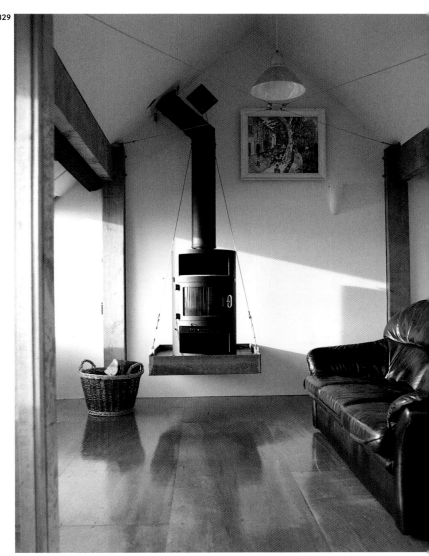

← Impossible to ignore, here the fireplace is reborn as modern sculpture. This suspended black steel design is called Bathyscafocus, and it is a part of the Focus fires collection, by Diligence.

→ Here is a modern interpretation of the large traditional ceramic-tiled stoves that are commonly found in homes throughout Continental Europe. The cast metal of the stove acts as an effective heat store, and so radiates warmth into the room long after the fire itself has been extinguished.

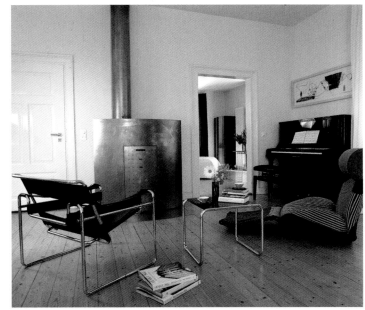

330

↑ Suspended well above the floor by steel cables fixed to its integral tray hearth, this attractive design is a contemporary version of the traditional cast-iron stove. Although it looks unusual raised off the ground in this fashion, this is in fact an extremely practical innovation, as it allows the heat to radiate all around the room. It also makes ergonomic sense – it is far easier to load with logs and empty of ash than stoves that sit directly on the floor.

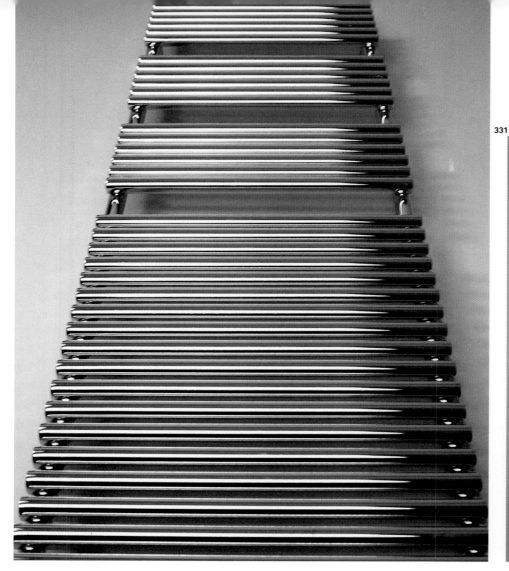

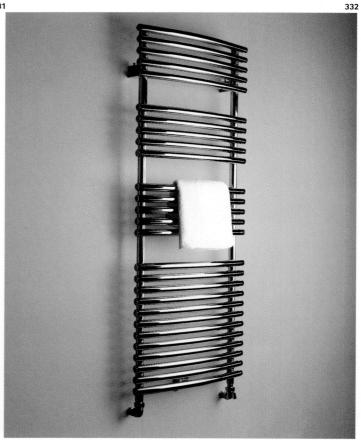

↑ Towel radiators are a practical addition to any bathroom, providing background heat as well as the luxury of warm towels. Even better, modern towel radiators look a great deal more stylish than ever before. This ladder-style straight-fronted design, from Bisque, is available as a plug-in electric model, or can be plumbed into your central heating system.

→ This extremely neat and compact tube style of radiator is ideal for small spaces. Despite its diminutive size, it is an effective heater owing to its design, which incorporates circular fins to radiate the heat. This model is called Flow Form, and is available from Bisque.

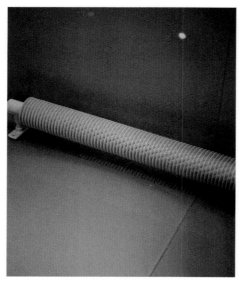

↑ For most of us, used to seeing the traditional, chunky, panelled radiator, is it possible for a radiator to look more different than this? Popular in kitchens and bathrooms, this bow-fronted towel radiator is available from Bisque in a range of sizes and a choice of more than 1,600 colours.

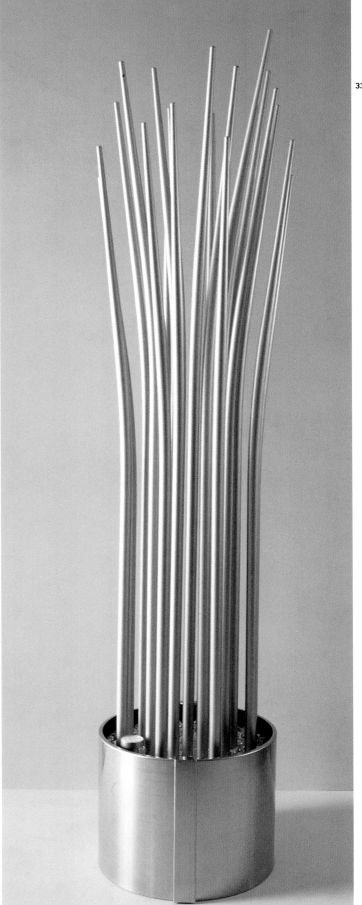

334

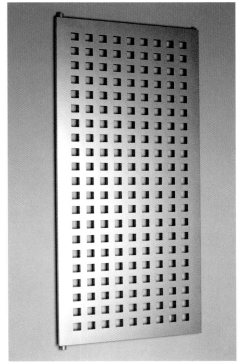

335

← This whimsical design of radiator, called Powerplant, has been inspired by sprouting branches and is made in Switzerland by Arbonia for Bisque. The radiator measures almost 2 m (6½ ft) tall and produces high levels of warmth. It is sold in a choice of colours and finishes, including the Metallica shown here.

↑ A real departure from the more familiar radiator is this design – the Bisque B2. It is a wall-mounted design with a distinctive pattern of square perforations. The radiator is available in more than a dozen sizes and shapes, as well as horizontal and vertical versions, and in a wide range of colours and metallic finishes.

Along with our fondness for the glow of real fires, we have also developed a taste for beautiful and unusual radiators. For decades, the choice of design was limited to the familiar, and now uninspiring, white-panelled variety. However, manufacturers have caught the mood of the market and have started to smarten up their act. Now, they employ the services of designers and offer glossy brochures full of tempting designs.

There are two main considerations when deciding on which radiator to buy. The first is whether a particular model of radiator is suitable for your design scheme – do you want the radiators to become an obvious part of the scheme, for example, so that they make some sort of design statement? And should they also be available in colours that complement your interior? Or do you favour the idea that radiators should be made to disappear out of sight? If you fall into the the latter category, then you might want to consider other options, such as underfloor heating.

The second consideration when choosing radiators is altogether more pragmatic – are they capable of producing the amount of heat required to warm a room or volume of space?

Any professional heating engineer will be able to provide a calculation based on the volume of space in your home and the potential heat output of the radiators. The results will provide guidelines concerning how many radiators you will need, what size they should be, and whether or not the boiler has the necessary muscle to run them at the required output.

handles and switches

It may be tempting to think that the final finishing touches, such as switches, sockets, and door handles, are not that important and so could be areas of a decorative scheme where attention to detail can be relaxed a little. Nothing could be further from the truth.

Our first impressions of any home are initially based on its superficial appearance – whether it appears inviting, whether we like the colour of the front door, and whether it seems well cared for. After that, we ring the bell or use the door knocker, which is a largely tactile experience. These things are small, but they are nevertheless significant.

If the door knocker feels heavy and substantial, it sets up positive expectations for the interior that lies beyond. It is likely that door handles and switches, and even items such as the stair handrail, perform in the same way.

A handle that is solid and fits well into your hand is reassuring and a pleasure to use. Grab hold of a flimsy, awkward, badly designed handle and it is slightly unsettling. In the same way that cheap handles will ruin a beautiful door, a well-balanced, exquisitely designed handle can transform an ordinary door by adding an all-important flourish. The same applies to light switches and electrical sockets – when these are well designed and thoughtfully chosen, they can add a sense of style and lift the overall quality of an interior.

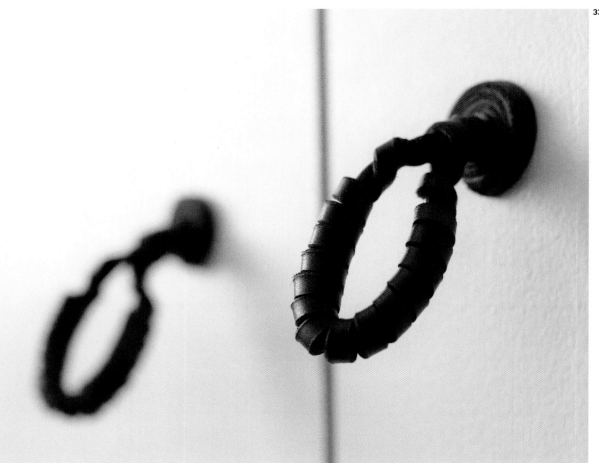

↑ The warmth and luxurious feel of leather is always pleasing, and when it is used like this, as a door handle, it scores extra points for novelty.

→ This jolly door handle, with its upturned end, is part of the Jedo collection from A Touch of Brass. This model has been given a polished-chrome finish and the generous curve fits comfortably into the hand.

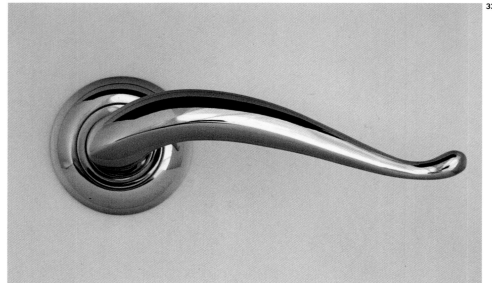

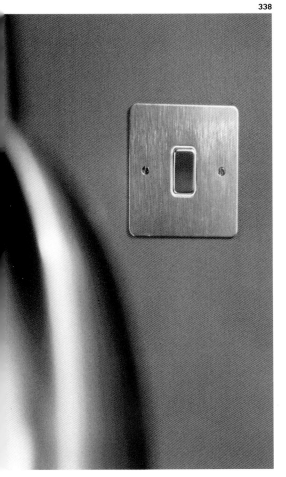

← A brushed stainless-steel light switch adds a wonderful finishing touch to this cerise-pink room. Importantly, the switch also picks up on a theme introduced by other materials used nearby, such as the stainless-steel pendant lampshade. The flush-fit switch is part of the New Edge range, from MK Electric.

→ A particularly pleasing detail in this contemporary-style bathroom is the shiny chrome finish of this shaver socket, which matches other metal accessories in the room. Available from MK Electric, the shaver socket is called Chroma.

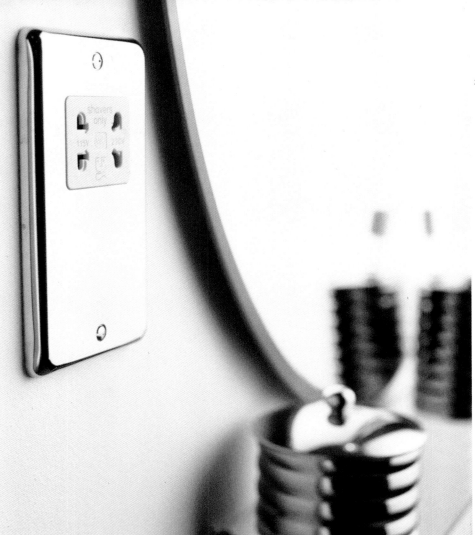

← This downturned handle in polished chrome is part of the Jedo collection from A Touch of Brass. This is a good example of a handle that is able to transmit a subtle, subconscious message — because it fits so neatly into the contours of the hand, it gives out reassuring signals that you are about to enter a well-considered, thoughtfully designed room. Such an elegant handle also has the ability to transform and enhance the appearance of an otherwise unremarkable door.

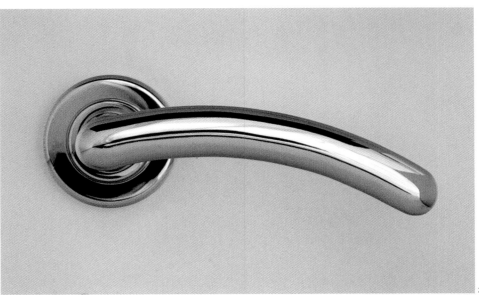

directory

walls

Altfield
Unit 2
22 Chelsea Harbour Design Centre
Chelsea Harbour
London SW10 0XE
UK
Tel: +44 (0)20 7351 5893
www.altfield.com

(M, R) Unusual wallpapers – such as
copies of ancient and antique designs
– and metallic, stone and wood
finishes.

Amabis Handmade Tiles
Shrewsbury SY1 3JE
UK
Tel: +44 (0)1743 461700 for
brochure
www.amabis.co.uk

(R) Range of colourful, handmade
tiles.

Anaglypta
UK
Tel: +44 (0)1254 870137 for
stockists
www.anaglypta.co.uk

(M) Maker of wallpaper of all types,
including those with a raised pattern.

Ardenbright
Tor Coatings Ltd
Potobello Industrial Estate
Birtley
Chester-le-Street
County Durham DH3 2RE, UK
Tel: +44 (0)191 410 6611
for stockists
email: enquiries@tor-coatings.com

(M) Maker of specialist paints,
including masonry, enamel, and
metallic types.

Auro Organic Paint Supplies
Unit 2
Pamphillions Farm
Purton End
Debden
Saffron Walden
Essex CB11 3JT
UK
Tel: +44 (0)1799 543077
www.auroorganic.co.uk

(I) Paints made with environment-
friendly components.

Bill Amberg
10 Chepstow Road
London W2 5BD
UK
Tel: +44 (0)20 7727 3560
www.billamberg.com

(D, R) A designer with a flair for using
leather for walls, floors, and furniture.
(See pictures 19, 21, 68, 149)

Bridge of Weir Leather Company
Clydesdale Works
Bridge of Weir
Renfrewshire PA11 3LF
UK
Tel: +44 (0)1505 612132

(D, M, R) Manufacturer and supplier
of leather upholstery and wall
panelling.

British Felt Company
Unit 14
Drakes Mews
Crownhill
Milton Keynes
Buckinghamshire MK8 0ER
UK
Tel: +44 (0)1908 263304
www.britishfelt.co.uk

(M, R) Maker of felts that can
be used as wall coverings.

Bruno Triplet
Unit 18/1
Chelsea Harbour Design Centre
Chelsea
London SW10 0XE
UK
Tel: +44 (0)20 7795 0395
www.brunotriplet.com
for suppliers

(M, trade only) Linen wallpapers

Brunschwig & Fils
10 The Chambers
Chelsea Harbour Drive
London SW10 0XF
UK
Tel: +44 (0)20 7351 5797
for stockists
www.brunschwig.com
and
979 Third Avenue
New York
NY 10022-1234
USA
Tel: +1 212 838 7878
www.brunschwig.com

(D, M, R) Traditional and
contemporary wallpapers.

C Brewer & Sons Ltd
327 Putney Bridge Road
London SW15 2PG
UK
Tel: +44 (0)20 8788 9335

(R) Specialist supplier of decorating
paints and glazes.

Coopers
Page House
33 Pages Walk
London SE1 4SF
UK
Tel: +44 (0)20 7237 1767

(M) Maker of a range of glass blocks.

Craig & Rose
Unit 8
Halbeath Industrial Estate
Crossgates Road
Dunfermline KY11 7EG
UK
Tel: +44 (0)1383 740 000
for stockists
email: Enquiries@craigandrose.com

(M, R) Decorative materials including
varnishes, glazes, and scumbles.

Crown Paints
Crown House
Hollins Road
Darwen
Lancashire BB3 0BG
UK
Tel: +44 (0)1254 704 951
www.crownpaint.co.uk

(M, R) Major producer of a wide
range of paints.

Cy-Pres
14 Bells Close
Brigstock
Kettering
Northamptonshire NN14 3JG
UK
Tel: +44 (0)1536 373431
for mail order

(M, R) Limewash and distemper
made to order.

Domus Tiles
33 Parkgate Road
London SW11 4NP
UK
Tel: +44 (0)20 7223 5555
www.domustiles.co.uk

(R) Ceramic and marble tiles.

Donghia
21 and 23 Chelsea Harbour Design
Centre
Chelsea
London SW10 0XE
UK
Tel: +44 (0)20 7823 3456

(D, M, R) Unusual wallpapers made
from raffia, grass cloth, and hemp as
well as furniture and lighting.

Dulux Paints
Wexham Road
Slough
Berkshire SL2 5DS
UK
Tel: +44 (0)1753 550000
www.dulux.co.uk

(M, R) Major paint maker producing
thousands of different colours.

Fantini Mosaici
Via A. Meucci 19
20128 Milano
Italy
Tel: +39 227 207 092
www.fantinimosaici.com

(R) Great mosaics.

Farrow and Ball
Uddens Estate
Wimborne
Dorset BH21 7NL
UK
Tel: +44 (0)1202 876141 for
stockists
www.farrow-ball.com

(M, R) Modern and traditional paints
and varnishes.

Fired Earth
Twyford Mill
Oxford Road
Adderbury Oxon OX17 3HP
UK
Tel: +44 (0)1295 812088 for stockists
www.firedearth.com

(R) Historic and modern paint colours,
plus natural wall and floor coverings,
bathrooms.
(See pictures 74, 306)

Graham & Brown
UK
Tel: + 44 0800 328 8452 (free phone
UK only)

(M, R) Amazing textured wallpapers.

Gustafs
Sweden
Tel: +46 243 792020
www.gustafs.com

(M) Maker of interesting perforated
acoustic wall panelling, most often
used in recording studios, finished in
beech or birch.

**Harlequin Fabrics
and Wallcoverings Ltd**
Ladybird House
Beeches Road
Loughborough
Leicestershire LE11 2HA
UK
Tel: +44 (0)1509 225000
www.harlequin.uk.com

(D, M) Traditional and contemporary
fabrics and wallcoverings.

Ineos Acrylics UK Ltd
PO Box 34
Duckworth Street
Darwen
Lancashire BB3 1QB
UK
Tel: +44 (0)1254 874 444 for
stockists
www.ineosacrylics.com

(M) Manufacturer of Perspex
sheeting.

JW Bollom & Co
Unit 1
Croydon Road
Beckenham
Kent BR3 4BL
UK
Tel: +44 (0)20 8658 2299 for
stockists
www.bollom.com

(M) High-quality paints, very popular
with professional decorators.

L Cornelissen & Son Ltd
105 Great Russell Street
London WC1B 3RY
UK
Tel: +44 (0)20 7636 1045
email: info@cornelissen.com

(M, R) Specialist decorating materials,
including raw pigment and gold leaf.

Lewis and Wood
5 The Green
Ulry
Gloucestershire
GL11 5SN
Tel: +44 (0)1453 860313
Fax: +44 (0)1453 860054

(M) Wallpapers including felt finish.

**Marco Crivello at
The Plateaux Gallery**
London
UK
Tel: +44 (0)20 7357 6880

(D, M, R) Maker of bespoke,
contemporary-style screens.

Metalkitsch
Unit 9 & 10
Ebbsfleet Industrial Estate
Stonebridge Road
Northfleet
Kent DA11 9DZ
UK
Tel: +44 (C)1474 568229
www.metalkitsch.co.uk

(M, R) Makers of beautiful and
unusual metal wall and floor tiles.

Muraspec
74–78 Wood Lane End
Hemel Hempstead
Hertfordshire HP2 4RF
UK
Tel: +44 (0)8705 117 118 for
stockists
www.muraspec.com

(D, M, R) Wallcoverings in suede,
hessian, and silk
(See pictures 34, 35, 39)

Nana Wall Systems
USA
Tel: +1 800 873 5673
www.nanawallsystems.com

(M) Maker of aluminium and
wood-framed door systems for
opening walls.

Natural Tile
150 Church Road
Redfield
Bristol BS5 9HN
UK
Tel: +44 (0)117 941 3707
www.naturaltile.co.uk

(M, R) A huge range of unusual tiles
available, including those made of
solid aluminium, glass, and resin.
(See picture 76)

Nobilis-Fontan
G3 Chelsea Harbour Design Centre
London SW10
UK
Tel: +44 (0)20 7351 7878

(R) Interesting wallpapers, including
an eye-catching concrete pattern.

Paint & Paper
11 Hellesdon Hall Industrial Park
Norwich
Norfolk NR6 5DR
UK
Tel: +44 (0)1603 400777
www.paint-paper.co.uk

(R) Traditional and modern paints by
leading producers, including Farrow &
Ball, Sanderson, Fired Earth, Laura
Ashley, and Morris and Co.

Paint & Paper Library
5 Elystan Street
London SW3 3NT
UK
Tel: +44 (0)20 7823 7755
www.paintlibrary.co.uk

(M, R) Specialist in beautiful paint
colours and finishes, as well as
individual wallpapers.

Pittsburgh Corning
USA
Tel: +1 724 327 6100
www.pittsburghcorning.com

(M) Maker of solid-glass blocks that
are ideal for walls and windows
openings.

Pittsburgh Paints
PPG Industries
1 PPG Place
Pittsburgh
PA 15272
USA
Tel: +1 888 774 1010
www.pittsburghpaints.com

(M, R) Leading paint manufacturer,
specializing in hard-wearing finishes.

Rose of Jericho
Horchester
Holywell
Dorchester
Dorset DT2 OLR
UK
Tel: +44 (0)1935 83676
www.rose-of-jericho.demon.co.uk

(M, R) Paints made to traditional recipes.

Screen Solutions Revolution
Beaufort House
Greenwich Way
Peacehaven
East Sussex BN10 8JQ
UK
Tel: +44 (0)1273 589 922 for stockists
Fax: +44 (0)1273 589 921
www.screensolutions.co.uk

(D, M) Maker of free-standing screens.

Steve Charles & Co
The Old Engineering Offices
2 Michael Road
London SW6 2AD
UK
Tel: +44 (0)20 7384 4424
www.stevecharles.com

(D, M, R) Stone and inlaid concrete for walls and floors.

Tantrum Design Ltd
UK
Tel: +44 (0)1832 226019
email: inquiries@tantrumdesign.com

(R) Seller of unusual tiles, including the pewter collection.

The Original Tile Company
23a Howe Street
Edinburgh EH3 6TF
UK
Tel: +44 (0)131 556 2013

(R) Specialist supplier of hand-made and hand-painted tiles from all over the world.

United Colors of Benetton Paint Colors with Imagica
(available through B&Q stores)
www.benetton.com

(M) Unusual textured paints.
(See picture 33)

Zoffany
Talbot House
17 Church Street
Rickmansworth
Hertfordshire WD3 1DE
UK
Tel: +44 (0)1923 710680
www.zoffany.com

(R) Beautiful but expensive wallpapers and a range of home accessories.

ceilings

Armstrong World Industries
Buildings Products Division
Armstrong House
38 Market Square
Uxbridge UB8 ING
UK
Tel: +44 0800 371 849 for stockists
(free phone UK only)
www.armstrong.com

(M) Customized ceilings in mineral/soft fibre, metal, and wood.

Cellbond Architectural
5 Stukeley Business Centre
Blackstone Road
Huntingdon
Cambridgeshire PE29 6EF
UK
Tel: +44 (0)1480 444725
www.cellbond.com

(M, R) Unusual architectural glass for ceilings, walls, floors, stairs, etc.

Cox Building Products
Unit 1
Shaw Road
Bushbury
Wolverhampton WV10 9LA
UK
Tel: +44 (0)1902 371800 for stockists
www.coxbp.com

(M) Producer of a huge range of rooflights, sunpipes, roof domes. etc.

Major Industries
PO Box 306
Wausau
Wisconsin 54402 0306
USA
Tel: +1 715 842 4616
www.majorskylights.com

(M, R) Maker of a huge range of skylights and glazed wall systems.

MM Systems
4520 Elmdale Drive
Tucker
GA 30084
USA
Tel: +1 800 241 3460
www.mmsystemscorp.com

(M, R) Makers of large barrel-vault and flat ceiling skylights.

Velux Company Ltd
Woodside Way
Glenrothes East
Fife KY7 4ND
Scotland
UK
Tel: +44 (0)1592 772 211
www.velux.com

(M, R) A very extensive range of rooflights.

floors

Altro Ltd
Works Road
Letchworth
Hertfordshire SG6 1NW
UK
Tel: +44 (0)1462 480480 for stockists
www.altro.co.uk

(D, M) Vinyl, PVC, and rubber flooring.

Bill Amberg
10 Chepstow Road
London W2 5BD
UK
Tel: +44 (0)20 7727 3560
www.billamberg.com

(D, R) A designer with a flair for using leather for walls, floors, and furniture.
(See pictures 19, 21, 68, 149)

Bisazza UK Ltd
UK
Tel: +44 (0)20 8640 7994
www.bisazza.it

(D, M) Ceramic flooring, including mosaics.
(See pictures 89, 91, 93)

Bragman Flett Ltd
Unit 4
193 Garth Road
Morden
Surrey SM4 4LZ
UK
Tel: +44 (0)20 8337 1934
www.bragmanflett.co.uk

(M, R) Aluminium sheet flooring made to customer's specifications.

Ceramic Tiles of Italy
Italian Trade Commission
Ceramic Tile Department
499 Park Avenue
New York
NY 10022
USA
Tel: +1 212 980 1500
www.italtrade.com

(M, R) A range of Italian tiles.

Classical Flagstones
The Old Dairy
Lower Ledge Farm
Dyrham
Nr Bath
UK
Tel: +44 (0)1225 316759
www.classical-flagstones.com

(M, R) Stone tiles, flags and cobbles – deliveries worldwide.

Compas Architectural Stone and Tile International Inc
767 North La Cienega Blvd
Los Angeles
CA 90069
USA
Tel: +1 310 854 3023

(R) Huge showroom of stone and tiles, modern and antique, as well as antique fireplaces and antique roof tiles.

Crucial Trading Ltd
79 Westbourne Park Road
London W2 5QH
UK
Tel: +44 (0)20 7221 9000
email: Sales@crucial-trading.com

(R) Retailer of natural flooring in sisal, coir, rush, jute, and even paper.

Dalsouple

PO Box 140

Bridgwater

Somerset TA5 1HT

UK

Tel: +44 (0)1984 667233

for stockists

www.dalsouple.com

(M) Maker of rubber flooring.

Delabole Slate

Pengelly Road

Delabole

Cornwall PL33 9AZ

UK

Tel: +44 (0)1840 212242

www.delaboleslate.com

(M, R) Slate floor tiles.

English Timbers

1a Main Street

Kirkburn

Driffield

East Yorkshire YO25 9DU

UK

Tel: +44 (0)1377 229301

www.englishtimbers.co.uk

(M) Hardwood flooring.

Exquisite Surfaces

731 North La Cienega Blvd

Los Angeles

CA 90069

USA

Tel: –1 310 659 4580

www.exquisitesurfaces.com

(R) Seller of great stone flooring –

from French limestone to antique

terracotta.

Fantini Mosaici

180 NE 39th Street

Suite 106

Miami

Florida 33137

USA

Tel: +1 305 572 0990

www.fantinimosaici.com

(R) Mosaic, marble,

and stone flooring.

Finewood Floors Ltd

Skillion Business Centre

1 Hawley Road

London N18 3SB

UK

Tel: +44 (0)20 8884 1515

(M) Specialist in all hardwood, strip

and parquet, in particular wide-plank

flooring.

Forbo-Nairn

PO Box 1

Kirkcaldy

Fife KY1 2SB

UK

Tel: +44 (0)1592 643777

for stockists

www.marmoleum.co.uk

(M) The UK's sole producer

of linoleum sheet and tile

and modular systems.

(See picture 97)

Georgia-Pacific

133 Peachtree Street NE

Atlanta

GA 30303

USA

Tel: +1 404 652 4000

www.gp.com

(M) Maker of high-quality plywood

flooring.

Gerbert Ltd

715 Fountain Avenue

PO Box 4944

Lancaster

PA 17406

USA

Tel: +1 717 299 5035

www.gerbertltd.com

(M) Producer of unusual recycled

rubber flooring.

Gerflor Ltd

UK

Tel: +44 (0)1926 401500

for stockists

(M) Vinyl and rubber flooring –

sheet and tile.

Gooding Aluminium

1 British Wharf

Landmann Way

London SE14 5RS

UK

Tel: +44 (0)20 8692 2255

Fax: +44 (0)20 8694 2004

for brochures and samples

www.goodingalum.com

www.gaproductfocus.com

(M, R) Aluminium sheet flooring.

Hard Rock Flooring

Fleet Marston Farm

Fleet Marston

Aylesbury

Buckinghamshire HP18 OPL

UK

Tel: +44 (0)1296 658 755

www.hardrockflooring.co.uk

(M, R) Natural stone flooring.

Harvey Maria

Trident Business Centre

89 Bickersteth Road

London SW17 9SH

UK

Tel: +44 (0)20 8516 7788

www.harveymaria.co.uk

(D, M, R) Laminated photographic

tiles in patterns of grass, pebbles,

leaves, and many more.

(See picture 98)

H&L Marble Ltd

Units 2–3

Abbey Wharf

Mount Pleasant

Alperton

Middlesex HAO 1NR

UK

Tel: +44 (0)20 8903 5811

(R) Supplier of granite, limestone,

and marble.

Hoboken Floors

70 Demarest Drive

Wayne

New Jersey 07470

USA

Tel: +1 973 694 2888

www.hobokenfloors.com

(R) Retailer of a range of hardwood,

laminate, ceramic, and vinyl flooring.

Innovative Floor Coverings Inc

767 Highway 98E

Suite #3

Destin

FL 32541

USA

Tel: +1 850 269 1385

www.innovativefloor.micronpcweb.com

(R) Wide range of different types of

flooring materials.

J Preedy and Sons

Lamb Works

North Road

London N7 9DA

UK

Tel: +44 (0)20 7700 0377

(M, R) Design and installation

of glass flooring and doors.

Junckers Ltd

Wheaton Court Commercial Centre

Wheaton Road

Witham

Essex CM8 3UJ

UK

Tel: +44 (0)1376 534700

for stockists

www.junckers.co.uk

(Distributor) Solid-hardwood flooring.

(See picture 63)

Kersaint Cobb

& Company Ltd

Gorsey Lane

Coleshill

Birmingham B46 1JU

UK

Tel: +44 (0)1675 430430

email: sales@kersaintcobb.co.uk

(I, R) Natural floor coverings

(New Zealand rugs).

(See picture 70)

Kahrs UK Ltd

Unit 2 West

68 Bognor Road

Chichester

West Sussex PO19 2NS

UK

Tel: +44 (0)1243 778747

for stockists

www.kahrs.se

(M) Producers of pre-laminated

wood floors.

Kirkstone

Skelworth Bridge

nr Ambleside

Cumbria LA22 9NN

UK

Tel: +44 (0)1539 433296

www.kirkstone.com

(R) Supplier of slate, granite, and

limestone for floors, walls, and

worktops, as well as Avalon Glass.

(See pictures 27, 71, 72, 77, 154, 266)

LASSCO Flooring
41 Maltby Street
London SE1 3PA
UK
Tel: +44 (0)20 7237 4488
www.lassco.co.uk

(R) New and reclaimed stone
and wood floors.

LBC Hardwood Flooring
Unit 9 Knutsford Way
Sealand Road Industrial Estate
Chester CH1 4NS
UK
Tel: +44 (0)1244 377811

(R) New and old plank, strip
and block flooring – installation
service also available.

Liberon Waxes
Mountfield Industrial Estate
Learoyd Road
New Romney
Kent TN28 8XU
UK
Tel: +44 (0)1797 367555

(M) Maker of specialist finishes
and treatments for wood.

Limestone Gallery
Arch 47
South Lambeth Road
London SW8 1SS
UK
Tel: +44 (0)20 7735 8555

(R) Antique and contemporary stone
flooring, and has UK's largest
selection of limestone flooring.

Lloyd of Bedwyn
91 Church Street
Great Bedwyn
Marlborough
Wiltshire SN8 3PF
UK
Tel: +44 (0)1672 870234
www.lloydofbedwyn.net

(M, R) All stone floors and surfaces –
especially granite, slate, and marble.

Mediterraneo Ltd
Studio C3
The Old Imperial Laundry
71 Warriner Gardens
London SW11 4XW
UK
www.mediterraneodesign.com

(R) Stocks a great range of
top-quality floor and wall tiles
including Bisazzi.
(See pictures 89, 91)

Mountain Lumber Co Inc
PO Box 289
Ruckersville
VA 22968
USA
Tel: +1 804 985 3646
www.mountainlumber.com

(R) Recycled and refurbished
floorboards in pine, oak, chestnut,
and many more.

Outdoor Deck Company
UK
www.outdoordeck.co.uk

(M, R) High-quality bespoke timber
decking.

Paris Ceramics
583 Kings Road
Chelsea
London SW6 2EH
UK
Tel: +44 (0)20 7371 7778
For US showrooms call
+1 888 845 3487
www.parisceramics.com

(R) Vast selection of flooring
materials, including tiles, stone, and
mosaics.

Pianeta Legno Floors USA
1100 Second Avenue
57th and 58th Street
New York
NY 10022
USA
Tel: +1 212 7555 1414
www.plfloors.com

(R) Offers a huge flooring collection in
hardwoods from Europe, the Far East,
Africa, and South America.

Quartzitec
15 Turner Court
Sussex
New Brunswick E4E 2S1
Canada
Tel: +1 877 255 9600
www.quartzitec.com

(M) Manufacturers of composite,
speckled quartz stone floor tiles and
paving stones.

Roger Oates Design
The Long Barn
Eastnor
Ledbury
Herefordshire HR8 1EL
UK
Tel: +44 (0)1531 631611
for mail order

(R) Suppliers of felt flooring material,
rugs, and runners.

Slate World Ltd
(in assoc with the American
Slate Company)
UK
Tel: +44 (0)20 7384 9595
www.slateworld.com

(R) Flooring and paving in a large
range of natural colours.

Steve Charles & Co
The Engineering Offices
2 Michael Road
London SW6 2AD
UK
Tel: +44 (0)20 7384 4424
www.stevecharles.com

(R) Supplier of unusual ceramic and
stone flooring from all over the world.

Stone Age
19 Filmer Road
London SW6 7BU
UK
Tel: +44 (0)20 7385 7954
www.estone.co.uk

(I, R) Importers of stone
from around the world.

Stonell
521–525 Battersea Park Road
London SW11 3BN
UK
Tel: +44 (0)20 7738 0606
www.stonell.co.uk

(I, R) Importers of a huge variety
of real stone flooring.

Stovax Original Style
Falcon Road
Sowton Industrial Estate
Exeter EX2 7LF
UK
Tel: +44 (0)1392 474011
for brochure
www.stovax.com

(M, Distributor) Floor
and wall tiles.

**The Alternative
Flooring Company**
Unit 3b Stephenson Close
East Portway
Andover
Hampshire SP10 3RU
UK
Tel: +44 (0)1264 335111
for stockists
www.alternative-flooring.co.uk

(I, M) Coir, sea grass, sisal, jute, and
bespoke rugs available.

The Amtico Company Ltd
Kingfield Road
Coventry CV6 5AA
UK
Tel: +44 (0)24 7686 1400
and in US:

Amtico International Inc
Amtico Studio
200 Lexington Avenue
32nd Street
New York
NY 10016
USA
Tel: +1 212 545 1127
and in Australia:

**Amtico International
Pty Ltd**
Amtico Studio
86–88 Dickson Avenue
Artarmon
Sydney
NSW 2064
Australia
Tel: +61 2 990 9494

(M) Maker of a huge range
of vinyl flooring.
(See pictures 95, 97)

**The Hardwood
Flooring Company**
146–152 West End Lane
London NW6 1SD
UK
Tel: +44 (0)20 7328 8481
and
151 Essex Road
Islington
London N1 2SN
UK
Tel: +44 (0)20 7354 3500
www.hardwood-flooring.uk.com

(R) Stockist of Junckers and Kahrs,
as well as reclaimed and new strip,
blocks, and planks.

Upofloor UK Ltd
Brook Farm
Horsham Road
Cowfold
Horsham
West Sussex RH13 8AH
UK
Tel: +44 (0)1403 860000

(M) Real wood floor systems.
(See picture 64)

Victorian Wood Works
54 River Road
Creekmouth
Barking IG11 0DW
UK
Tel: +44 (0)20 8534 1000
www.victorianwoodworks.co.uk

(R) Reclaimed wood flooring.

Walcot Reclamation
108 Walcot Street
Bath BA1 5BG
UK
Tel: +44 (0)1225 444404
www.walcot.com

(R) Salvaged and resawn oak flooring,
boards, tongue-and-groove, and
parquet block.

Wicanders
Amorim UK Ltd
Amorim House
Star Road
Partridge Green
Horsham
West Sussex RH13 8RA
UK
Tel: +44 (0)1403 710001
for stockists
www.amorim.com

(M) Makers of cork and interlocking
wood flooring.
(See pictures 61, 66)

windows

American Shutters
72 Station Road
London SW13 0LS
UK
Tel: +44 (0)20 8876 5905
www.americanshutters.co.uk

(I, M, R) Importers and makers
of American shutters for windows
and doors.

Andersen Windows
Andersen Corp
100 Fourth Avenue North
Bayport MN 55003
USA
Tel: +1 651 264 5150
www.andersenwindows.com

(M) Makers of windows, available in
more than 200,000 shapes and sizes.

**Clement Windows
Group Ltd**
Clement House
Haslemere
Surrey GU27 1HR
UK
Tel: +44 (0)1428 643393
www.clementwg.co.uk

(M, R) Manufacturer of windows in
all shapes and sizes – in aluminium,
upvc, and steel.

Crittall Windows Ltd
Springwood Drive
Springwood Industrial Estate
Braintree
Essex CM7 2YN
UK
Tel: +44 (0)1376 324106
www.crittal-windows.co.uk

(M, R) Specialists in steel-framed
windows.

Draks
Draks Industries Limited
Unit 316
Heyford Park
Upper Heyford
Oxfordshire OX25 5HA
UK
Tel: +44 (0)1869 232989

(M) Makers of bespoke shutters
and blinds.

Fusion Glass Designs Ltd
365 Clapham Road
London SW9 9BT
UK
Tel: +44 (0)20 7738 5888
www.fusionglass.co.uk

(D, M) Architectural decorative glass.

Luxaflex
Mersey Industrial Estate
Heaton Mersey
Stockport
Cheshire SK4 3EQ
UK
Tel: +44 08000 399 399
for stockists (free phone UK only)
www.luxaflex.com

(M) Unusual blinds, including soft
suede effects.

**Marvin Windows
and Doors**
USA
Tel: +1 800 236 9690
www.marvin.com

(M) Maker of doors
and windows.

Norco
811 Factory Street
Hawkins
WI 54530
USA
Tel: +1 888 476 6726
www.norcowindows.com

(M) Huge range of wood windows.

North 4 Design
52 Victoria Road
London N4 3SL
UK
Tel: +44 (0)870 74 24 596
www.north4.co.uk

(D, M, R) Produces a range of smart-
looking stainless-steel porthole vision
panels for doors and walls.

Pilkington
PO Box 799
Toledo
OH 43697-0799
USA
Tel: +1 419 247 3731
www.pilkington.com

(M) Innovative glass manufacturer,
including solar-control glass.

Pilkington PLC
Prescot Road
St Helens WA10 3TT
UK
Tel: +44 (0)1744 28882
www.pilkington.co.uk

(M) Innovative glass manufacturer,
including solar-control glass.

**The London Stained
Glass Company**
UK
Tel: +44 (0)20 7252 5706

(D, M, R) Contemporary and
traditional stained glass.

The Metal Window Company
Unit 8
Wychwood Business Centre
Milton Road
Shipton-under-Wychwood OX7 6XU
UK
Tel: +44 (0)1993 830613
www.metalwindow.co.uk

(M) Specialist in glass walls
and barn conversions.

Velux
Woodside Way
Glenrothes East Fife
Scotland KY7 4ND
UK
Tel: +44 (0)1592 772211
www.velux.com

(M, R) Specialists in roof windows.

doors

Cotswold Doors
5 Hampden Way
London N14 5DJ
UK
Tel: +44 (0)20 8368 1664

(R) Huge range of timber doors.

Handmade Door Company
12–14 Brook Road
Redhill
Surrey RH1
UK
Tel: +44 (0)1737 773133

(D, M, R) Thousands of doors from
which to choose.

Just Doors
UK
Tel: +44 (0)870 200 1010
www.justdoors.co.uk

(D, M, R) Doors of all designs, shapes,
and sizes.

Loewen USA
USA
Tel: +1 800 245 2295
www.loewen.com

(M) Traditional and modern
terrace doors.

Original Door Specialists
93 Endwell Road
London SE4 2NF
UK
Tel: +44 (0)20 7252 8109

(R) Supplier of doors, windows,
floors, and handles.

**The Designer
Door Company**
Bow Wharf
Grove Road
London E3 5SN
UK
Tel: +44 (0)20 8880 6739
www.designerdoorcompany.co.uk

(M) Doors produced in all shapes,
sizes, and styles.

**The London
Door Company**
155 St Johns Hill
London SW11
UK
Tel: +44 (0)20 7801 0877

(D, M, R) Hand-made doors built
to order.

Timely
10241 Norris Avenue
Pacoima
California 91331
USA
Tel: +1 818 896 3094
www.timelyframes.com

(M) Steel door specialist.

Weather Shield Mfg Inc
USA
Tel: +1 800 477 6808
www.weathershield.com

(M) Huge collection of windows
and doors.

stairs

**Albion Design
of Cambridge Ltd**
Unit H3
Dales Manor Business Park
Babraham Road
Sawston
Cambridge CB2 4TJ
UK
Tel: +44 (0)1223 836128
www.albionspirals.co.uk

(D, M) Cast-iron, steel,
and timber spirals.

Bayfield Joinery
Praed Road
Trafford Park
Manchester M17 1PQ
UK
Tel: +44 (0)161 848 0700
www.bayfieldstairs.co.uk

(D, M) Maker of bespoke staircases.

Blanc de Bierges
Eastrea Road
Whittlesey
Peterborough
Cambridgeshire PE7 2AG
UK
Tel: +44 (0)1733 202566
www.blancdebierges.com

(M, R) Straight and spiral stairs in
stone.

Crescent of Cambridge Ltd
Edison Road
St Ives
Cambridgeshire PE27 3LG
UK
Tel: +44 (0)1480 301522
www.crescentstairs.co.uk

(D, M) Specialists in spiral
and straight stairs.

KDA
Unit 8
38–40 Upper Clapton Road
London E5 8BQ
UK
Tel: +44 (0)20 8806 8399

(D, M, R) Builder and designer of
bespoke contemporary staircases and
installation service.

Spiral Staircase Systems
Lewes Design Contracts
The Mill
Glynde
East Sussex BN8 6SS
UK
Tel: +44 (0)1273 858 341
www.spiralstairs.co.uk

(D, M, R) Maker of unusual staircases.

Stairway Products
UK
Tel: +44 (0)20 8559 9226

(D, M, R) Staircase maker.

storage

Aero Ltd
96 Westbourne Grove
London W2 5RT
UK
Tel: +44 (0)20 7221 1950

(R) Modern furniture.

Alias
Grumello del Monte
Bergamo
Italy
Tel: +39 035 44 22 511
www.aliasdesign.it

(M) Maker of fine contemporary
furniture.

Aram Designs
3 Kean Street
London WC2B 4AT
UK
Tel: +44 (0)20 7240 3933

(R) Modern furniture.

Atrium
Centrepoint
22–24 St Giles High Street
London WC2H 8LN
UK
Tel: +44 (0)20 7379 7288
for stockists
www.atrium.ltd.uk

(R) Showrooms of contemporary
furniture.

B&B Italia
150 East 58th Street
New York
NY 10155
USA
Tel: +1 800 872 1697
for nearest stockist
www.bebitalia.it

(M) Maker of fine-quality
contemporary Italian furniture.

**Blue Dot Design
& Manufacturing Inc**
Minneapolis
USA
Tel: +1 612 782 1844

(D, M) Designer and maker
of unusual contemporary-style
modular storage systems.

Bo Concept
158 Tottenham Court Road
London W1 7NH
UK
Tel: +44 (0)20 7388 2447
www.boconcept.copm

(D, M, R) Elegant minimal furniture
and modular shelving systems.

California Closets
227 Kings Road
London SW3 5EJ
UK
Tel: +44 (0)20 7349 1450
www.calclosets.co.uk

(D, M, R) Modular storage solutions
for anywhere in the home.

Cassina
Via Busnelli 1
20036 Meda Milano
Italy
Tel: +39 0362 3721
Fax: +39 0362 32246
www.cassina.it

(M, R) Contemporary furniture
including storage systems

Claudia Leu

Cologne

Germany

Tel: +49 221 31 38 33

email: Claudialeu@netcologne.de

(D) Designer, with Antje Mehnert, of
an intriguing modular shelving system
– Kleine3 – that glows in the dark.

**Design Centre
of the Americas**

1885 Griffin Road

Dania Beach

Florida 33004

USA

Tel: +1 954 920 7997

www.dcota.com

(R) Vast array of designer goodies,
including lighting, furniture, and
furnishings.

Domus Design Collection

181 Madison Avenue

New York

NY 10016

USA

Tel: +1 212 685 0800

www.ddcnyc.com

(R) The latest in contemporary
furnishings.

Driade

Via Padana Inferiore 12

29012 Fossadello di Caorso PC

Italy

in the UK at Viaduct Furniture

Tel: +44 (0)20 7278 8456

(M) Maker of chic Italian furniture.
(See pictures 252, 264, 265)

EmmeBi

Via C Monteverdi 28

20031 Cesano Maderno

Milan

Italy

Tel: +39 0362 502 296

www.emmebidesign.com

(M) Cool storage solutions,
wardrobes, and furniture.
(See pictures 17, 183)

Former

Via per Cant 43

22060 Montesolaro di Carimate

Como

Italy

Tel: +39 031 780 252

www.former.it

(D, M) Modular storage units of all
types and sizes and bedroom
furniture, available worldwide.

Furniture Craft International

Rays House

North Circular Road

London NW10 7XP

UK

Tel: +44 (0)20 8961 7780

www.fci.uk.com

(R) Vast warehouse full
of modern, classic, and contemporary
furniture and accessories.

Geoffrey Drayton

85 Hampstead Road

London NW1 2PL

UK

Tel: +44 (0)20 7387 5840

www.geoffrey-drayton.co.uk

(R) Modern, classic storage
and furniture, featuring names
including Cassina.

Habitat UK Ltd

196 Tottenham Court Road

London W1P 9LD

UK

Tel: +44 (0)845 601 0740

www.habitat.net

(M, R) Good value, contemporary
furniture, lighting, and home accessories.

Heal's

196 Tottenham Court Road

London W1P 9LQ

UK

Tel: +44 (0)20 7636 1666

(R) Storage, furniture, lighting,
and accessories for the home.

Huelsta Furniture UK Ltd

22 Bruton Street

London W1X 7DA

UK

Tel: +44 (0)20 7629 4881

www.huelsta.co.uk

(M, R) Blond wood fitted furniture,
particularly suitable for bedrooms.

John Barnard

The Granary

Trowse Bridge

Norwich

Norfolk NR1 2EG

UK

Tel: +44 (0)1603 623959

www.norfolk-furnituremakers.co.uk

(D, M, R) Contemporary fitted
and free-standing furniture.

Kate Wiggin

39 St Stephens Street

Edinburgh EH3 5AH

UK

Tel: +44 (0)131 225 2606

(R) Inspirational modern furniture.

Ligne Roset (Roset UK)

95 High Street

Great Missenden

Bucks HP16 OAL

UK

Tel: +44 (0)1494 865 001

for stockists

www.ligne-roset.co.uk

(M, R) Contemporary furniture
and storage designs.

Maxalto

Strada Provinciale 32

22060 Novedrate (Co)

Italy

Tel: +39 031 795 213

UK contact:

Keith de la Plain

Tel: +44 (0)1233 770 555

and

Australia Space Furniture

Sydney

Tel: +61 29380 6000

and

USA

New York

150 East 58th Street

Tel: +1 800 872 1697

(M) Great modern furniture ideas.

MDF Italia

Via Morimondo 5/7

20143 Milan

Italy

Tel: +39 0281 804 100

for suppliers in all countries

www.mdfitalia.it

(M) Chic, sleek Italian furniture.

Molteni & C

Via Rossini 50

20034 Giussano

Milan

Italy

UK agent:

Interiors Plus

Tel: +44 (0)1484 530334

USA agent:

Ernest Stoecklin International
Furniture

Tel: +1 877 665 8364

www.molteni.it

(D, M) Contemporary furniture designs.

Moroso spa

Via Nazionale 60

Cavalicco 33010

Udine

Italy

Tel: +39 0432 577111

UK at Atrium Ltd

Tel: +44 (0)20 7379 7288

Scandinavia at Interstudio

Tel: +45 3526 3100

USA at Stoecklin

Tel: +1 201 585 9420

www.moroso.it

(D, M) Seat wear.

Oxo Tower Wharf

Barge House Street

London SE1 9PH

UK

Tel: +44 (0)20 7401 2255

www.oxotower.co.uk

(D, M, R) Shops, studios, and café/
bars dedicated to home furnishings.

Plastic Buddha

63 Albert Street

Winnipeg

Manitoba

Canada

Tel: +1 204 452 3131

(D, M) Complex geometric furniture
by designer Craig Alun Smith.

Porro
Via per Cantu 35
22060 Montesolaro (Co)
Italy
Tel: +39 031 780237
www.porro.com
and UK agent:
Clemente Cavigioli
5 Walmer Studios
235–239 Walmer Road
London W11 4EY
UK
Tel: +44 (0)20 7792 2522
and in US:
(Los Angeles) at Modern Living
Tel: +1 310 657 877
(Chicago) at Luminaire
Tel: +1 312 664 9582

M) Modern furniture and storage.

Room by Wellis
Ettiswilerstrasse 24
CH-6130 Willisau
Switzerland
In UK:
Key London
Tel: +44 (0)20 7499 9461
In US:
Menzie International
Pacific Design Center
Los Angeles CA
Tel: +1 310 475 2331
www.roombywellis.com

(D, M) Individual furniture and storage.

SCP
135–139 Curtain Road
London EC2A 3BX
UK
and
SCP at Selfridges
4th Floor
400 Oxford Street
London W1A 1AB
UK
Tel: +44 (0)20 7739 1869
www.scp.co.uk

(D, M, R) Contemporary storage,
furniture and lighting.

Spacecraft
1205 Manhattan Avenue
Brooklyn
New York
NY 11222
USA
Tel: +1 718 383 9600 or
349 8833
www.spacecraftnyc.com

(R) Huge range of sleek, modern
storage shelving and cabinets.

Stone Circle
Tor House
45 Chapel Lane
Crich
Matlock
Derbyshire DE4 5BU
UK
Tel: +44 (0)1773 850081
www.stonecircle.co.uk

(D, M, R) Maker of an amazing
circular shelving system.

Stua
Poligono 26
E 20115 Astigarraga
San Sebastian
Spain
Fax: +34 943 556 002
www.stua.com

(D, M) Maker of contemporary
furniture sold around the world.

System 180
387 Kings Street
London W6 9NJ
UK
Tel: +44 (0)20 8748 6200
www.system180.co.uk

(D, M, R) Award-winning modular
metal construction systems for
shelving and furniture.

The Bachelor Pad
36 St Stephens Street
Edinburgh EH3 5AL
UK
Tel: +44 (0)131 226 6355
www.thebachelorpad.org

(R) A modernist haven.

The Conran Shop
81 Fulham Road
London SW3 6RD
UK
Tel: +44 (0)20 7589 7401
www.conran.com

(R) Contemporary design classics.

The Holding Company
241–245 Kings Road
London SW3 5EL
UK
Tel: +44 (0)20 7352 1600
www.theholdingcompany.co.uk

(R) Huge range of storage systems.

The Loft
Via Pegoraro 24
21013 Gallarate
VA
Italy
Tel: +39 0331 776 578
www.illoft.com

(M) Loft-style modern furniture that is
available worldwide.

The Morson Collection
31 St James Avenue
Boston MA 02116
USA
Tel: +1 617 482 2335 or +1 800
204 2514
www.themorsoncollection.com

(M, R) European contemporary
furniture, rugs, lighting, and
accessories.

Theodore's
2233 Wisconsin Avenue
NW
Washington DC
USA
Tel: +1 202 333 2300
www.theodores.com

(R) Modern masterpieces
of furniture design.

USM U. Schaerer Sons Inc
150 East 58th Street
New York
NY 10155
USA
Tel: +1 212 371 1230
www.usm.com

(M, R) Crisply detailed modern
modular furniture.

Valentini Mobili
Via Garibaldi 17
25081 Bedizzole
Italy
Tel: +39 030 687 0773

(R) Modern furniture, including
elegant shelving and storage systems.

Viaduct Furniture Ltd
1–10 Summers Street
London EC1R 5BD
UK
Tel: +44 (0)20 7278 8456
www.viaduct.co.uk

(I, R) Suppliers of contemporary
European furniture.

Vitra Ltd
Clerkenwell Road
London EC1M 5PQ
UK
Tel: +44 (0)20 7608 6200
or +41 61 377 1507
for details of retailers
www.vitra.com

(D, M, R) Fantastic office furniture,
including interesting storage systems,
that also works well in a
contemporary-style home.

Wallbed Workshop
290 Battersea Park Road
London SW11 3BT
UK
Tel: +44 (0)20 7924 1323
for brochure

(M, R) Great storage solutions,
including wallbeds.

lighting

Aero
96 Westbourne Grove
London W2 5RT
UK
Tel: +44 (0)20 7221 1950

(R) Range of contemporary-style
furniture and lamps.

After Noah
121 Upper Street
London N1 1QP
UK
Tel: +44 (0)20 7359 4281
www.afternoah.com

(R) Home decor store that also stocks
unusual secondhand lighting.

Aktiva Ltd
Spring House
10b Spring Place
London NW5 3BH
UK
Tel: +44 (0)20 7428 9325
www.aktiva.co.uk

(M) Producer of low-voltage modern
light fittings.

Aram Designs

3 Kean Street

London WC2 4AT

UK

Tel: +44 (0)20 7240 3933

(R) Offers a range of high-quality contemporary designs, including furniture and lighting.

Aria

133 Upper Street

London N1 1QP

UK

Tel: +44 (0)20 7226 1021

www.aria-shop.co.uk

(R) Contemporary interior design shop with lighting.

Artemide

323 City Road

London EC1

UK

Tel: +44 (0)20 7833 1755

(D, M) Renowned Italian lighting designer and manufacturer.

Atrium

Centrepoint

22–24 St Giles High Street

London WC2H 8LN

UK

Tel: +44 (0)20 7379 7288

for stockists

www.atrium.ltd.uk

(R) Specialist in contemporary classical lighting.

Babylon Design

301 Fulham Road

London SW10 9QH

UK

Tel: +44 (0)20 7376 7233 or 7376 7255

(D) Lights by adventurous contemporary designers.

Black + Blum

2.07 Oxo Tower Wharf

Barge House

London SE1 9PH

UK

Tel: +44 (0)20 7385 4216

email: design@black-blum.com

www.black-blum.com

(D) Unusual contemporary lighting designs. (See pictures 232, 233, 239)

Box Products

The Lodge

3 Russell House

Cambridge Street

London SW1V 4EQ

UK

Tel: +44 (0)20 7976 6791

(D, M, R) Box-designed lighting products, plus a bespoke lighting design service.

Bruck Lighting Systems

Costa Mesa

CA 92626

USA

Tel: +1 714 424 0500

www.brucklightingsystems.com

(D, M) Leading innovator in track and cable lighting technology.

Central

33–35 Little Clarendon Street

Oxford OX1

UK

Tel: +44 (0)1865 311141

(R) Interiors shop with lighting section.

Christopher Wray

591–593 Kings Road

London SW6 2YW

UK

Tel: +44 (0)20 7736 8434

www.christopher-wray.com

(R) Massive showrooms, stocking mostly traditional-style fittings.

Coexistence

288 Upper Street

London N1 2TZ

UK

Tel: +44 (0)20 7354 8817

www.coexistence.co.uk

(D, R) Contemporary furniture and fittings.

Cotterell Lighting

28–30 Carnoustie Place

Glasgow

UK

Tel: +44 (0)141 492 5648

and

122 Causewayside

Edinburgh EH9 1PU

UK

Tel: +44 (0)131 662 0000

www.theinternetpages/Scotland/Edin/light1/cl.htm

(R) Supplier of designer lighting.

Cowley Designs

Clifton Road

Blackpool

Lancashire FY4 4QE

UK

Tel: +44 (0)1253 831500

(D, M, R) Warehouse supplying a wide range of interior goods, including lighting.

Creative Element

2 King Lane

Clitheroe

Lancashire BB7 1AA

UK

Tel: +44 (0)1200 427313

www.design-conscious.co.uk

(R) Contemporary interior design, including lighting.

Denis Smitka

Australia

Tel: +61 3 9419 1219

www.smitka.com.au

(D) Designer of some amazing new lights, including the award-winning sinuous shapes of the Poli.

El Ultimo Gritto

4 Peacock Yard

Iliffe

London SE17 3LH

UK

Tel: +44 (0)20 7732 6614

(D) Contemporary designers.

Erco Lighting Ltd

38 Dover Street

London W1S 4NL

UK

Tel: +44 (0)20 7408 0320

for sales and stockists

www.erco.com

(D, M, R) Leading manufacturer of high-quality light fittings, very popular with architects.

Fillamento

2185 Fillmore Street

San Francisco

CA 94115

USA

Tel: +1 415 931 2224

(R) Emporium of home furnishings.

Flos

(Mcinnes Cook)

31 Lisson Grove

London NW1 6UV

UK

Tel: +44 (0)20 7258 0600

www.flos.net

(D, M, R) Great range of contemporary light designs. (See pictures 208, 226, 237)

Fontana Arte

(in UK at Clemente Cavigioli)

Walmer Studios

235–239 Walmer Road

London W11 4EY

UK

Tel: +44 (0)20 7792 2522

(M, R) Classic modern Italian lighting.

Foscarini

Italy

Tel: +39 041 595 1199

www.foscarini.com

(R) Amazing, warm, domestic, charming contemporary lamps.

George Kovacs Lighting

USA

Tel: +1 718 628 5201

(R) Remarkable lighting store featuring pieces by designers, including Harry Allen.

Habitat UK Ltd

196 Tottenham Court Road

London W1P 9LD

UK

Tel: +44 (0)845 601 0740

www.habitat.net

(R) Extensive range of good value contemporary domestic lamps and home furnishings.

Helvar Ltd

Hawley Mill

Hawley Road

Dartford

Kent DA2 7SY

UK

Tel: +44 (0)1322 282258

for stockists

www.helvar.co.uk

(M) High-tech lighting control systems.

Hessamerica
PO Box 430
Shelby
North Carolina 28151
USA
Tel: +1 704 471 2211
www.hessamerica.com

(M) Contemporary lighting.

IKEA
UK
Tel: +44 (0)20 8208 5600
for nearest store
www.ikea.co.uk

(R) Range of good value
contemporary domestic lamps,
and a lot more besides.

Inflate
11 Northburgh Street
London EC1V OAH
UK
Tel: +44 (0)20 7251 5453
www.inflate.co.uk

(D, M, R) Innovative designers
of furniture and lighting.

Ingo Maurer
Kaiserstrasse 47
80801 Munich
Germany
Tel: +49 89 381 6060
www.ingo-maurer.com

(D, M) Impressively inventive designer
of contemporary lighting.

John Cullen Lighting
585 Kings Road
London SW6 2EH
UK
Tel: +44 (0)20 7371 5400
www.johncullenlighting.co.uk

(D, M, R) Designers and makers
of contemporary fittings for all
applications.

John Lewis
Oxford Street
London W1
UK
Tel: +44 (0)20 7629 7711
ext 4800
www.johnlewis.co.uk

(R) A mix of traditional and modern
lighting styles.

Jo Whiting
UK
Tel: +44 (0)7973 829698
Fax: +44 (0)2087 152759

(D, M) Designer of one-off lighting
pieces.

Lighting Design Supplies
118 Duncrue Street
Belfast BT3 9AR
UK
Tel: +44 (0)28 9035 1435

(R) Great choice of lighting designs.

Lindsay Bloxham Design
1.03 Oxo Tower Wharf
Bargehouse Street
London SE1 9PH
UK
Tel: +44 (0)20 7633 9494

(D, M, R) Lighting designer.
(See picture 235)

Lloyd Davies
14 John Dalton Street
Manchester M2 6JR
UK
Tel: +44 (0)161 832 3700
www.lloyddavies.co.uk

(R) Shop selling contemporary
designs.

Louis Poulsen Lighting Inc
3260 Meridan Parkway
Fort Lauderdale
FL 33331
USA
Tel: +1 954 349 2525
www.louispoulsen.com

(M, R) Retailer of chic contemporary
lighting.

Mathmos
20–24 Old Street
London EC1V 9AP
UK
Tel: +44 (0)20 7549 2743
www.mathmos.com.uk

(M, R) Famous for the ever-popular
lava lamp, but there is more besdes.

Mint
70 Wigmore Street
London W1U 2SQ
UK
Tel: +44 (0)20 7224 4406

(R) Contemporary furniture and
lighting.

New Rooms
51 High Street
Cheltenham
Gloucestershire GL50 1DX
UK
Tel: +44 (0)1242 237977
www.newrooms.net

(R) Contemporary interior designs,
including lighting.

Purves & Purves
220–224 Tottenham Court Road
London W1T 7QE
UK
Tel: +44 (0)20 7580 8223
www.purves.co.uk

(R) Suppliers of a large range
of modern furniture with wide
selection of lamps.

Ralph Capper Interiors
10a Little Peter Street
Manchester M15 4PS
UK
Tel: +44 (0)161 236 6929
www.ralphcapper.com

(M) Contemporary furniture
and lighting made to order.

SCP
135–139 Curtain Road
London EC2A 3BX
UK
and

SCP at Selfridges
4th Floor
Oxford Street
London W1A 1AB
UK
Tel: +44 (0)20 7739 1869
www.scp.co.uk

(D, M, R) Contemporary lighting.

Selfridges
400 Oxford Street
London W1A 1AB
UK
Tel: +44 (0)20 7629 1234
www.selfridges.com

(R) Department store with
a strong lighting department stocking
lots of contemporary designs.

Set Design
100 High Street
Leicester LE1 5YP
UK
Tel: +44 (0)116 251 0161

(R) Contemporary furnishings,
including examples of great Italian
lighting.

SKK
34 Lexington Street
London W1F OLH
UK
Tel: +44 (0)20 7434 4095
www.skk.net

(D, M, R) Wild stuff from the
innovative lighting designer Shiu
Kay Khan.

Targetti Sankey
Via Pratese 164
50145 Florence
Italy
Tel: +39 055 37911
www.targetti.it

(M) Maker of beautiful contemporary
lighting.

The Colour Light Company
Unit 28
Riverside Business Centre
Victoria Street
High Wycombe
Bucks HP11 2LT
UK
Tel: +44 (0)1494 462112
Fax: +44 (0)1494 462612
www.colourlight.com

(D, M, R) Extraordinary colourful
lights as art.
(See picture 230)

The Conran Shop
81 Fulham Road
London SW3 6RD
UK
Tel: +44 (0)20 7589 7401
www.conran.com

(R) A range of contemporary lighting
and home furnishings.

The London Lighting Company
135 Fulham Road
London SW3 6RT
UK
Tel: +44 (0)20 7589 3612

(R) Extensive range of lighting.

Viaduct Furniture Ltd
1–10 Summers Street
London EC1R 5BD
UK
Tel: +44 (0)20 7278 8456
www.viaduct.co.uk

(R) Chic contemporary lamps
and furniture.

fittings

KITCHENS

AEG Domestic Appliances
55–77 High Street
Slough
Berkshire SL1 1DZ
UK
Tel: +44 (0)8705 158158

(M) Maker of high-performance
kitchen appliances.

Allmilmo
Unit 5
Rivermead
Pipers Way
Thatcham
Berkshire RG19 4EP
UK
Tel: +44 (0)1635 868181
for stockists

(D) Contemporary kitchen designs.

Alno (UK)
Unit 10
Hampton Farm Estate
Hampton Road
West Hanworth
Middlesex TW13 6DB
UK
Tel: +44 (0)20 8898 4781
for stockists
www.alno.co.uk

(M) Modern unit designs.

Appliances On Line
Morris Green Business Park
Bolton
BL3 3PE
UK
Tel: +44 (0)870 9001 636
www.appliancesonline.co.uk

(R) Just as the name suggests,
leading brand kitchen appliances
sold direct.

Baumatic UK
UK
Tel: +44 (0)118 933 6900
www.baumatic.com

(M) Industrial-style ovens and cookers
intended for serious cooks.

Belling Appliances
Talbot Road
Mexborough
Swinton
South Yorkshire S64 8AQ
UK
Tel: +44 (0)1709 579902

(M, R) Maker and supplier
of cooking appliances.

Binova Spa
06086
Assisi Loc Petrignano
Perugia
Italy
Tel: +39 075809701
www.binova.com

(D, M) Technological kitchens.

Blanco UK Ltd
Oxgate Lane
Cricklewood
London NW2 7JN
UK
Tel: +44 (0)20 8450 9100
and
Blanco
Cinnaminson
NJ
USA
Tel: +1 800 451 5782

(M) State-of-the-art kitchen sinks.

Boffi spa
Via Oberdan 70
20030 Lentate s/S
Italy
Tel: +39 0362 5341
www.boffi.it
Sold in the UK at

Alternative Plans
Tel: +44 (0)20 7228 6460)
and in the US at
Boffi Soho
New York
USA
Tel: +1 212 431 8282

(D, M) Maker of some of the coolest
looking kitchens around.

Bordercraft
The Old Forge
Peterchurch
Herefordshire HR2 0SD
UK
Tel: +44 (0)1981 550251
www.bordercraft.co.uk

(R) Supplier of hardwood worktops.

Bosch
UK
Tel: +44 (0)870 727 0446 brochure
line
www.boschappliances.com

(M) Fast, smart ovens.

Brabantia UK
Blackfriars Road
Nailsea
Bristol BS48 4SB
UK
Tel: +44 (0)800 316 1110
www.brabantia.com

(M, R) State-of-the-art kitchen
accessories.

Bradshaw UK
UK
Tel: +44 (0)1275 343000
www.bradshaw.co.uk

(R) UK distributor for genuine
American Amana refrigerators, Asko
Swedish washing machines and
dishwashers, Viking professional
cookers, and Atag cooking appliances.

Bulthaup
The Kitchen People Ltd
37 Wigmore Street
London W1H 9LD
UK
Tel: +44 (0)20 7495 3663
www.bulthaup.com

(D, M, R) Cutting-edge contemporary
designs.
(See pictures 260, 263)
and
Bulthaup USA
Tel: +1 800 808 2923
www.bulthaup.com

(D, M, R) Leading contemporary
kitchen design.

Buddy Rhodes Studio
San Francisco
USA
Tel: +1 877 706 5303
www.buddyrhodes.com

(M, R) Bespoke concrete casting for
worktops, fireplaces, garden furniture.

Buyers and Sellers
120–122 Ladbroke Grove
London W10 5NE
UK
Tel: +44 (0)845 080 2207

(R) Seller of all major brands
of cooker appliances.

Cider House Furniture
UK
Tel: +44 (0)1395 443111
www.ciderhouse.co.uk

(D, M, R) Traditionally crafted wood
kitchens with a twist.

Classic Granites
UK
Tel: +44 (0)1777 710366

(M, R) Custom-designed worktops
in granite, marble, and slate.

CP Hart
Newnham Terrace
Hercules Road
London SE1 7DR
UK
Tel: +44 (0)20 7902 1000
for branches

(R) Vast showroom of traditional
and contemporary designs.

Czech & Speake
39c Jermyn Street
London SW1Y 6DN
UK
Tel: +44 (0)20 7439 0216
www.czechspeake.com

(M, R) Great taps, kitchen sink mixers
and accessories, available worldwide.

De Dietrich
Brandt Group UK
Intec 4
Wade Road
Basingstoke
Hampshire RG24 8NE
UK
Tel: +44 (0)8707 503503

(R) Classy cookers.

DuPont Corian
Maylands Avenue
Hemel Hempstead
Hertfordshire HP2 7DP
UK
Tel: +44 (0)800 96 21 16
www.corian.com

(M) Super-tough, stain- and heat-
resistant, man-made work counter
and surfacing material.
(See pictures 254, 256, 257, 269, 270)

Dornbracht
Kbbingser Muhle 6
D-58640 Iserlohn
Germany
Tel: +49 2371 4330
Fax: +49 2371 433135
www.dornbracht.com

(M) High-quality contemporary taps.
(See pictures 255, 303, 307, 308)

Elon
12 Silver Road
London W12 7SG
UK
Tel: +44 (0)20 8932 3000
www.kitchensinks.co.uk

(M) Contemporary-style ceramic sinks.

Formica
Coast Road
North Shields
Tyne and Wear NE29 8RE
UK
Tel: +44 (0)191 259 3000
for stockists

(D, M) Tough laminated surface
material for worktops and doors,
available in an extensive range of
different colours and patterns.

Forneaux de France
30 Albion Close
Newtown Business Park
Poole
Dorset BH12 3LL
UK
Tel: +44 (0)1202 733011
www.lacanche.co.uk

(M, R) Made in France, serious
cookers for serious cooks.

Franke UK Ltd
East Park
Manchester International Office
Centre
Styal Road
Manchester M22 5WB
UK
Tel: +44 (0)161 436 6280
for stockists
www.franke.co.uk

(M, R) Stainless-steel and ceramic
sinks and taps.
(See pictures 246, 250)

Fulham Kitchens
19 Carnwath Road
London SW6 3HR
UK
Tel: +44 (0)20 7736 6458

(D, M, R) Design and build bespoke
kitchens.
(See pictures 201, 204, 251, 268)

Gaggenau USA
USA
Tel: +1 800 828 9165
www.gaggenau.com/us

(M) Beautifully engineered
contemporary-style kitchen
appliances.

GEC Anderson Ltd
Oakengrove
Shire Lane
Hastoe
Tring HP223 6LY
UK
Tel: +44 (0)1442 826999
www.gecanderson.co.uk

(M, R) Bespoke stainless-steel
products.

Italian Appliances
UK
Tel: +44 0800 9520711
(free phone UK only)
www.italianappliances.com

(R) Seller of the latest Italian cookers
and refrigerators.

Kayode Lipede
6 Iroko House
Lithos Road NW3 6ER
UK
Tel: +44 (0)20 7794 7535

(M) Polished concrete work surfaces.

Kohler Kitchen Sinks
At Elon Ltd
66 Fulham Road
London SW3 6HH
UK
Tel: +44 (0)20 7460 4600
www.kitchensinks.co.uk

(D, M) Novel, contemporary kitchen
sink designs.

Laminex
Australia
Tel: +61 3 9581 3930
www.fusionsurfaces.com

(D, M) Amazing collection of laminate
designs – look out for the Fusion
range in particular.

Merchants
Unit C
Olmar Wharf
Malt Street
London SE1 5AY
UK
Tel: +44 (0)20 7237 0060

(M, R) Stainless-steel finishes.

Miele UK
UK
Tel: +44 (0)1235 233533
for stockists
www.miele.co.uk

(D, M) Smart kitchens
and appliances.
and

Miele
USA
Tel: +1 888 643 5372
www.miele.com

(M) Stylish kitchen equipment.

Neff Domestic Appliances
Milton Keynes
UK
Tel: +44 (0)8705 133090
for brochures
www.neff.co.uk

(M, R) Sturdy and smart kitchen
appliances.
(See picture 213)

Norbert Wangen
Germany
Tel: +49 89 4900 1572
www.norbert-wangen.com

(M) Maker of an extraordinary
stainless-steel-clad all-in one kitchen
unit, which has a sliding top-cum-table.

Poggenpohl
Lloyds Court
681–685 Silbury Boulevard
Milton Keynes MK9 3AZ
UK
Tel: +44 0800 243781 for stockists
(free phone UK only)
email: kitchens@poggenpohl-group.co.uk
www.poggenpohl.de
and

Poggenpohl USA
www.poggenpohl-usa.com

(M) Modern German kitchen designs.
(See picture 271)

Rhode Design
137–139 Essex Road
London N1 2NR
UK
Tel: +44 (0)20 7354 9933
email: Sales@rhodedesign.com

(D, M, R) Makers of bespoke kitchens
and showroom of units and
accessories.

Roundhouse Design
25 Chalk Farm Road
London NW1 8AG
UK
Tel: +44 (0)20 7428 9955
www.roundhousedesign.com

(D, M, R) Team of architects and
designer creating kitchens and free-
standing furniture.
(See pictures 253, 258)

Samsung
UK
Tel: +44 0800 52 16 52 for
brochures (free phone UK only)
www.samsungelectronics.co.uk

(M) Mostly associated with sound
equipment, this company is now
making smart, low-energy, side-by-
side, two-door-wide refrigerators with
built-in water and ice dispensers.

SieMatic
Osprey House
Rookery Court
Primett Road
Stevenage
Hertfordshire SG1 3EE
UK
Tel +44 (0)1438 369327

(M) Smart modern kitchens.
and

SieMatic
D-32584 Lohne
Germany
Tel: +49 5732 670
www.siematic.com

(M) Maker of the chic, award-winning, modular and linear 6006 kitchen.

Smeg UK Ltd
Tel: +44 (0)8708 437373
www.smeguk.com

(M) Kitchen technology with style – available worldwide.
(See picture 258)

Space Savers Ltd
222 Kentish Town Road
London NW5 2AD
UK
Tel: +44 (0)20 7485 3266

(D, M, R) Specialist makers of space-saving kitchens.
(See pictures 244, 249, 274)

StileStone
at Domus Tiles
London
UK
Tel: +44 (0)20 7223 5555

(M) Amazing quartz-composite worktops.

Stoves
UK
Tel: +44 (0)151 430 8497
www.stoves.co.uk

(M) Big, range-style, free-standing cookers.

Strato
Italy
www.stratocucine.com

(M) The smoothest fitted kitchens around – sold worldwide.

The Range Cooker Company
Range House
281 Bristol Avenue
Blackpool FY2 0JF
UK
Tel: +44 (0)1253 471117
www.rangecooker.co.uk

(M, R) Maker of handsome professional-style cookers, including the Britannia.

UK Marble
21 Burcott Road
Hereford HR4 9LW
UK
Tel: +44 (0)1432 352178
www.ukmarble.co.uk

(M) Granite and marble surfaces. Installation service available.

Viaduct Furniture Ltd
1–10 Summers Street
London EC1R 5BD
UK
Tel: +44 (0)20 7278 8456
www.viaduct.co.uk

(R) Supplier of cutting-edge Driade kitchens, contemporary furniture, and storage systems.

Viking Designer Kitchens
USA
Tel: +1 888 845 4641
www.vikingrange.com

(M) High-design, professional-style kitchens.

Whirlpool UK
UK
Tel: +44 (0)870 600 8989
www.whirlpool.co.uk

(M) Modern cooking technology.

Whitehall Fabrications Ltd
Exhibition House
Grape Street
Leeds LS10 1BX
UK
Tel: +44 (0)113 222 3000
www.whitehall-uk.com

(M, R) Man-made surfaces in granite or Corian.

BATHROOMS

Acorn Powell
4 Barratt Industrial Park
St Oswalds Road
Gloucester GL1 2SH
UK
Tel: +44 (0)1452 332224

(M, R) Maker and supplier of smart stainless-steel bathroom fittings, including shower cubicles, lavatories, column showers, and basins.

Aero
96 Westbourne Grove
London W2 5RT
UK
Tel: +44 (0)20 7221 1950

(R) Supplier of bathroom accessories.

Alternative Plans
9 Hester Road
London SW11 4AN
UK
Tel: +44 (0)20 7228 6460
www.alternative-plans.co.uk

(R) Bathroom fittings, especially those by Italian manufacturers.

Ambiance Bain
France
www.ambiancebain.com

(M) Modern fitted and unfitted units.

American Standard
PO Box 6820
NJ 08855 680
USA
Tel: +1 800 524 9797
www.americanstandard-us.com

(M) Huge range of bathroom fittings.

Andreoli Alide Curvatura Laminati Plastici
Italy
Tel: +39 03 6250 6897
www.andreoli.it

(D, M) Chic wash basins, including the Star Vanity.

Ann Sacks
204 East 58th Street
New York
USA
Tel: +1 800 278 8453
www.annsacks.com

(R) Tiles, fittings, and accessories.

Anne Hunter Interiors
Catchpell House
Carpet Lane
Bernard Street
Edinburgh EH6 6SP
UK
Tel: +44 (0)131 468 7444
Fax: +44 (0)131 468 7445
www.annehunter.co.uk

(D) Flexible design solutions for the whole house including bathrooms.
(See pictures page 17 and number 293)

Aqata Shower Enclosures
Nuffield Road
Hinckley
Leicestershire LE10 3DT
UK
Tel: +44 (0)1455 890078
www.aqata.co.uk

(R) Contemporary shower enclosures.

Armitage Shanks
Armitage
Rugeley
Staffordshire WS15 4BT
UK
Tel: +44 (0)1543 490253
www.armitage-shanks.co.uk

(M, R) Maker and supplier of classic bathroom ranges.

Aston Matthews
141–147a Essex Road
London N1 2SN
UK
Tel: +44 (0)20 7226 7220
www.astonmatthews.co.uk

(M, R) Large showroom of bathroom fixtures and fittings, including own-brand.

Avante Bathroom Products
Unit 2 Dragon Court
Springwell Road
Leeds LS12 1EY
UK
Tel: +44 (0)113 244 5337
www.avante-bathroom-products.co.uk

(M) Contemporary basins, units, and accessories in glass and Corian.
(See picture 298)

Bathaus
92 Brompton Road
London SW3 1ER
UK
Tel: +44 (0)20 7225 7620
www.bathaus.co.uk

(R) Contemporary bathrooms,
including products by Durat.

Bathrooms International
54 The Burroughs
London NW4 4AN
UK
Tel: +44 (0)20 8202 8288
for stockists
www.bathroomsint.com

(R) Specialist in stylish bathroom
products.
(See pictures 294, 296, 304, 305, 309)

Cesana
Via Dalmazia
3 Vimercate 20059
Milan
Italy
Tel: +39 039 608 2441
www.cesana.it

(M) Beautiful shower enclosures.

Cifial
UK
Tel: +44 (0)1933 402008
www.cifial.co.uk

(R) Unusual bathroom taps
and accessories.

Cloakroom Solutions Ltd
Unit 8
The Courtyard
Holmbush Farm
Faygate
Nr Horsham
West Sussex RH12 4SE
UK
Tel: +44 (0)1293 852 503
www.cloakroomsolutions.co.uk

(R) Brilliant contemporary designs,
including basins in glass and
stainless steel.
(See picture 292)

Colombo Design
Via Baccanello 22
24030 Terno D'Isola
Italy
Tel: + 39 035 4949 001
www.colombodesign.it

(D, M) Huge range of door furniture
and hooks and bathroom furniture.
(See picture 196)

CP Hart
Newnham Terrace
Hercules Road
London SE1 7DR
UK
Tel: +44 (0)20 7902 1000
for branches

(R) Vast showroom of traditional and
contemporary bathroom designs.

Czech & Speake
39c Jermyn Street
London SW1Y 6DN
UK
Tel: +44 (0)20 7439 0216
www.czechspeake.com

(D, M, R) Bathroom suites
and accessories.

Diamond Spas Inc
760 South 104th Street
Broomfield
Colorado 80020
USA
Tel: +1 800 951 7727
email:
customerservice@diamondspas.com

(M) Maker of spa baths, including one
in stainless steel.

Durante International
Bathrooms
266 Brompton Road
London SW3 2AS
UK
Tel: +44 (0)20 7589 9990
www.durante.co.uk

(R) Contemporary designs from US
and Europe, and specialist in the
supply of Jacuzzi whirlpool baths.

Durat
Tonester Ltd
Huhdantie 4
21140 Rymattyle
Finland
Tel: +358 (0) 2252 1000
Fax: +358 (0) 2252 1022
www.durat.com

(M) Polyester-based surface material.
(See picture 279)

Duravit SA
Route de Marienthal
F-67241 Bischwiller Cedex
Germany
Tel: +49 889061 00
and

Duravit
UK
Tel: +44 (0)20 7902 1000
for stockists
www.duravtit.com

(M) Contemporary sanitaryware.
and

Duravit USA
1750 Breckinridge Parkway
Suite 500
Duluth
GA 30096
USA
Tel: +1 888 387 2848
www.duravit.com

(M) High-quality contemporary-style
bathroom ware and accessories.
(See picture 31)

Ekesi
Sweden
Tel: +46 8728 92000
www.ekesioo.se

(R) Seller of probably the world's
most stylish drain covers in
shiny steel.

Florestone
2851 Falcon Drive
Madera
CA 93637-9287
USA
Tel: +1 559 661 4171
www.florestone.com

(M, R) Producers and suppliers of
shower and bathroom products.

GEC Anderson
Oakengrove
Shire Lane
Hastoe
Tring HP23 6LY
UK
Tel: +44 (0)1442 826999
www.gecanderson.co.uk

(D, M, R) Bespoke stainless-steel
work, including baths, basins,
and WCs.

H2O
At Fired Earth
Twyford Mill
Oxford Road
Adderbury Oxon OX17 3HP
UK
Tel: +44 (0)1295 812088
for stockists
www.firedearth.com

(M, R) Bathroom fittings and
accessories, plus historic and modern
paint colours, and wall and floor tiles.

Hansgrohe
Units D1 and 2
Sandown Park trading Estate
Royal Mills
Esher
Surrey KT10 8BL
UK
Tel: +44 (0)1372 465655 for
stockists
www.hansdgrohe.co.uk

(M, R) Contemporary taps and
showers.

Hansgrohe Inc
1490 Bluegrass Lakes
Parkway Suite 209
Alpharetta
GA 30004
USA
Tel: +1 770 360 9880
www.hansgrohe-usa.com

(M) Manufacturer of contemporary-
style taps and showers.

HighTec and Vola
Landsbergerstrasse 146
D-80339 Munich
Germany
Tel: +49 (0)8954 09450
Fax: +49 (0)8950 6009
www.hightec-vola.de

(M, D) Taps, showers, and accessories.
(See pictures 292, 300)

Home
UK
Tel: +44 0800 9522 022
(free phone UK only)

(R) Specialist in water technology,
including glass baths.

Hueppe
RSJ Associates
Unit 5
Greenfield Road
Greenfield Farm Industrial Estate
Congleton
Cheshire CW12 4TR
UK
Tel: +44 (0)1260 276188
www.hueppe.com

(M) Specialist shower maker.

**Ideal Standard
and Sottini**
National Avenue
Hull
East Yorkshire HU5 4HS
UK
Tel: +44 (0)1482 346461
for stockists
www.ideal-standard.co.uk

(D, M, R) Huge manufacturer
of bathroom ware.

Jacob Delafon
Unit 1
Churchward South Mead Park
Didcot
Oxfordshire OX11 7HB
UK
Tel: +44 (0)1235 510511
for stockists
www.jacobdelafon.com

(M) French bathrooms – traditional
and contemporary styles.

Jeff Bell Glass Casts
299 Haggerston Road
Dalston
London E8 4EN
UK
Tel: +44 (0)20 7275 8481
www.glasscasts.co.uk

(D, M) Cast-glass baths, basins,
and shower screens.
(See picture 27)

Kallista Inc
444 Highland Drive
Mailstop 032
Kohler WI 53044
USA
Fax: + 1 888 272 3094
www.kallistainc.com

(M) Luxury kitchen and bath products
(See picture 309)

Kayode Lipede
6 Iroko House
Lithos Road NW3 6ER
UK
Tel: +44 (0)20 7794 7535

(D, M, R) Polished concrete
mouldings, basins, and work surfaces.

Kroin
180 Fawcett Street
Cambridge
Massachusetts 02138
USA
Tel: +1 617 492 4000

(M) Maker of high-quality sanitary
fittings and polished stainless-steel
sinks.

**Mantaleda Bathroom Company
Ltd**
Unit 10 & 11
Willford Mill
Station Road
Brompton
Northallerton
North Yorkshire DL6 2RE
UK
Tel: +44 (0)1609 771211
www.mantaleda.fsnet.co.uk

(M, R) Makers of dozens of bath
shapes and sizes, including unusual
square tubs and deep soaking tubs.

Max Pike Bathrooms
70–71 Patcham Terrace
London SW8 4BP
UK
Tel: +44 (0)20 7720 9136
www.maxpike.com

(D, M, R) Leading bathroom designer
and supplier of products including the
stainless-steel Kan bath and WC.

Mira Showers Ltd
Cromwell Road
Cheltenham
Gloucestershire GL52 5EP
UK
Tel: +44 (0)1242 221221 for
stockists
www.mirashowers.co.uk

(M) Manufacturer of top-brand
showers.

Moen USA
USA
Tel: +1 800 289 6636
www.moen.com

(M) Water filtering taps and
equipment, including showers.

Original Bathrooms
143–145 Kew Road
Richmond
Surrey TW9 2PN
UK
Tel: +44 (0)20 8940 7554

(R) Retailer of innovative bathroom
products.
(See pictures 81, 298)

Original Style Ltd
Falcon Road
Sowton Industrial Estate
Exeter
Devon EX2 7LF
UK
Tel: +44 (0)1392 473000
www.originalstyle.com

(D, M, R) Design and supply
of novel bathroom tiles.

Papema Spas
UK
Tel: +44 (0)1254 278991
www.papema-spas.co.uk

(M, R) Bespoke spa baths, made in
the UK.

Pegler Ltd
St Catherines Avenue
Doncaster
South Yorkshire DN4 8DF
UK
Tel: +44 (0)1302 560560
www.pegler.com

(D, M, R) High-quality taps and
showers.

Porcelanosa
UK
Tel: +44 (0)800 915 4000 for nearest
showroom

(M) Maker of contemporary ranges of
ceramic tiles and bathroom
accessories.

Ripples
18–20 Regent Street
Clifton
Bristol BS8 4HG
UK
Tel: +44 (0)117 973 1144
for branches

(R) Large showrooms of
contemporary fixtures and fittings

Samuel Heath & Sons Plc
Leopold Street
Birmingham B12 0UJ
UK
Tel: +44 (0)121 772 2303
www.samuel-heath.com

(R) Top-quality bathroom accessories.

Showeristic Ltd
Unit 10
Manor Industrial Estate
Flint
Clwyd CH6 5UY
UK
Tel: +44 (0)1352 735381

(M, R) Made-to-measure showers.

Soft Options
Polished Metal Products Ltd
Devauden Green
Chepstow
Monmouthshire NP16 6PL
UK
Tel: +44 (0)1291 650455
www.sinks.co.uk

(R) A fine collection of stainless-steel
sinks and taps.

Sottini
UK
Tel: +44 0800 591586 (free phone
UK only)
www.sottini.co.uk

(M) Italian manufacturer of classic
and contemporary sanitary ware.

Submarine
8 Lanark Street
Glasgow G1 5PY
UK
Tel: +44 (0)141 564 9867

(R) Contemporary stainless-steel
baths, basins, and WCs.

Svedbergs of Sweden
717 Fulham Road
London SW6 5UL
UK
Tel: +44 (0)20 7371 9214
www.svedbergs.co.uk

(M) Manufacturer of everything for
the bathroom.

Teuco UK
Suite 314
Business Design Centre
52 Upper Street
London N1 0QH
UK
Tel: +44 (0)20 7704 2190 for
stockists
www.teuco.com

(D, M) Whirlpool baths and
multifunction showers and
hydroshowers.

The Albion Bath Company UK
Tel: +44 (0)7000 422847

(R) Seller of baths of all types, plus
showers, taps, lavatories, and basins.

The Water Monopoly
16–18 Lonsdale Road
London NW6 6RD
UK
Tel: +44 (0)20 7624 2636

(R) Fine French and English antique
and reproduction sanitary ware.

Villeroy & Boch
267 Merton Road
London SW18 5JS
UK
Tel: +44 (0)20 8871 0011

(M, R) Beautiful bathrooms.
(See picture 287)

Vola UK Ltd
Unit 12
Ampthill Business Park
Station Road
Ampthill
Bedfordshire MK45 2QW
UK
Tel: +44 (0)1525 841155 for stockists
www.vola.co.uk

(M) Taps, showers, and accessories.
(See picture 312)

Water Front Ltd
20 Lakesmere Close
North Oxford Business Centre
Kidlington
Oxfordshire OX5
UK
Tel: +44 (0)1865 371571

(M) Bathroom accessories.

William Garvey
Leyhill
Payhembury
Nr Honiton EX14 OJG
UK
Tel: +44 (0)1404 841430
www.williamgarvey.co.uk

(D, M, R) Maker of teak baths, basins,
and shower trays.

HEATING

ACR Heat Products
UK
Tel: +44 (0)121 706 8266
www.franco-belge.co.uk

(R) UK distributor of stylish Franco-
Belge cast-iron stoves.

**Anglia Fireplaces
and Design**
UK
Tel: +44 (0)1223 234713
www.fireplaces.co.uk

(M, R) Astonishing modern fireplaces.

Bisque Radiators
244 Belsize Road
London NW6 4BT
UK
Tel: +44 (0)20 7328 2225
and
23 Queen's Square
Bath BA1 2HX
UK
Tel: +44 (0)1225 478 500
www.bisque.co.uk

(R) Radiators and towel heaters.
(See pictures 277, 331, 332, 333,
334, 335)

Chesneys
194–202 Battersea Park Road
London SW11 4ND
UK
Tel: +44 (0)20 7627 1410
www.chesneys.co.uk

(R) Traditional and contemporary
fireplaces. (See picture 322)

CVO Firevault
36 Great Titchfield Street
London W1W 8BQ
UK
Tel: +44 (0)20 7580 5333
www.cvo.co.uk

Contemporary fireplaces.

Diligence
UK
Tel: +44 (0)1794 388812

(R) Importer of unusual, ceiling-
suspended Focus fires in steel and
glass.
(See pictures 327, 328)

Douvre Castings Ltd
UK
Tel: +44 (0)121 706 7600
www.douvre.co.uk

(R) Supplier of classic cast-iron,
multi-fuel stoves.

Eco Hometec UK Ltd
UK
Tel: +44 (0)1302 722266
www.eco-hometec.co.uk

(M) Underfloor heating specialist.

Ecolec
Sharrocks Street
Wolverhampton
West Midlands WV1 3RP
UK
Tel: +44 01902 353752
www.thama.co.uk

(M) Stylish contemporary radiators.

Ecotecht UK
UK
Tel: +44 (0)845 601 4115
www.ecotecht.com

(R) Fire furniture, including high-tech
wood-burning stoves.

Faral Radiators
Tropical House
Charlwoods Road
East Grinstead
West Sussex RH19 2HJ
UK
Tel: +44 (0)1342 315757

(M) Contemporary-style aluminium
radiators.

Heatlink UK
UK
Tel: +44 (0)0353 5062 4062
www.hlinkirl.com

(M) Underfloor heating specialist.

MFT
Unit 5b
Estate Road No 6
South Humberside Industrial Estate
Grimsby
Lincolnshire DN31 2TG
UK
Tel: +44 (0)1472 350771

(M) Makers of finned tube radiators,
up to 6 m (20 ft) in length.

Nu-Heat UK
UK
Tel: +44 01404 549770
www.nu-heat.co.uk

(M) Underfloor heating specialist.

Pither Studio Stoves
UK
Tel: +44 (0)1784 457896

(R) Sells the classic Studio No 2
stainless-steel, anthracite-burning
stove.

Powertech Solar Systems
UK
Tel: +44 (0)8707 300111
www.eco-shop.co.uk

(M, R) Environment-friendly heating
systems.

Radiating Style
UK
Tel: +44 (0)20 8577 9111

(R) Seller of great radiators.

The Ceramic Stove Company
UK
Tel: +44 (0)1865 245077
www.ceramicstove.com

(M, R) Hugely efficient, rapid-firing,
heat-retaining wood stoves.

**The Platonic
Fireplace Company**
Phoenix Wharf
Eel Pie Island
Twickenham
Middlesex TW1 3DY
UK
Tel: +44 (0)20 8891 5904
www.platonicfireplaces.co.uk

(D, M, R) Contemporary fireplaces.
(See pictures 319, 320)

HANDLES AND SWITCHES

Allgood
297 Euston Road
London NW1 3AQ
UK
Tel: +44 (0)20 7255 9321

(M, R) Solid, contemporary handles by
star designers, including Starck and
Rogers, plus security equipment.

Architectural Components
4–8 Exhibition Road
London SW7 2HF
UK
Tel: +44 (0)20 7581 2401

(R) Architectural hardware for doors,
from traditional to modern.

A Touch of Brass
210 Fulham Road
London SW10 9PJ
UK
Tel: +44 (0)20 7351 2255

(R) Brass and chrome switches
and sockets.
(See pictures 337, 340)

Bombay Duck
Mail order
UK
Tel: +44 (0)20 8749 8001
for brochure

(R) More than a hundred styles of
handles and knobs.

Charles Mason Ltd
UK
Tel: +44 0800 085 3616 (free phone
UK only)
www.charles-mason.com

(R) Door handles, window fixings,
and quality ironmongery.

Colombo Design
Via Baccanello 22
24030 Terno D'Isola
Italy
Tel: +39 035 49 49 001
www.colombodesign.it

(D, M) Huge range of door furniture
and hooks.

Danico Brass Ltd
31–35 Winchester Road
London NW3
UK
Tel: +44 (0)20 7483 4477

(R) Brass letterplates, handles, knobs,
and more.

David Wainwright
61–63 Portobello Road
London W11
UK
Tel: +44 (0)20 7727 0707

(R) Handles and knobs of all types
in glass, china, bone, and iron.

Forbes & Lomax
205a St John's Hill
Battersea
London SW11 1TH
UK
Tel: +44 (0)20 7738 0202
www.forbesandlomax.co.uk

(M, R) Interesting range of light
switches.

HAF Ltd
HAF House
Mead Lane
Hertford
Hertfordshire SG13 7AP
UK
Tel: +44 (0)1992 512 566
www.hafinternational.com

(M, R) Handles, light switches, and
bathroom fittings.

HEWI UK Ltd
Scimitar Close
Gillingham Business Park
Gillingham
Kent ME8 ORN
UK
Tel: +44 (0)1634 377 688
www.hewi.com

(M) Leading manufacturer of
contemporary handles and door
furniture.

JD Beardmore & Co
17 Pall Mall
London SW1Y 5LU
UK
Tel: +44 (0)20 7670 1000

(M, R) Architectural ironmongery, and
will also copy existing designs.

Knobs and Knockers
567 Kings Road
London SW6
UK
Tel: +44 (0)20 7384 2884

(R) Vast range of brass, iron,
and ceramic door furniture.

McKinney & Co
Studio P
The Old Imperial Laundry
71 Warriner Gardens
London SW11
UK
Tel: +44 (0)20 7627 5077

(M, R) Door and window accessories,
including finger plates.

Manital
Via Provinciale 80
25079 Vobarno
Brescia
Italy
Tel: +39 0365 599999
www.manitalsrl.it

(M) Contemporary door handles.

MK Electric
The Arnold Centre
Paycocke Road
Basildon
Essex
UK
Tel: +44 (0)1268 563000
www.ec-ic-sg.com/mkelectric/-
index.htm

(M) Contemporary light switches and
sockets.
(See pictures 338, 339)

Nanz Custom Hardware
USA
Tel: +1 212 367 7000
www.nanz.com

(R) Contemporary door handles, locks,
and hinges.

Primalite
Triangle Business Park
Wendover
Bucks HP22 5BL
UK
Tel: +44 (0)1296 611800

(M) Maker of a range of switches,
sockets, and door furniture.

Rocky Mountain Hardware
USA
Tel: +1 888 788 2013
www.rockymountainhardware.com

(M, R) Handcrafted architectural
hardware, including handsome
handles.

Shopkit Designs Ltd
100 Cecil Street
Watford
Hertfordshire WD24 5AD
UK
Tel: +44 (0)1923 818282
www.shopkit.com

(D, M, R) Producer and supplier of a
handles, knobs, shelving, and accessories.

Silent Gliss Ltd
Star Lane
Margate
Kent CT9 4EF
UK
Tel: +44 (0)1843 863571
www.silentgliss.co.uk

(D, M) Perfect curtain railing.

Trimco
USA
Tel: +1 323 262 4191
www.trimcobbw.com

(M) Maker of contemporary-style
locks and door handles.

architects

AAB architects
Fourth Floor
Linton House
39-51 Highgate Road
London NW5 1RT
UK
Tel: +44 (0)20 7267 0636
(See picture page 11)

Alan Power
5 Haydens Place
London W11 1LY
UK
Tel: +44 (0)20 7229 9375
(See picture 179)

Alberto Campo Baeza
Spain
Tel: +34 91 521 7061

Allford Hall Monaghan
Morris Architects
5–23 Old Street
London EC1V 9HL
UK
Tel: +44 (0)20 7251 5261
(See pictures 283, 321)

Arthur Collin Architect
1A Berry Place
London EC1V OJD
UK
Tel: +44 (0)20 7490 3520
(See pictures 47, 123, 181)

Aukett Tytherleigh
Atlantic Court
Kings Road
London SW3
UK
Tel: +44 (0)20 7352 3622
(See pictures 217, 241)

Barbara Weiss Architects
4 Offord Street
London N1 1OH
UK
Tel: +44 (0)20 7609 1867
(See picture 194)

Belmont Freeman Architects
110 West 40th Street
Suite 2401
New York
NY 10018
USA
Tel: +1 212 382 3311

Belsize Architects
48 Parkhill Road
London NW3
UK
Tel: +44 (0)20 7482 4420
(See pictures 56, 58)

Bill Amberg
10 Chepstow Road
London W2 5BD
UK
Tel: +44 (0)20 7727 3560
www.billamberg.com
(See pictures 19, 21, 68, 149)

Birds Portchmouth Russum
8 New North Place
London EC2A 4JA
UK
Tel: +44 (0)20 7613 1777
(See picture 161)

Brookes Stacey Randall
New Hibernia House
Winchester Walk
London SE1 9AG
UK
Tel: +44 (0)20 7403 0707
(See pictures 73, 78, 166, 168)

Buckley Gray
2–8 Scrutton Street
London EC2A 4RT
UK
Tel: +44 (0)20 7426 0303
(See pictures 224, 316)

Charles Barclay
74 Josephine Road
London SW2 2LA
UK
Tel: +44 (0)20 8674 0037
(See picture 142)

D'Soto Architects
38 Mount Pleasant
London WC1X 0AP
UK
Tel: +44 (0)20 7278 5100
(See picture 7)

Eric Owen Moss
Culver City
CA
USA
Tel: +1 310 839 1199

51% Studios
1–5 Clerkenwell Road
London EC1M 5PA
UK
Tel: +44 (0)20 7251 6963
(See pictures 45, 156)

Frankl + Luty
1 Kite Yard
Cambridge Road
London SW11 4TA
UK
Tel: +44 (0)20 7924 2261
(See picture 9)

Fraser Brown McKenna
2 St John's Place
London EC1M 4 NP
UK
Tel: +44 (0)20 7251 0543
(See pictures 6, 188)

Freeland Rees Roberts
25 City Road
Cambridge CB1
UK
Tel: +44 (0)1223 366555
(See pictures 158, 160)

Fulham Kitchens
9 Carnwath Road
London SW6 3HR
UK
Tel: +44 (0)20 7736 6458

Glenn Murcutt
Australia
Tel: +61 2 9969 7797

Gluckman Mayner Architects
145 Hudson Street
New York
NY 10013
USA
Tel: +1 212 925 8967

Hanrahan Meyers Architects
22 West 21st Street
New York
NY 10010
USA
Tel: +1 212 989 6026

Harrison Ince
UK
Tel: +44 (0)161 236 3650

Hawkins Brown Architects
60 Bastwick Street
London EC1V 3TN
UK
Tel: +44 (0)20 7336 8030
Fax: +44 (0)20 7336 8851
(See pictures 16, 57)

Ian Simpson Architects
Manchester
UK
Tel: +44 (0)161 839 4804

Jim Jennings Architecture
USA
Tel: +1 415 551 0827
(See picture 85)

John Kerr Associates
53a Bayham Street
London NW1 0AA
UK
Tel: +44 (0)20 7209 2784
(See pictures 132, 133, 134,135)

John Pawson
Unit B
70–78 York Way
London N1 QAG
Tel: +44 (0)20 7837 2929
(See pictures 211, 278)

John Wardle
Sydney
Australia
Tel: +61 39421 0700

Jonathan Woolf
39–51 Highgate Road
London NW5 1RS
UK
Tel: +44 (0)20 7428 9500
(See picture 169)

Kuth/Ranieri Architects
340 Bryant Street
San Francisco CA 94107
Tel: +1 415 543 9235
(See pictures 136, 227)

Lighting Design International
Lighting Design House
Ellaine Road
London W6
UK
Tel: 020 7381 8999
(See picture 213)

Littman Goddard Hogarth Architects
12 Chelsea Wharf
15 Lots Road
London SW10 0QJ
UK
Tel: +44 (0)20 7351 7871
(See pictures 87, 259)

London Basement Company
Unit B
Innovation House
292 Worton Road
Isleworth
London TW7 6EL
UK
Tel: +44 (0)20 7255 1577
(See picture 243)

McDowell & Benedetti
62 Rosebery Avenue
London EC1R
UK
Tel: +44 (0)207 278 8810
(See pictures 11, 12)

McLean Quinlan Architects
2a Bellevue Parade
London SW17 7EQ
UK
Tel: +44 (0)20 8767 1633
(See pictures 27, 105, 124, 184)

Mark Guard Architects
161 Whitfield Street
London W1P 5RY
UK
Tel: +44 (0)207 380 1199
(See picture 4)

MoreySmith
Greencoat House
Francis Street
London SW1P 1DH
UK
Tel: +44 (0)20 7931 8598
(See pictures 284, 302)

Morphosis
2041 Colorado Avenue
Santa Monica
CA 90404
USA
Tel: +1 310 453 2247

Munkenbeck + Marshall
135 Curtain Road,
London EC2A 3BX
UK
Tel: +44 (0)20 7739 3300
(See pictures 32, 325)

Nicolette & Martin Baines
6A South Street
Leominster
Herefordshire HR6 8JB
UK
Tel: +44 (0)1568 615406

Olson Sundberg
108 First Avenue South
4th floor
Seattle
Washington 98104
USA
Tel: +1 206 624 5670

Patel Taylor
85 Royal College Street
London NW1
UK
Tel: +44 (0)20 7388 3223
(See pictures 22, 25)

Peter Barber Architects
11–12 Great Sutton Street
London EC1V 0BX
UK
Tel/Fax: +44 (0)20 7689 3555
(See picture 112)

Peter Bernamont
Wharf Studios
Baldwin Terrace,
London N1 7RU
UK
Tel: +44 (0)20 7704 6859
(See pictures 46, 54)

Procter:Rihl
63 Cross Street
London N1 2BB
UK
Tel: +44 (0)20 7704 6003
(See pictures 73, 78, 189)

Reed Creative Services
151a Sydney Street
London SW3 6NT
UK
Tel: +44 (0)20 7565 0066
(See pictures 150, 281)

Roundhouse Design
25 Chalk Farm Road
London NW1 8AG
UK
Tel: +44 (0)20 7428 9955

Sergison Bates Architects
44 Newman Street
London W1
UK
Tel: +44 (0)20 7255 1564
(See picture 143)

Seth Stein
52 Kelso Place
London W8 5QQ
UK
Tel: +44 (0)20 7376 0005
(See pictures 210, 289)

Shed KM
Liverpool
UK
Tel: +44 (0)151 709 8211

Siegel Diamond Architecture
605 West Olympic Boulevard 820
Los Angeles
CA 90015
USA
Tel: +1 213 627 7170

Simon Conder
8 Nile Street
London N1
UK
Tel: +44 (0)20 7251 2144
(See pictures 131, 170)

Soren Robert Lund Associates
St Kongensgade 110E 1
1264 Copenhagen
Denmark
Tel: +45 33 91 01 00

Spencer Fung
3 Pine Mews
London NW10 3JA
UK
Tel: +44 (0)208 960 9883
(See picture 323)

Stephane Beel
Koningin Astridlaan 7/19
8200 Bruges
Belgium
Tel: +32 50 30 19 50

Stickland Coombe Architecture
258 Lavender Hill
London SW11 1LJ
UK
Tel: +44 (0)20 7924 1699
(See pictures 106, 107, 109,
198, 285)

Studio Baad
Linden Mill
Linden Road
Hebden Bridge
West Yorkshire HX7 7DN
UK
Tel: +44 (0)1422 843045
(See picture 129)

Studio M G
101 Turnmill Street
London EC1M 5QP
UK
Tel: +44 (0)20 7251 2648
(See picture 23)

The Architects Practice
23 Beacon Hill
London N7 9LY
UK
Tel: +44 (0)20 7607 3333
(See pictures 8, 44, 77)

**The Douglas Stephen
Partnership**
140–142 St John Street
London EC1
UK
Tel: +44 (0)20 7336 7884
(See pictures 60, 185)

Thinking Space
First Floor North
Rutland House
42–46 New Road
London E1 2AX
UK
Tel: +44 (0)20 7422 0085
(See picture 120)

Thomas de Cruz Architects
80–82 Chiswick High Road
London W4 1SY
UK
Tel: +44 (0)20 8995 8100
(See pictures 36, 55)

Tsao & McKown
20 Vandam Street
10th floor
New York
NY 10013
USA
Tel: +1 212 337 3800
(See picture 176)

Walters & Cohen
400 Highgate Studios
53–79 Highgate Road
London NW5 ITL
UK
Tel: +44 (0)20 7428 9751
(See picture 147)

Wells Mackereth Architects
10–11 Archer Street
London W1
UK
Tel: +44 (0)20 7287 5504
(See picture 207)

Will White Design
326 Portobello Road
London W10 5RU
UK
Tel: +44 (0)20 8964 8052
(See picture 152)

index

acknowledgments

PICTURE CREDITS

1 Camera Press

2 Richard Davies/ Brookes Stacey Randall

3 David Wakely/ Kuth/ Ranieri Architects

5 Ray Main/ Mainstream

6–7 The Douglas Stephen Partnership

8 Mike Redfern/ Charles Barclay Architect

10 Ray Main/ Mainstream

11 AAB Architects (Joiners: Edsons, Nottingham, tel: 0115 9372247)

12–13 Geoffrey Drayton for Cassina

14 Richard Davies/ Brookes Stacey Randall

15 Peter Cook/ VIEW/ Tugman Partnership

16 Dornbracht

17 Iain Peter McGregor/ Anne Hunter Interiors

18–19 Cesar Rubio/ Kuth/ Ranieri Architects

20 Ray Main/ Mainstream/ Grant Architects

22 above, below left Ray Main/ Mainstream

22 below right Ianthe Ruthven/ The Interior Archive/ Architect: Mark Guard

23 left Camera Press/ Schöner Wohnen

23 above right Nick Hufton/ VIEW/ Fraser Brown McKenna

23 below left Richard Bryant/ www.arcaid.co.uk

23 below right The Architects Practice

24 above left Frankl + Luty

24 above centre Brian Harrison/ Red Cover

24 above right Nick Hufton/ VIEW/ Renato Benedetti

24 below left Ray Main/ Mainstream/ McDowell & Benedetti

24 below right Ed Reeve/ The Interior Archive/ Designer: Ou Baholydin

25 Henry Wilson/ The Interior Archive/ Architect: Ian Chee

26 above left Ray Main/ Mainstream

26 above right Hawkins Brown Architects

26 below EmmeBi

27 above left Ray Main/ Mainstream/ Eltham Palace

27 above right Tim Beddow/ The Interior Archive/ Designer: Bill Amberg

27 below left Camera Press/ Schöner Wohnen

27 below right Modus for Bill Amberg

28 above left Chris Gascoigne/ VIEW/ Patel Taylor Architects

28 above right Studio MG Architects

28 below left Luke White/ The Interior Archive/ Owner: Keith Wainwright

28 below right Chris Gascoigne/ VIEW/Patel Taylor Architects

29 above left Richard Bryant/ www.arcaid.co.uk

29 right Peter Cook/ VIEW/ Quinlan McLean Architects

29 below left Ryno/ Camera Press/ Sarie Visi, Interior: The House of Manning

30 Winfried Heinze/ Red Cover

31 above left Wayne Vincent/ The Interior Archive/ Designer: Martin Walker

31 above right Ray Main/ Mainstream/ Architects: Littman Goddard Hogarth

31 below Ken Hayden/ Red Cover

32 above left Modus for United Colors of Benetton Paint Colors and Effects

32 above right Peter Thomas de Cruz

32 below Muraspec

33 above Lewis & Wood

33 below left Richard Bryant/ www.arcaid.co.uk

33 right Muraspec

34 Ray Main/ Mainstream

36 above left Ray Main/ Mainstream/ Martin Lee Associates

36 above right Ray Main/ Mainstream

36 below 51% Studios

37 above left Chris Gascoigne/ VIEW/ The Architects Practice

37 above right designed by Arthur Collin Architect

37 below left Peter Bernamont

37 below right 51% Studios

38 above left Andreas von Einsiedel/ Red Cover

38 above right Camera Press/ Neues Wohnen

38 below Ryno/ Camera Press/ Sarie Visi, Architects: Anya van der Merwe Miszewski & Macio Miszewski

39 above left Ryno/ Camera Press/ Sarie Visi, interior: The House of Manning

39 above right Ray Main/ Mainstream

39 below Camera Press/ Schöner Wohnen

40 Paul Tyagi/ VIEW/ Peter Bernamont

41 above left Peter Thomas de Cruz

41 above, & below right Nicholas Kane/ Belsize Architects

41 below left Hawkins Brown Architects

42 Ken Hayden/ Red Cover

44 above left The Douglas Stephen Partnership

44 above right Wicanders/ Amorim

44 below Ken Hayden/ Red Cover

45 above Junckers Ltd

45 below left Upofloor UK Ltd

45 below right Andreas von Einsiedel/ Red Cover

46 Wicanders/ Amorim

47 above left Camera Press/ Zuhause Wöhnen

47 above right Modus for Bill Amberg

47 below left Chris

Gascoigne/ VIEW/ Circus Architects

47 below right Hillgate PR for Kersaint Cobb

48 above & below left Kirkstone Quarries Ltd

48 below right Brookes Stacey Randall/ Rylands Peters & Small

49 above left Fired Earth

49 above right Verity Welstead/ Red Cover

49 below left Natural Tile

49 below right Kirkstone Quarries Ltd

50 above left Nathan Willock/ Procter:Rihl

50 above right Kearney

50 below left Trevor Richards/ Red Cover

50 below right Original Bathrooms

51 Camera Press/ Neues Wohnen

52 Richard Powers @redback/ www.arcaid.co.uk

53 above left Ray Main/ Mainstream

53 above right Alan Weintraub/ www.arcaid.co.uk

53 below Lu Jeffery

54 above left Littman Goddard Hogarth Architects

54 above right Dennis Gilbert/ VIEW/ Brian Housden

54 below left Bisazza

54 below right Simon Kenny/ Belle/ www.arcaid.co.uk

55 above and below left Bisazza

55 below right Ray Main/ Mainstream/ Eltham Palace

56 above, below right The Amtico Company

56 below left Ray Main/ Mainstream

57 left Ray Main/ Mainstream

58 above left Camera Press/ Schöner Wohnen

58 above right Henry Wilson/ The Interior Archive/ Architect: Voon Wong

58 below left Camera Press/ Brigitte

58 below right Verity Welstead/ Red Cover

59 Ray Main/ Mainstream/ Sergison Bates Architects

60 Peter Cook/ VIEW/ Quinlan McLean Architects

62 Stickland Coombe Architecture/ David Churchill/ www.arcaid.co.uk

63 above, below left Stickland Coombe Architecture/ David Churchill/ www.arcaid.co.uk

63 below right Winfried Heinze/ Red Cover

64 above left Dennis Gilbert/ VIEW/KNTA Architects

64 above right Peter Barber

64 below left Ray Main/ Mainstream/ Architect: John Broome

64 below right Ray Main/ Mainstream

65 left Stickland Coombe Architecture/ David Churchill/ www.arcaid.co.uk

65 right Tim Beddow/ The

Interior Archive/ Architect: Dennis Mires

66 Ray Main/ Mainstream

67 above left Paul Ratigan/ VIEW/ Carter Reynolds

67 above right Alan Weintraub/ www.arcaid.co.uk

67 below Dennis Gilbert/ VIEW/ KNTA Architects

68 above left Christian Nicholas/ designed by Arthur Collin Architect

68 above right Dennis Gilbert/ VIEW/KNTA Architects

68 below left Henry Wilson/ The Interior Archive

68 below right Peter Cock/ VIEW/ Quinlan McLean Architects

69 above Ray Main/ Mainstream

69 below Jeremy Cockayne/ www.arcaid.co.uk

70 Henry Wilson/ The Interior Archive/ Architect: Ian Chee

72 Ray Main/ Mainstream/ Architect: Simon Conder

73 above left Ray Main/ Mainstream

73 above right, below left Chris Gascoigne/ VIEW/ John Kerr

73 below right Nick Hufton/ VIEW/ Anelius Design

74 above left Kuth/ Ranieri Architects/ Cesar Rubio

74 above right Trevor Mein/ www.arcaid.co.uk

74 below left Geoffrey Drayton for Cassina

74 below right Richard Bryant/ www.arcaid.co.uk

75 above left Camera Press/ Laura Ellenberger

75 above right Winfried Heinze/ Red Cover

75 below Mike Redfern/ Charles Barclay Architects

76 Ray Main/ Mainstream/ Sergison Bates Architects

77 above left Ray Main/ Mainstream/ Architect: Chris Cowper

77 above right Edina van der Wyck/ The Interior Archive/ Owner: Ann Hatch

77 below left Ray Main/ Mainstream

77 below right Dennis Gilbert/ VIEW/Walters & Cohen

78 above left Ray Main/ Mainstream

78 above right Tim Beddow/ The Interior Archive/ Designer: Bill Amberg

78 below Ken Hayden/T he Interior Archive/ Designer: Jonathan Reed

79 above Richard Bryant/ www.arcaid.co.uk

79 below left James Morris/ Axiom

79 below right Nick Hufton/ VIEW/ Anelius Design

80 Kirkstone Quarries Ltd

82 above left Ray Main/ Mainstream/ Nash Architects

82 right 51% Studios

82 below Ray Main/ Mainstream/ Architect: Chris Cowper

83 above & below left Peter Cook/ VIEW/ Freeland Rees Roberts

83 above right Tim Beddow/The Interior Archive/ Architect: Garrett O'Hagan

83 below right Morely von Sternberg

84 Dennis Gilbert/ VIEW/ Rick Mather Architects

85 above left Tim James/ VIEW/ Julian Arenot Associates

85 above right Andrea Ferrari/ Geoffrey Drayton for Cassina

85 below left Ryno/ Camera Press/ Sarie Visi, Interior: Uschi Stuart

85 below right Camera Press/ Max Jourdan

86 above left James Mitchell/ Red Cover

86 above right Graham Atkins Hughes/ Red Cover

86 below left Peter Cook/ VIEW

86 below right Ray Main/ Mainstream/ Architect: Simon Conder

87 above left Henry Wilson/ The Interior Archive/ Designer: Vincent Mazzucci

87 above right James Mitchell/ Red Cover

87 below left James Morris/ Axiom/ Architect: Pip Horne

87 below right Winfried Heinze/ Red Cover

88 left Peter Cook/ VIEW/ Magyar Marsoni

88 above Richard Bryant/ www.arcaid.co.uk

88 below centre Chris Gascoigne/ VIEW/ Fletcher Priest Architects

88 below right Henry Wilson/ The Interior Archive/ Architect: Ian Chee

89 Chris Gascoigne/ VIEW/Alan Power Architects

90 Ryno/ Camera Press/ Sarie Visis, Architect: Anya van der Merwe Miszewski & Macio Miszweski

92 above left Jeremy Young/ designed by Arthur Collin Architect

92 above right Ray Main/ Mainstream

92 below left Geoffrey Drayton for EmmeBi

92 below right Peter Cook/ VIEW/ Quinlan MacLean Architects

93 The Douglas Stephen Partnership

94 above left Lu Jeffery

94 above right Dennis Gilbert/ VIEW/ Sanya Polescuk Associates

94 below right Procter:Rihl

95 left Albert Piovanno/ www.arcaid.co.uk

95 left Richard Powers/ www.arcaid.co.uk

96 above Marianne Majers/ Barbara Weiss Architects

96 below left Richard Bryant/ www.arcaid.co.uk

96 below right Andrew Wood/ The Interior Archive/ Stylist: Polly Dickens

97 above left Parker Hobart Associates

97 above right Colombo Design

97 below Living/ Zenit

98 left Stickland Coombe Architecture/ David Churchill/ www.arcaid.co.uk

98 above right Ray Main/ Mainstream

98 below right Kim Sayer/ Red Cover

99 above left, below right Jake Fitzjones/ Red Cover

99 above right Camera Press/ Brigitte

99 below left Kim Sayer/ Red Cover

100 Stickland Coombe Architecture/ David Churchill/ www.arcaid.co.uk

102 above left Ray Main/ Mainstream/ UsickHeal Associates

102 above right Chris Gascoigne/ VIEW/ Wells Mackereth

102 below Flos

103 above left Ken Hayden/ Red Cover

103 above right Chris Gascoigne/ VIEW/ Seth Stein

103 below Ken Hayden/ Red Cover

104 Chris Gascoigne/ VIEW/ Circus Architects

105 above left James Morris/ Axiom/ Lighting Design International

105 above right Camera Press/ Schöner Wohnen

105 below left James Morris/ Axiom

105 below right Ray Main/ Mainstream

106 above left Dennis Gilbert/ VIEW/ Aukett Tytherleigh

106 above right Ray Main/ Mainstream

106 below left Ray Main/ Mainstream

016 below right Ken Hayden/ Red Cover

107 above left Nick Hufton/ VIEW/ Anelius Design

107 above right Ray Main/ Mainstream

107 below Luke White/ The Interior Archive/ Owner: Detmar Blow

108 above left Nathan Willock/ Buckley Gray

108 above right Ed Reeve/ The Interior Archive

108 below left Flos

108 below right Sharon Risedorph/ Kuth/ Ranieri Architect

109 Graham Atkins Hughes/ Red Cover

110 above left Ray Main/ Mainstream

110 above right The Colour Light Company

110 below Kim Sayer/ Red Cover

111 above Black + Blum

111 below left Ed Reeve/ The Interior Archive

111 below right Lindsay Bloxham

112 above right James Morris/ Axiom/ Designer: Andrea Mendelson

112 above right Flos

112 below left Guy Drayton/ Geoffrey Drayton for Tocs Design

112 below right Black + Blum

113 Fernando Bengoechea/ The Interior Archive/ Designer: Gaston Marticorena

114 Dennis Gilbert/ VIEW/Aukett Tytherleigh

116 above left Wayne Vincent/ The Interior Archive/ Designer: The London Basement Co.

116 below Space Savers/ Quantum 2K

117 above right Franke

117 below left Jake Fitzjones/ Red Cover

118 Space Savers/ Quantum 2K

119 above left Franke

119 above right Jake Fitzjones/ Red Cover

119 below left Viaduct/ Antonia Astori

119 below right Roundhouse Design

120 above Corian

120 below Dornbracht

121 above Corian

121 below Roundhouse Design

122 above left Littman Goddard Hogarth

122 above right, & below left Bulthaup

122 below right Nivk Hufton/ VIEW/ Renato Benedetti

123 above Bulthaup

123 below Viaduct/ Antonia Astori

124 Kirkstone Quarries Ltd

125 above left James Morris/ Axiom

125 above right Jake Fitzjones/ Red Cover

125 below left Corian

125 below right Nick Kane/ www.arcaid.co.uk

126 above left Camera Press/ Schöner Wohnen

126 above right Ray Main/ Mainstream

126 below left Andrew Wood/ The Interior Archive/ Owner: Antonio Carluccio

126 below right Space Savers/ Quantum 2K

127 Luke White/ The Interior Archive/ Owner: George Hammer

128 above Ray Main/ Mainstream

128 below left Bisque

128 below right Ken Hayden/ Red Cover

129 above Hillgate PR for Durat

129 below right Ken Hayden/ The Interior Archive/ Designer: Jonathan Reed

130 above left Original Bathrooms

130 above right James Morris/ Axiom/ Architect: AHMM

130 below left MoreySmith/ Patrick Burrows

130 below right Stickland Coombe Architecture/ David Churchill/ www.arcaid.co.uk
131 above left Original Bathrooms
131 above right Villeroy & Boch
131 below left Andrew Wood/ The Interior Archive/ Owner: Brix Smith
131 below right Richard Bryant/ www.arcaid.co.uk
132 Dennis Gilbert/ VIEW/ Rick Mather Architects
133 above left Camera Press/ Schöner Wohnen
133 above right High Tec + Vola AG
133 below Iain Peter

McGregor/ Anne Hunter Interiors
134 left Taylor Alden Ltd for Bathrooms International
134 above right Ed Reeve/ The Interior Archive/ Cabinet Maker: Neil Blackwell
134 below right Winfried Heinze/ Red Cover
135 above left Avante Bathroom Products
135 above right Original Bathrooms
135 below left High Tec + Vola AG
135 below right Winfried Heinze/ Red Cover
136 above left Patrick Burrows/ MoreySmith

136 above left, below Taylor Alden for Bathrooms International
137 above left Fired Earth
137 above right Kallista
137 below Sigurd Kranenbonk/ Dornbracht
138 left Ray Main/ Mainstream
138 above right Patrick Burrows/ MoreySmith
138 below right David Wakely/ Kuth/ Ranieri Architects
139 above left Original Bathrooms
140 above left Chris Gascoigne/ VIEW/ Buckley Gray Architects
140 above right Verity

Welstead/ Red Cover
140 below James Mitchell/ Red Cover
141 left Jake Fitzjones/ Red Cover
141 right Platonic Fireplace Company
142 left Dennis Gilbert/ VIEW/Alford Hall Monaghan Morris
142 above right Parker Hobart for Chesneys
142 below right Andrew Wood/ The Interior Archive/ Architect: Spencer Fung
143 above Ed Reeve/ The Interior Archive/ Cabinet Maker: Mathew Carver
143 below right Ed Reeve/

The Interior Archive/ Architect: Unique Environments
144 Diligence/ Beazley
145 above left Diligence
145 above right Ray Main/ Mainstream/ Nash Architects
145 below Camera Press/ Schöner Wohnen
146 above Bisque
146 below Richard Powers
147 Bisque
148 above Andreas von Einsiedel/ Red Cover
148 below Parker Hobart for A Touch of Brass
149 above MK Electric
149 below Parker Hobart for A Touch of Brass

AUTHOR'S ACKNOWLEDGMENTS

I'd like to thank every architect and designer who has contributed to this volume. You really are doing your bit to make the world a more beautiful place. I salute you. I'd also like to thank everyone who has worked on this book – it is a vast and complex project and stands, I hope, as a triumph of teamwork.